Piagetian Research

Volume Eight

PIAGETIAN RESEARCH:
Compilation and Commentary

Volume Eight

Cross-Cultural Studies

Sohan Modgil, PhD and Celia Modgil, MPhil

Foreword by Professor Bärbel Inhelder
The University of Geneva

NFER Publishing Company Ltd

Published by the NFER Publishing Company Ltd.,
2 Jennings Buildings, Thames Avenue,
Windsor, Berks. SL4 1QS
Registered Office: The Mere, Upton Park, Slough, Berks. SL1 2DQ
First Published 1976
© Sohan and Celia Modgil, 1976
ISBN 0 85633 108 2

Printed in Great Britain by
Staples Printers Ltd., Rochester, Kent.
Distributed in the USA by Humanities Press Inc.,
Atlantic Highlands, New Jersey, 07716, USA.

Contents

To Gita and Ramayana

With Love

FOREWORD

I most sincerely thank Dr Sohan and Celia Modgil for asking me to write a foreword to the series of eight volumes which they are at present compiling. We all know the interest that was shown in, and the success of, the previous book, *Piagetian Research: A Handbook of Recent Studies*. Now, two years later, eight follow-up volumes are being published. We are well aware of what this represents in terms of continuity and devotion to such a long-term task.

The rapid extension of Piaget-inspired research is very impressive; in this series 3700 references are mentioned. It would seem that such an extension is explained by the need for a general theory in fundamental psychology. Another possible explanation is the growing awareness of the gaps in strictly behaviourist theory, on the one hand, and on the other, the continued emergence of new applications for the work carried out in Geneva in the fields of education and psychopathology. Recent studies confirm this trend.

Pleasing though this extension is, however, we are somewhat disturbed by the fact that the replication of our experiments does not always show a sufficient understanding of Piagetian theory on the part of the authors of these new works. We are of course the first to admit that such understanding is not easy to acquire, especially since this form of psychology is closely linked to a certain form of epistemology. Once understood, this form of epistemology appears to be that which best suits genetic psychology, as both are essentially constructivist. Constructivism implies that knowledge is not acquired merely under the impact of empirical experience, as suggested by behaviourist theory, although of course such impact is not entirely excluded from the process. It is also opposed to innate theory, to which, it seems, recourse is frequently had today (maturation being a factor which intervenes, but not exclusively). Constructivism emphasizes the child's or the subject's activity during the course of cognitive development: in other words, everything derives from actions and is eventually translated into coherent and logical thought operations.

In order to promote the necessary understanding, Sohan and Celia Modgil have systematically encouraged the reader to return to the original texts. If authors who have an excellent knowledge of the work of Piaget and his colleagues slightly misunderstand our theoretical position — which is in no way maturationist but rather epigenetic — one can easily imagine the misunderstanding of researchers who are less well informed and further away from Geneva. It is one thing to recognize the necessary sequence of the stages, but another thing altogether to explain them by invoking an innate 'programme'. Piaget's explanation, which is best presented in constructivist terms, deals with the sequence of stages by a process of equilibration or autoregulation. This regulatory activity enables the subject truly to construct knowledge — something which simple maturation does not do.

This point of view is fundamental to the understanding of Piagetian psychology; but more than that, it seems to us to constitute a particularly useful approach to questions of educational application since this form of autoconstruction corresponds more than any other perspective to the ideal called 'the active school', an ideal rarely carried out in practice.

In a constructivist perspective of this kind, it is clearly the sequence of stages which is important and not the chronological ages; the latter vary considerably from one environment to another and also depend on the experimental procedures being used. It is not astonishing that Bryant obtains convservation responses at earlier ages than those noted by us: we ourselves have obtained notable accelerations using operatory learning procedures developed in collaboration with H. Sinclair and M. Bovet (1974). We have recently published the results of a study (Inhelder *et al.*, 1975) which show stable acquisition of conservation notions as of age 5 if the following procedure is used: rather than merely deforming an object such as a ball of clay or modifying a collection of discrete elements, one removes part of or an element of the object(s) and moves it to another spot. In this case conservation appears earlier because the child understands two things he did not grasp during the simple deformations: firstly, that changes in shape are the result of displacements, and secondly, that in the course of these displacements what appears at the end is identical to what was removed at the start (this is what Piaget calls 'commutability'). We highlight this piece of work in order to show the much lesser importance of chronological age which can so easily be accelerated or delayed according to circumstances. The main point is the mode of construction which obeys constant laws and this characteristic is best exemplified by constructivism as we have defined it earlier.

We would also like to add that the recent discoveries of T. Bower and others concerning the innateness of certain behaviours which Piaget had not observed at the sensorimotor level do not contradict constructivism, since these primitive reactions do not directly result in higher-order behaviours but are reconstructed on different levels. These reconstructions are themselves not innate, but evidence of the constructive activities we have already observed elsewhere.

I should like to congratulate Dr Sohan and Celia Modgil on their fine effort in bringing together in these eight volumes the numerous pieces of work, thus rendering them accessible to researchers. We sincerely hope that this will encourage further progress in genetic psychology and all its applications.

Bärbel Inhelder,
University of Geneva

PREFACE

The eight volumes in the present series, *Piagetian Research*, together with the previous publication, *Piagetian Research: A Handbook of Recent Studies*, 1974, are intended to serve a wide range of needs for both teacher and learner at all levels: for university and college lecturers; post-graduate research students; those training to be educational psychologists; teachers and others following a wide range of advanced diploma courses; and education and psychology students at undergraduate level, following Educational and Developmental Psychology options. Research projects have been included which have implications for psychiatrists, paediatricians, rehabilitation and social workers.

In one sense, there are many authors to these volumes. The research evidence included is dependent on the countless efforts of Piaget's followers. In fairness, our gratitude is extended to those followers whose researches contribute immeasurably to the contents of these volumes. In particular, we acknowledge the cooperation of the many researchers personally communicating and forwarding papers for inclusion. Some collaborators have contributed material previously unpublished. These contributions, together with their accompanying correspondence, have resulted in a more comprehensive output.

We owe a very special debt of gratitude to Geneva University, and to universities here and abroad. Likewise, the inspiration of Professors Piaget and Inhelder, together with the general support of Professor Ruth Beard, Dr Gordon Cross, and Professor Marcel Goldschmid, are acknowledged.

It is an honour to have received such distinguished recognition for the volumes from Professor Bärbel Inhelder's gracious Foreword. We offer sincere thanks and gratitude for her interest and involvement and for the pleasant meeting in Geneva.

Enver Carim, an author in his own right as well as a perceptive editor, has provided the expertise necessary for such an ambitious series. Further to these more direct qualities Enver Carim has a profound philosophy with respect to a number of areas of knowledge including psychology and unusual drive and energy. We are indebted to him for all his support and acknowledge with gratitude the tremendous contributions he has made to this series.

Sohan Modgil
Celia Modgil
July 1976

INTRODUCTION

The eight volumes in the present series *Piagetian Research* together with the previous publication *Piagetian Research: A Handbook of Recent Studies*, 1974, are designed to make available a substantial number of Piaget-oriented researches that may be useful for immediate information as well as for long-term reference. The accelerating expansion of Piagetian research has led to an acute need for a source book more comprehensive than the ordinary textbook but more focused than the scattered periodical literature. More specifically, it should give the reader access to source materials that elaborate upon most Piagetian topics. Likewise, such volumes should offer students examples of a variety of approaches utilized by researchers in their efforts to investigate cognitive development. The numerous researches assembled present experimental subjects whose chronological ages range from birth to 98 years. The intended readership is therefore broad, from those interested in the very young, in adolescents, in the elderly.

The present volumes, as well as recording the replications and extensions of Piaget's work, include reflections on, speculations about, and analyses of the various problems of the theory. Hopefully, this should in turn provide inspiration for further elaboration, extension and revision. The research worker is provided with a broad spectrum of original sources from which an appreciation in depth of the theoretical, methodological and practical questions relevant to a Piagetian framework can be obtained. While it is conceded that a secondary source is not the ideal way to comprehend the theory, nevertheless it can provide the reader with a basic direction to the problem at hand.

The material gathered has been heavily drawn from University degree theses, published and unpublished researches up to and as recent as July 1976.* It became apparent that the subject matter was voluminous and that there were many ways to subdivide the Piagetian cognitive researches. In choosing the articles, the criteria were made as

---

*   The authors have been alert to studies appearing up to August 1976 (after the completion of the main manuscript) and brief details of further selected researches have been added in order to enrich particular areas of inquiry and discussion. Hopefully, researches within this category will receive full treatment in anticipated follow-up volumes.

objective as possible, while recognizing that a personal slant is bound to influence the selection. Despite an extensive search it is not unlikely that valuable articles have been overlooked. To these researchers apologies are extended. In assembling these researches the principal objective was to include only those which satisfy one of the following criteria: Piaget-oriented (replications or extensions); developmental in nature; or those which have discussed their findings within the Piagetian framework.

The tables of content reflect a broad range of studies, and represent most of the major subdivisions of Piagetian literature. It must be pointed out that while some articles fall naturally into certain specific volumes, others would have fitted simultaneously into more than one volume, this being in part due to the inability to distinguish between the analytic and synthetic. Consequently, it was difficult to select one single scheme that would satisfy all readers and many arbitrary decisions had to be made. There is obviously considerable reliance on the use of cross references.

The compilation covers fifteen areas, assembled in eight volumes — each volume focuses on one/two major aspects of Piaget's work. The main areas covered are: Piaget's Cognitive Theory and his major works, Sensorimotor Intelligence, Conservation, Training Techniques, Logic, Space, Handicapped Children, Cross-Cultural Research, The School Curriculum, Morality, Socialization, Test Development, Animism, Imagery and Memory.

Each volume consists of an integrated review of the range of recent studies followed by abstracts of these researches arranged, in the main, alphabetically. Where details of early research are essential to illustrate the evolution of a particular area of study, these are not represented by a full abstract, but are included in the introductory review. Although many cross references to related abstracts are included, the reviews preceding the abstracts are not intended to be fully critical of the validity and reliability of experimental design. This is partly due to the fact that, unless full details are available (sometimes these have neither been published fully, nor the definition of concepts made meaningful), this would be inimical, and partly because the amount of work involved in a critical evaluation of every study in a work of this breadth would be prohibitive.

In comparison to most publications, an unusual amount of detail of researches is made available, and to accompany this with an equal amount of discussion, although essential, could introduce complexity in the aims of the volumes. Some of the abstracts (indicated by an asterisk) have been written by the authors themselves and reproduced in their entirety. It is realized that some abstracts are of only marginal importance, yet their inclusion is essential to show general developmental patterns.

It is the authors' intention that the reader, having investigated the range of available material, would then consult the original research according to his specific interests. Advanced research depends a great deal on what sources and data are available for study, and there is a consequent tendency for some parts of the field to be ploughed over and over again, while others remain virtually untouched.

The list of references included at the end of each volume together form a comprehensive bibliography encompassing over 3,500 references. Volume One additionally includes a comprehensive survey of Piaget's works, arranged chronologically.

Every care has been taken to report the results of the researches as accurately as possible — any misinterpretation of the results is accidental. It must be conceded that all the studies included do not receive equal coverage. While the overall response to the circulated requests was excellent, some shortcomings in the volumes are due partly to some failure of response. While deficiencies of the final product are our own responsibility, they exist in spite of a number of advisers who gave their time generously.

Cross-Cultural Studies

a. Introduction

Piaget's views are that 'Cross-cultural research which is most important does not only concern child development but development in general including the final adult stages', (1966). However, with the evidence available so far, it is difficult to make any sweeping statements about the cross-cultural replication of Piaget's findings. Perhaps in no other area of psychology is there so much cross-cultural and cross-social class empirical research data available as on the Piagetian tasks. For example, Piagetian problems have been given to subjects in Alaska (Feldman, Lee, McLean, Pillemer, and Murray, 1974); Algeria (Bovet, 1972); Arabia (Hyde, 1959); Australia (De Lemos, 1969; Dasen 1972, 1974; Kelly, Tenezakis and Huntsman, 1973; Keats and Keats, 1974; Dasen, de Lacey and Seagrim, 1974; Philp and Kelly, 1974; Taylor and de Lacey, 1974); Canada (Dodwell, 1960, 1961; Laurendeau and Pinard, 1962); Central Africa (Heron and Simonsson, 1969; Heron, 1971; Deregowski and Serpell, 1972; Heron and Dowel, 1973, 1974); China (Cheng and Lee 1964); England (Lovell and Ogilvie, 1961; Modgil 1965a,b,c),; Guatemala (Lester and Klein, 1973); Holland (Goldschmid, Bentler and Modgil *et al.*, 1973); Hong Kong (Goodnow and Bethon, 1962); India (Jahoda, Deregowski and Sinha, 1974; Kale, 1974 / 1975; Abravanel, 1975); Iran (Mohseni, 1966; Al-Shaikh, 1973; Safar, 1974; Al-Fakhri, 1975); Israel (Furby, 1976); Italy (Peluffo, 1962); Jamaica (Vernon, 1965); Japan (Noro, 1961; Fujinaga, Saiga and Hosoya, 1963); Kenya (Mwangangi, 1975); Korea and Costa Rica (Youniss and Dean, 1974); Lebanon (Za'rour, 1971); Libya (Hamza, 1976); Mexico (Price-Williams, 1968); New Guinea (Prince, 1968; Waddell, 1968); New Zealand (Goldschmid, Bentler, Modgil *et al.*, 1973); Poland (Goldschmid, Bentler, Modgil *et al.* 1973); Senegal (Greenfield, 1966); Southern Mexico (Dempsey, 1971; Greenfield, 1974); Tanzania (Omari, 1975); Uganda (Goldschmid, Bentler, Modgil *et al.* 1973; Otaala, 1973); USA (Mermelstein and Shulman, 1967); West Africa (Price-Williams, 1961; Okonji, 1971; Lloyd, 1971; Piller, 1971) and West Berlin (Heron and Kroeger, 1974).

The major periods in the cognitive development of the child were regarded by Piaget as universal progressions through which all children move at about the same pace. However, studies of cross-cultural and subcultural variations have not always substantiated such an interpretation. This led Piaget (1972) to suggest that the speed of progression is not the same under all social conditions, but may produce retardation in deprived and accelerations in stimulating environments. Differences are generally marked at the later periods of development. In the early periods, the progression seems to be most uniform.

Dasen (1973) analysed the question of the universality of Piagetian cognitive structures and concluded that 'the development of the sensorimotor and concrete operational stage is universal, at least from a qualitative point of view (the structure of the stages and their succession). On the other hand, ... studies ... show the cultural relativism of Piagetian cognitive structures; ... speed of development of concrete operations change as a function of acculturation and ecological and cultural needs, which enhance certain cognitive areas over others', p. 149.

Dasen (1975) extended Berry's (1971) model of ecological functionalism to Piagetian developmental psychology. It was hypothesized that the rate of development of concrete operations was partly determined by ecological and cultural factors. 'In particular, if three subsistence-economy populations are placed on an ecocultural scale, with low food-accumulating, nomadic, hunting groups at one extreme, and high food-accumulating, sedentary, agriculturalist groups at the other extreme, the former are expected to develop spatial concepts more rapidly than will the latter, whereas the sedentary group is expected to attain concepts of conservation of quantity, weight, and volume more rapidly than nomadic groups will', p. 156. The results generally supported the model in a study involving 190 children, aged six through 14 years from three cultural groups: Canadian Eskimos, Australian Aborigines, and Ebrié Africans. (Details are given later.)

Likewise Heron (1974) concluded, 'I find myself increasingly inclined to the view that the apparent unity of (the concrete operational) stage has been generated by the cognitively-relevant cultural homogeneity in development of the children serving as subjects in most European and North American studies', p. 100. In continuation, Heron and Dowel (1974) maintained, 'There seems a good case for not regarding the concrete operations stages as a formal unity: it may be more productive to view it as a set of structures without necessary interdependence', p. 8.

More recently, Dasen (1976, personal communication)* maintains, 'Two difficulties remain with the universalist position. Even if studies with more adequate experimental situations or studies taking an emic approach were to demonstrate the universal existence of Piaget's last stage (and the same is true of the other stages), the cultural relativists could maintain the following objections: (i) Working from within Piaget's theory, and with the usual methodology linked to it, it seems difficult to find anything but data supporting the theory. The typical research demonstrates either the presence of a certain structure, or its absence (but negative results are conspicuously non-interpretable), and there is little room to find an alternative structure. Preiswerk (1976), for example, doubts the validity of the universal sequence of stages on the following grounds: In the cross-cultural situation, the validity of a finding cannot be judged from its multiple verification. The researchers are all from the same Western macro-culture and even the recent work of their non-Western colleagues suffers from the same induced ethnocentrism. (ii) The demonstration that all individuals are able to reason according to a certain structure does not prove that this is their usual or preferred mode of reasoning. In fact we may not be adequately sampling the culturally relevant skills (Berry, 1974). What we may be asking, is the question "How well can *they* do *our* tricks?", whereas what we should be asking is "How well can *they* do *their* tricks?" (Wober, 1969, as quoted in Berry, 1974)', pp. 10–11.

Likewise, Price-Williams (1975) suggested, ' . . . that a mode of thought may exist which does in fact not sharply distinguish intellect and emotion, logic and rhetoric and so forth. It does not follow from this theory that such thought processes are primitive, nor that people who adopt this thinking cannot adopt strict logical criteria when the situation warrants . . . What seems to be at the bottom of the difficulty of understanding this type of thought is that "logic", "intellect", and "abstraction" are in fact terms which obey certain rules. We like to think that these rules fall along a continuum of development, both phylogenetic and ontogenetic. In addition, this path of development is regarded as unilineal, and any deviation from it perceived as inferior. Some people are now suspecting that parallel lines of development exist: that certain spheres of human activity require one kind of thinking, others demand other kinds of thinking, and each has its own set of rules . . . further suspicion arises that what has been hitherto demanded as "primitive thinking" may indeed be quite sophisticated, and that the reason such thought has been labelled inferior is that we have no understanding of it', p. 82.

---

* Gratitude is extended to Dr P.R. Dasen of Geneva University for sending the work to be referenced.

There are problems in interpreting results from cross-cultural studies, partly because of the differences in language and partly due to experience and cultural values. If differences are observed, it is not easy to interpret or account for the cause of the differences. Furby (1971) has provided a theoretical framework for interpreting cross-cultural studies of conservation by distinguishing between manual and automated environments, on the one hand, and empirical and magical types of reasoning on the other.

b. Conservation

Among the early attempts to replicate Piaget's contentions on a cross-cultural basis, is Hyde's (1959) study. She repeated many of Piaget's tasks with a multiracial group of children in Aden. The results described by Piaget were generally confirmed. In her study there was some indication that quantity (substance and liquid) was easier than weight and volume, but the results of individual subjects suggested that the sequence was not invariable. There was therefore no support for the theory that the concepts of substance, weight and volume were invariably acquired in that order. (Fuller details appear in Hyde, 1959; Lunzer, 1960 and Flavell, 1963, pp. 383, 387.)

An experimental study of the development of the concept of quantitative conservation of substance, weight and volume was investigated in 264 Iraqi children aged from four to 14 years by Al-Shaikh (1973). The tasks were administered individually and the general procedure was identical to Elkind (1961). The general tendency of the results confirmed Piaget's findings with regard to the development of the concept of conservation progressively with age. No sex differences were computed. The F-ratio for the type of question was 8.02 and was significant beyond the .01 level. T-tests indicated that explanation was more difficult than judgment or prediction for small children. The F-ratio for the type of quantity obtained was better than chance expectations (F = 42.64; $p > .01$). T-tests for the means of conservation responses of substance, weight and volume revealed that they were significantly different from each other ($p > .01$). Differences among age-level were found to be significant beyond the .01 level (F = 31.92). Analysis of variance for the interaction between type of quantity and age-level supported Piaget's theory concerning the development of the concept of conservation of substance, weight and volume in three stages (F = 6.93, $p > .01$). Iraqi children exhibited mental operations similar to those stated by Piaget such as reversibility, identity and composition. (Details are given later.)

The Concept Assessment Kit Conservation (Goldschmid and Bentler, 1968b) was administered to 250 children — 25 boys and girls from each age group from four to eight years — in each of the following countries: Australia, England, Holland, New Zealand, Poland, and Uganda (Goldschmid, Bentler, Debus, Kohnstamm, Modgil *et al.*, 1973). Age trends in conservation development for both males and females were fairly consistent from culture to culture. The rate of conservation acquisition differed somewhat across the samples studied. These variations were most likely due to specific environmental differences among the groups compared. The Concept Assessment Kit appeared to be a reliable indicator of conservation across several cultural groups. (Details appear later.)

Swize (1972) was intent to determine the relationship between Piagetian conservation operativity and the resulting composite score and the predictor variables of SES, ethnic background, primary language used in the home, nursery school, New Nursery School, Head Start, kindergarten, CA, MA, IQ, sex, arithmetic, spelling, and reading achievement. The sample consisted of 70 second grade Mexican — American and Anglo-American children who were administered the following tests: Columbia Mental Maturity Scale; Concept Assessment Kit Conservation (Goldschmid and Bentler, 1968b); and the Metropolitan Achievement Test. Socioeconomic level of the family of each of the Ss was determined by the administration of Warner's Index of Status Characteristics. The data was subjected to the Pearson product-moment correlation and the multiple linear regression. Results indicated that enrolment in the New Nursery School and Head Start correlated significantly but negatively at the .05 level with the ability to conserve two-dimensional space. No predictor variables related significantly with number conservation operativity. High scores on Arithmetic and Reading Achievement correlated significantly at the .05 level with continuous quantity conservation operativity. Attendance in Head Start related significantly positively at the .05 level with continuous quantity conservation operativity. Enrolment in nursery school and higher MA related significantly with weight conservation operativity. Enrolment in the New Nursery School and Head Start related negatively and significantly at the .05 level with the ability to conserve discontinuous quantity. Higher scores on reading achievement related significantly at the .05 level with the composite score. (Details are given later.)

The relationship between age-grouping of subjects and performance on Piagetian conservation tasks was studied by Firlik (1975) in 108 children between the ages of six and seven drawn from Britain and the United States. The Ss were pre-tested on the Goldschmid and Bentler (1968b) Conservation Kit. In each country equal numbers of children were randomly assigned to either mixed-age, same-age, or independent treatments. The three-member groups, both same-age and mixed-age, were asked to reach consensus on their responses. Ss working independently answered the same questions. After receiving the treatment for seven days, Ss were post-tested on an alternate form of the Conservation Kit. A significant relationship existed between mixed-age grouping and performance on conservation tasks. The mixed-age groups performed significantly better than same-age and independent Ss. However, no significant relationship was computed between performance on the criterion measure and country of residence. (Details follow.)

Heron and Simonsson (1969) demonstrated that between 40 and 50 per cent of a sample of urban Zambian subjects could not demonstrate the ability to conserve weight by the time they left primary school (median stated age 15 years). Heron and Dowel (1973) corroborated this finding in a sample of Papuan high school children (median stated age 13 years). These authors also confirmed the findings by Heron (1971) that there appeared to be little connection in the Zambian sample between the presence or absence of weight conservation performance and independent measures of achievement and logical thinking. In continuation therefore, to obtain data in a different cultural setting from that of Zambia (Heron, 1971) concerning the ability of children to conserve weight and to explore the relationship between this conservation performance and that on reasoning tasks of the kind used in non-verbal psychometric tests, Heron and Dowel (*op. cit.*) tested 109 children (Papuan) ranging in age from 10 to 16 years. Conservation of weight was patterned after Heron and Simonsson (1969). Reasoning was evaluated by three sets of six matrix tasks. No sex differences were noted. Fifty per cent of the sample demonstrated weight operativity (as in Zambian sample). Little relationship between weight conservation and matrix-reasoning performance was observed. (Details appear later.) With respect to Heron's (1971) study, Ashton (1975) argued, 'The validity of Heron's study is questionable, considering the small number of subjects and the lack of comparability of tests and procedures', p. 480.

Heron and Dowel's (1974) study showed a 45 per cent operativity for the conservation of volume and may be compared with those of Peluffo (1967): children aged 11–12 years living in 'an underdeveloped milieu' in Sardinia demonstrated 30 per cent conserving volume, while in children immigrated to Genoa from Southern Italy — for at least three years the nine-year-old figure was 40 per cent; 'very recent' immigrants gave 35 per cent at both nine and 11 years. With respect to multiple classification in the Heron and Dowel study the overall percentage of operativity performances for the four two-attribute tasks was 69. For the four three-attribute it reached 47 per cent. De Lacey's (1969) results for children aged eight years five months and seven years five months are comparable to Heron and Dowel's.

Bowd (1975) administered Piagetian tasks for the conservation of length and volume to two groups of seven- and eight-year-old Canadian Indian and white children (ns = 35, 33). No significant difference across groups for the conservation of length was computed. However, conservation of volume and the ability to conserve both length and volume resulted in a higher proportion of successful performances for the white group. (Details follow.)

A comparative study of Libyan and American children's conservation status in a sample of 86 Libyan children was undertaken by Hamza (1976) and 25 first, second, and third grade teachers assigned to teach in these schools. Libyan boys' and girls' status of conservation was equivalent, and American normative scores were higher than the scores of Libyan children. Further, the Libyan teachers advanced accurate descriptions as to the age at which Libyan children demonstrated conservation operativity. (Details follow.)

i. Conservation and language

Studies such as Darcy (1963), Lambert and Macnamara (1969), Peel and Lambert (1962), and Macnamara (1966) have examined the performance of bilingual children in which language development has been related to varied aspects of intellectual functioning. However, 'the problem of the role of language in the acquisition of concepts of conservation in bilinguals has usually been examined in a static situation rather than in one which attempts to manipulate the child's knowledge of concepts (Gallagher, 1971; Kelly, 1970). However, there are now sufficient studies to show that methods exist for inducing the acceptance of conservation in a considerable proportion of children who are of an appropriate age but who did not accept this concept before training. The method used by Bearison (1969) has by now been replicated sufficiently to produce some confidence in its effectiveness (see, for example, Gow, 1971)', Keats and Keats (1974, p. 81). Keats and Keats were therefore intent to determine whether and to what extent logical concepts acquired by bilingual Ss in one language can be generalized to a second language. All children were non-conservers on the concept of weight and included 35 Ss bilingual in Polish and English, 31 children bilingual in German and English, and a control group of 34 Australian children. Pre-testing in one language followed training in the acquisition of the concept of weight using the other, then post-testing in the previous language. Delayed post-tests were administered four weeks later in both languages. The results demonstrated 'that the concept was acquired in either language and with some transfer to other concepts thereby substantiating the Piagetian standpoint that a concept may be considered independently from the language by which it is acquired.' 'Interference between language was indicated in the German group in that the earlier they had learned English, the poorer was their final performance in both languages', p. 80. (Fuller details of the study appear later.) In extending their 1974 work, Keats, Keats and Rafaei (1976) pre-tested in both languages, a group of five-year-old Malaysian children bilingual in English and Malay and English and Chinese. They were then trained in one language on the conservation of weight, post-tested on their other language, and again from one to two months later in both languages. 'Immediate improvements were obtained after training, but other untrained control groups also showed improvement on the delayed post-test.' It was concluded that 'language plays a minor part in the acquisition of cognitive concepts and that young children will perform at a slightly higher level on these tasks if tested in their native language.' (Details follow.)

Conservation behaviour in children exposed to two cultures was examined by Kelly, Tenezakis, and Huntsman (1973). Greek migrant children in Sydney (NSW) schools taught with English as the medium of instruction were administered the test of conservation of number and length. The tests were given in both English and Greek. The Ss were pre-tested in both languages to make sure that the children understood the relational terms used in the conservation tests. 'Twenty-five per cent of children who passed the language pre-tests and failed to conserve in English, did show conservation when subsequently tested in Greek but again failed to conserve in a post-test in English. This finding is not in accord with Piaget's view of the interrelationships of language and cognition' p. 181. (Details are given later.).

The results of Kelly and Philp, 1975, (discussed in a later section) are similar to the findings of Kelly, Tenezakis and Huntsman (*op. cit.*) and Keats and Keats (*op. cit.*), though children in both these studies possessed equivalent terms in both their languages. 'It points to the importance of the choice of language of instruction in the school both for adequacy of vocabulary and "generalizability" to life outside the school where a different language is used. It may be that here, too, a great awareness of the structures of the vernacular language and culture can assist generalization for the school life to the community life', (Kelly and Philp, p. 197).

Tenezakis (1975) compared data obtained in Australia among Greek—English bilinguals and English monoglots with Sinclair-de-Zwart's (1967, 1969) findings on the relationship between cognitive and linguistic development. The major results were concerned with '(1) The equivalence of all groups on the conservation task; (2) The infrequent use of relational terms and the frequent use of coordinated syntax, by both conservers and non-conservers in all groups; (3) for Greek children in grades one and two the better performance on the comprehension task when tested in English rather than in Greek; and (4) the pattern of relationships between language and conservation tasks.' (Details follow.)

At the University of Southern California School for Early Childhood Education, the primary goal of research has been to identify ways of enhancing the acquisition of representational thought in young children. Smart, Dahl and Wetzstein's (1975) study involved 82 three-, four-, and five-year-olds (38 Mexican-Americans, 35 Black, 9 White / Other). Among the results, there was significance in the amount of spontaneous language as a function of ethnicity: Mexican-American children verbalized less than the other groups. There was a tendency to verbalize spontaneously more frequently during 'water play' for Blacks and during 'cooking' for Mexican-Americans. (Details follow.)

In continuation, Wetzstein and Smart (1976) in a study entitled, 'Mexican–American preschoolers' acquistion of English in a Piagetian oriented school', argued that there was little evidence in the literature on the acquisition of English by monolingual Spanish speaking children from a Piagetian view point. Among the findings, there was evidence which suggested that language used for egocentric purposes was typically in English and that when the child communicated with others, he used English or Spanish depending on whom he addressed and on the topic discussed. (Details follow later.)

In an ongoing study entitled, 'A cross-ethnic study of language and cognitive ability', Klippel's (1976) study has been evolved from Piaget's theory that classification and seriation are prerequisites for the development of logical thinking and from Bruner's emphasis on the categorical and hierarchical properties of language. Two ethnic groups (N = 120) are being studied: Maori (Polynesian, native of New Zealand) and European. 'Each child will be assessed on his (her) ability to classify and seriate and analyses will be carried out on the recorded language related to these tasks'. (Details follow.)

c. Spatial and Geometric Concepts

Beard's (1963) study (Part One) drew a sample of Ghanaian children ranging in age from eight to 11 years. A comparison was made with a sample of English children. She points out that the ages of the English children were somewhat younger than those of the Ghanaians. She argues, 'if maturity rather than schooling or experience, was an important factor in the acquisition of mathematical concepts we would expect the Ghanaian sample to excel'. The results indicated that in tests of concepts of number, quantity and of mechanical arithmetic, the range of mean scores for the schools in the two samples was roughly the same. However, the mean for all the English sample significantly exceeded the mean for all the Ghanaian sample. The increase in score with age was significantly greater for the English than for the Ghanaian sample. In tests of spatial concepts, the English sample greatly excelled the Ghanaian children and it was suggested that the environment of English children favoured the development of spatial concepts. Similarly Vernon's (1966) Eskimo subjects performed at higher levels of perceptual-spatial operativity in relation to West Indians and Canadian Indians. Vernon argues that the training that the Eskimo children have in tracking and in locating objects may have been a contributory factor in this respect. This kind of result may suggest that good spatial performances may occur without a high level of schooling. Such a finding gives impetus to the question as to the kinds of experiences which contribute to the particular kinds of skills. This lends credence to Piaget and Inhelder's statement (1967, p. 296), 'the child who is familiar with folding and unfolding paper shapes through his work at school is two or three years in advance of children who lack this experience'. Vernon (1969) administered a battery of individual and group tests to 50 Canadian Eskimo boys within the age range from 10 to 12 years. He attempted to delineate meaningful clusters of abilities as reflected in the test results and to relate performance to environmental factors. The poor performance of both Indians and Eskimos on an arithmetic achievement test was attributed to the use of the highly verbal new mathematics in the schools. The Eskimos were only slightly below average on spelling, comprehension and usage and group vocabulary tests. However, their scores on the Terman-Merill individual vocabulary test were quite low. Vernon stated that, despite the verbal fluency they showed, the Eskimos were impaired in their ability to think and learn in English. The Eskimos performed at the higher levels on a set of spatial tests, including Kohs Blocks, picture recognition, and an embedded figures test. (Fuller details are given in *Intelligence and Cultural Environment*, 1969.)

Some pictorial artifacts in studies of African children's pictorial depth perception were studied by Omari and MacGinitie (1974) using two versions of Hudson's (1960) pictures — the original version used in previous studies of pictorial depth perception in developing countries, and a revised version, using the same depth cues but with familiar characters in neutral poses. Results demonstrated that the revised-version scores were higher and increased with grade level. Original version scores were low for children in all grades (one, three, five, and seven). Urban children scored higher than remote area children. (Details appear later.)

Cousins and Abravanel (1971) administered children with a standard and two comparison shapes so constructed that matching could be either on a topological or a Euclidean basis. 'One series comprised regular geometrical shapes, while the other, irregular forms. With the former, testing children between three years 10 months and five years four months, a large majority of matches was according to Euclidean features; in the case of the irregular series there was a trend, falling short of significance, away from topological matches with increasing age. Unfortunately these findings are difficult to interpret, for each choice was bound to appear either topological or Euclidean, when in fact the even split among the youngest children looks suspiciously like random behaviour. Moreover, the instruction to select the picture "most like" the standard is of doubtful validity with such young Ss, as indicated by the work of Taylor and Wales (1970) . . . Cousins and Abravanel made the suggestion that the tendency to respond differentially to the two series may have been a function of experience, i.e., greater familiarity with Euclidean shapes in the nursery school environment . . . Further explanation of the possibility calls for a cross-cultural approach with children of widely varying backgrounds. So far very little seems to have been done along these lines. Cowley and Murray (1962) dealt with the development of spatial concepts in Zulu children, and their work was followed up by Page (1973) who studied concepts of length and distance among schooled and unschooled Zulu youths. He suggested that rural youths were more likely to retain a topological concept of space', Jahoda, Deregowski, and Sinha (1974, p. 160). These latter authors, therefore were intent to investigate 'whether the spatial-perceptual difficulties experienced in some cultures could be partly accounted for in terms of a persistence of predominantly topological functioning. An oddity-choice task was devised consisting of one set of regular and another of irregular figures such that responses could be classified as topological (T), Euclidean (E), or "unrelated" (U), the last indicating failure to categorize figures consistently'. The sample comprised 415 children aged from four to twelve years and were drawn from Hong Kong, India, Scotland and Zambia. Highly significant cultural and subcultural differences were computed but few significant age trends were noted. 'Contrary to expectation, T responses were roughly constant while the proportion of both E and U responses showed systematic cross-cultural variations. There was evidence that it is U responses rather than the proportions of E responses which directly reflect spatial ability', (*ibid.*, p. 159). (Details appear later.)

The developmental order of spatial concepts among 240 school children (grades one, three, five, and seven) were studied by Omari (1975). The Piagetian concepts involved conservation of area, conservation of distance, and the concept of horizontality in the coordinate reference system. The developmental sequence at nearly all grade levels was: conservation of distance, conservation of area, and the acquisition of the concept of horizontality in the coordinate reference system. A stagewise progression was computed, but each stage was achieved at a later age as compared to the Geneva norms. Omari argued, 'that the acquisition of these concepts in children is a function of the spatial dimensions involved in each concept, and that environmental factors retard the developmental tempo of spatial concepts among the African children', p. 444. (Details follow.)

The results of the concept of horizontal and vertical demonstrated that the Iraqi children pass through the same stages designated by Piaget and Inhelder (1956) but with a lag of three years when compared with the Genevan subjects, Al-Fakhri (1975). This lag was attributed to cultural factors.

Children's conception of territory: a study of Piaget's spatial stages was undertaken by Stoltman (1972). A sample of 204 North Georgia children stratified by grade (one–six), sex, race, and urban–rural residence were administered 'an evaluation instrument incorporating Piagetian tasks'. The Ss did not conform to the Piagetian stages. 'Significant differences (p < .001) were found between observed frequencies of children and the theoretically expected. Closest conformity between the observed and expected occurred with those children eight years of age and younger ... the decentration of the American sample was slower than that theorized by Piaget ... No significant differences were attributed to the main effects of sex and rural—urban residence. A significant difference (p < .01) was found between the black and white Ss ... this difference is probably attributed to the socioeconomic variable rather than an effect of race. Age of the child and socioeconomic status of parents were significantly related to the children's conception of territory (p < .01). The multiple relationship between the independent variables, age, and SES, and performance on the evaluation instrument was .71 (p < .01)'. (Details appear later.)

The development of the concept of conservation of length among 235 Iraqi school children aged between five and 13 years was investigated by Al-Shaikh (1974). The tasks, individually administered were the conservation of length (the length of lines and the coincidence of their extremities); and the conservation of length (comparison of length and change of position). No sex differences were noted. The mean of the conservation responses were significantly different with regard to explanation *vs.* judgment (p > .01). Iraqi children lagged about three years behind Swiss and English children with regard to the acquisition of the concept. The three stages were discovered. The onset of the first stage was about five to six years, the onset of the second stage was about seven to eight and the onset of the third stage was about 10 years. It was found that Iraqi children had used the same arguments which were described by Piaget to explain their judgments. (Details follow.)

A series of studies were conducted by Al-Fakhri (1975a, 1975c) to investigate the development of the Piagetian concepts of length, and continuous quantity, among 180 Iraqi children, aged from four to 12 years. Three stages were distinguished in the development of the concept of length. The first stage was characterized by the non-conservation of length, which was noted among children ages four to eight years. The second stage was a transitional stage where the children exhibited hesitation regarding the conservation of length in one case but not another, and even when they denied conservation, they remained hesitant and took a different stance when compared to the younger children. During the third stage, children exhibited conservation of length. This phenomenon appeared at the age of 10 amongst 50 per cent of the sample, and it rose to 85 per cent at the age of 11. The remaining 15 per cent were in the transitional stage. The onset of the formation of the concept of length seemed to lag about two years when compared to the Swiss children. The results of the concept of the conservation of continuous quantity were similar to the general studies with regard to the sequence of stages. Al-Fakhri's results were similar to those of Za'rour (1971) in Lebanon where the concept was found to appear during the age of nine. This indicated that Iraqi children like the Lebanese children seemed to lag about two years behind the Genevan children. This lag was attributed to cultural differences including education.

d. Logic

Results of the concept of class-inclusion demonstrated that the concept was formed in accordance with the stages designated by Piaget (Al-Fakhri, 1975b). The onset of the formation of the concept, however, showed a lag of two years when compared to the Genevan children. (Details follow.)

The development of some logical concepts among Iraqi children was examined by Safar (1974) from lower middle class within the age range from four to 12 years. Piagetian tasks of serial correspondence and seriation were used. Results indicated that the concept of seriation and serial correspondence developed gradually in children. The process of growth demonstrated three stages: the first stage was between four- to eight-years-old where the concept was not acquired; the second, between eight to 11, was a transitional stage, while the third stage, in which the concept formation was complete, started at 11 years of age. Results obtained through following a special teaching method confirmed the possibility of accelerating the growth of the seriation concept provided the child was in a transitional stage. The sample group lagged about three years of growth behind the western children of the same age. (Details follow.)

Conservation, seriation and classification as factors in the acquisition of mathematics in 120 Nigerian children aged between four and eight years were examined by Omotoso (1975). Two teacher-made tests were administered to children of age groups five, six and seven years. The Piagetian tests included length, volume, number, seriation and classification. A strong relationship was computed between mathematics achievement and all the Piagetian tasks — the latter tasks predicted mathematics achievement better for boys than for girls. Nigerian children demonstrated operativity around CA eight years.

Whether verbal ability, sex, grade, and age predicted success on Piagetian classification and seriation skills in a sample of Mexican-American and Anglo-American children (N = 60), was examined by

Wisener (1976). These predictor variables were successful in predicting the composite classification score only. However, when taken in isolation such variables proved ineffective. The single best predictor of classification performance was found to be verbal ability. (Details follow.)

The development of logical thinking (classification) in 128, three- to six-year-old Zambian children from two different socioeconomic groups was studied by Okonji (1974). The stimuli comprised pieces of wooden geometric shapes which also varied in colour and size. Sorting was done under two conditions: free sorting and guided sorting. Results demonstrated that 'these children were not yet able to form true classes as expected in the light of Piaget's theory. It was observed, however, that "graphic collections" were not a dominant feature of these children's classificatory performance. The usefulness of designating a substage of the growth of logic as the stage of graphic collections is questioned, especially if it is intended to be a universal descriptive category. The need for longitudinal studies or cross-sectional studies covering from age two to beyond 11 is stressed to streamline and strengthen the evidence from Africa suggesting that in overall pattern it is not different from the pattern observed elsewhere by Piaget and others'.

In a study entitled, 'Perceptual set induction in young children: cross-cultural support for the role of active classification', Abravanel (1975) tested four-and five-year-old Indian children (N = 120) where the method of perceptual-set induction involved a procedure of contrastive classification that had been attempted only once before with an American sample of subjects. The results demonstrated the formation of perceptual sets in pre-school age children. The evidence provided a firmer basis for conceptualization and the author considered the findings in connection with contemporary ideas about symbolic mediation and production deficiencies in children's memory and thinking. Abravanel asserted, 'Likewise, many of Piaget's (1952, 1967) demonstrations of how young children fail to conserve quantitative properties of matter (such as length, mass or weight) illustrate a propensity to consider successive events in a rather unrelated fashion that ignores important interconnections. Instead of attending to changing events and integrating successive transformations of length or mass, non-conserving children appear to treat each state of a sequence as a detached "tableau". Thus, we note findings from a number of diverse investigations indicating that the young child does not as readily forge links among segments of new information, even when they might provide a way of ordering and organizing information. Yet, a few years later, rehearsal strategies for recall, easy acquisition of perceptual sets, and ability to coordinate changes in fundamental properties of matter, become much more evident', pp. 162—163. (Details follow.)

The reported capacity of weight non-conservers to deal successfully with tasks involving multiple classification was undertaken by Heron and Dowel (1974). Forty-nine Yugoslav children (median age 10.5 years) in Australian schools, were tested on the Piagetian tests of seriation, class-inclusion, conservation of quantity, weight and volume, and eight multiple classification tasks. The language of administration was Serbo-Croat. 'Performance on most of these tests of concrete operational behaviour was found to be about two years retarded as compared with Genevan data. On seven of the eight multiple classification tasks, not less than one-third of non-conservers of weight were able to give operational solutions. No differences were found in this group of 22 non-conservers, in terms of success *vs.* non-success in multiple classification, in age, sex, urban / rural domicile of origin, more / less recent arrival in Australia, or Macedonian / Serbian ethnicity. It is concluded that a case can be made for not regarding the concrete operations stage as a formal unity, but instead (following Flavell and Wohlwill) as a set of structures without necessary interdependence', (*ibid.*, p. 1). (Details of the study are given later.)

In continuing the study of Heron and Dowel, Heron and Kroeger (1974) investigated the effects of training on uneven concrete operational development in 109 Yugoslav migrant children (age range nine to 13 years) who had been in West Berlin between six months and five years (median 3.4 years). The sample was pre-tested in Piagetian tasks of conservation (quantity, weight, volume); class-inclusion; dichotomous and multiple classification. Experimental and control groups were formed for training and post-testing (nine weeks) on conservation and multiple classification, as required. 'On conservation training no training effect claimed, as gains by experimental and control groups were not significantly different: on multiple classification a highly significant training effect was evident at nine weeks, with significant generalization to selected items from Raven's Progressive Matrices'. At the conclusion of the experiment the presence or absence of weight conservation performance was 'both unaccounted for, and essentially independent of cognitive performance in other domains (including school mathematics grades)'. Previous findings by Heron and Dowel (1974, *op. cit.*) were confirmed in respect of length of residence in the host country on performance in multiple classification. (Details are given later.)

e. Familiarity with the Stimulus Materials/Experience

Price-Williams' (1961) study with West African Bush children of the Tiv tribe comprised five groups each of nine illiterate children. Ss were tested on the question of conservation of continuous and discontinuous quantities. Price-Williams admits some difficulties in ascertaining the child's exact chronological age. He stresses too, that mastery of the language was not sufficient to allow follow-up questions of the type which the Piagetian tasks demand, other than the question 'why?' Results indicated that the progression of the idea of conservation paralleled that found in European and other Western children. However, Furby (1971, p. 244) maintains that, 'there is a very common game among the Tiv children which seems very much like a conservation task — in fact, the child may learn task-specific responses that allow him to perform well in the conservation task since it is so similar'. Okonji (1971a, p. 127) elaborates on this common game and maintains 'Price-Williams (1961) might not have claimed that as Tiv children had no formal instruction in concepts of abstract numbers, there is much to be said for the neurophysiological interpretation of readiness for dealing with such concepts if he had taken into account the possible effect of engaging in a game involving the placing of seeds in rows of six holes which is common in most parts of Africa (it is called Omweso or Ekyeso in Uganda, Owar in Ghana and Okwe in Iboland). Such a game enjoyed by both adults and children requires some understanding of number concepts'. Uzgiris (1964) found that there were appreciable differences in the ability to conserve when the tasks dealt with different materials and that these differences were not constant across individuals and materials. Lloyd (1971, described later) argues that in Price-Williams' study standard Western materials were not employed as a control in investigating conservation of quantity. (Price-Williams', 1961, study is described more fully in *Cross-Cultural*

Studies, edited by Price-Williams, 1969.)

In another investigation, Price-Williams (1962) found moderate differences due to length of schooling in tasks requiring classificatory strategies. He stresses familiarity of materials as influencing level of performance. Nigerian children performed at a higher level of operating relative to English children in classifying and abstracting the common features of indigenous plants. However, the Nigerian subjects performed at a lower level of Piagetian operativity with animals which were considered to play a less meaningful role in everyday living. Okonji (1971) comments, 'Price-Williams (1962) used familiar indigenous objects for studying classification among the Tiv of Northern Nigeria. Following this example, Kellaghan (1965) used local materials for the investigation of classificatory behaviour among some western Nigerian Yoruba children. These studies showed for the first time that when appropriate test materials are used the African children involved were not qualitatively different from their European counterparts in their abstract attitude. Although the results of these studies are important they do not throw any light on the nature of the effect of familiarity on test performance in different cultural groups'. Okonji's study attempted to fulfil such an objective. He examined the effects of familiarity on classificatory behaviour. Two hundred and forty-three Ibusa and Glasgow children (CA six to 12 years) were administered two classificatory tasks. Although the degrees of familiarity influenced classificatory behaviour in some aspects, the overall developmental trends in both the tasks were similar in both samples. (Details are given in Modgil, 1974, pp. 248–249.)

The finding of no differences between Western and non-Western partly-related study. Deregowski and Serpell (1972) demonstrated that Zambian children did not differ significantly from the Scots on re-sorting of toys. However, the Zambian subjects performed at the lower levels of classification than the Scots, when re-sorting colour or black-and-white photographs of these toys.

Uzgiris, (1964, *op. cit.*) found that performance varied with changes in stimulus materials for several conservation tasks (substance, weight, and volume) and suggested that past experiences may account for such situational specific responses. In continuation, Calhoun (1971) and Lovell, Healey, and Rowland (1962) have employed the concept of stimulus familiarity to account for discrepancies in the sequence of development of conservation as advanced by the Geneva school.

Goodnow and Bethon's (1966) study (described in the 'schooled' / 'unschooled' variable section) found bright children matched for MA performing equally well as normal and retarded children. However this result was not corroborated by Brown (1973). She argues that 'The difference in results may be attributed to the fact that in . . . (her) study a critical MA (six years) was established and then used to determine the MA match. The effects of lack of experience may have been masked in the Goodnow and Bethon study by the selection of MA levels not critically related to the conservation tasks studied', p. 379.

Issues concerning the effect of familiar and alien materials, age, and culture on conservation behaviour of Yoruba children were investigated by Lloyd (1971). Conservation operativity among Yoruba subjects was observed at the same age as their counterparts in other cultures. Performance was similar with familiar and with alien materials, 'although it improved with practice'. (Details appear in Modgil, 1974, pp. 245–247.)

The developmental ability of 224 Lebanese children to conserve number and liquid was examined with regard to the effect of age, sex, religion, socioeconomic status, scholastic level and mother's literacy (Za'rour, 1971). Such an ability increased significantly with age. Sex was the only other variable which yielded a difference significant at the .05 level in number conservation. This contradicted Dodwell's (1961) study and the Almy *et al.* (1966) study but confirmed Goldschmid's (1967) possible explanation that ' . . . boys in their play activities have more opportunity to manipulate objects and perceive them after different transformations than girls do'. (Details are given in Modgil, 1974, pp. 251–253.)

In continuation, Za'rour's (1971a) study was designed to investigate the effects of materials, age, sex, scholastic level and mother's literacy on weight conservation behaviour of Lebanese children. The results indicated that for the seven- to nine-year-old children, it was easier to conserve weight on plasticine rather than on a rubber band or on alcohol in a thermometer. (Details given in Modgil, 1974, pp. 253–254.)

Price-Williams and Gordon (1969) reported that children from pottery-making families in Mexico conserved at earlier ages on a conservation of matter task using clay than did children from similar but non-pottery making families. Lester and Klein (1973) asserted 'it is not clear, however, whether these differences in performance were due to differential familiarity with the stimulus materials or to basic differences in cognitive capacity stemming from the greater experience of the children from the pottery-making families in the manipulation of clay', p. 198. Lester and Klein therefore studied the effect of stimulus familiarity on the conservation performance of rural Guatemalan children. The 40 Ss at five and seven years of age were tested and then retested four weeks later on conservation tasks of continuous quantity, matter, area (familiar stimulus material), and area (unfamiliar stimulus material). Performance on the area conservation task with familiar stimulus materials was observed to be at higher levels of operativity when compared to the area task with unfamiliar materials, as well as to the other conservation tasks. Conservation performance likewise showed enhancement from first to second testing. The age at which conservation operativity occurs and the sequence of development of different conservation abilities was affected by the use of familiar stimulus materials. The authors discussed the importance of retesting in cross-cultural research. (Fuller details are given later.)

Otaala (1973) administered a battery of conservation, seriation, and classification tasks to 160 rural Iteso children of Uganda. Four age groups of children were tested in their native language and all tasks comprised test materials from the immediate area (clay, pebbles, etc). Results provided better support for Piaget's claim regarding the sequential achievement of logical thought than it did for the synchronous development of abilities within major stages. The most interesting aspect of this research concerned the influence of Iteso belief in magic and superstition upon their children's performance on the Piagetian tasks. Otaala pointed out, for example, the children's conservation performance involving clay might well have been influenced by the prevalent belief that if children used clay excessively, they would develop hunchbacks.

Greenfield's (1974) study on cognitive processes among the Zinacantecos of Southern Mexico focused on the role of familiarity and cultural relevance in the development of categorization behaviour. Results demonstrated that, 'The ability to use verbal concepts in sorting and resorting an array of objects developed with age in both schooled and unschooled Zinacantecos. No aspect of sorting behaviour showed a positive effect of familiarity of object domain. On the contrary, grouping and regrouping familiar objects (flowers) by colour sometimes was done more poorly than grouping and regrouping unfamiliar objects (rods) because of the irrelevance of the colour dimension to flower bouquets in the context of Zinacanteco culture. Flower sellers, moreover, did not sort flowers better than other subjects. Although the species dimension is relevant to categorizing the culturally familiar flowers, its use as a basis for grouping developed after all other dimensions used in the experiment — colour, length, and circumference — probably because of its multidimensional perceptual qualities', p. 158. (Details follow.)

The cognitive development of Kenya African children as shown by their performance on selected Piagetian tasks of conservation was studied by Mwangangi (1975). The sample comprised 160 children, aged from six to 10 years six months drawn from rural and city schools. Ss were matched on both age and sex and were administered the Piagetian tasks of clay, water, number and area. Results demonstrated that the variables of parents earning wages, type of house, number of siblings, chores done before and after school, and news media in the home were not good predictors of children's performance on conservation tasks. Rural Ss performed at the higher levels of clay conservation than city school children. No such trends were computed for the tasks of conservation of water, number, and area. Likewise, no sex differences were noted. Conservation operativity increased as a function of age and the ages of acquisition of conservation were found to closely parallel those of children from Western cultures. The role of familiarity with the stimulus materials and experience were stressed. Implications of the findings for education and research in Kenya were discussed. (Details appear later.)

Support may therefore be inferred (e.g. Goodnow, 1969; Price-Williams, 1969) for Piaget's contention that the biological conserving process which applies to free actions — reflective abstraction (Piaget, 1971) — plays a role in development equal to that of material experience, which may differ across milieus.

f. The 'Schooled'/'Unschooled' Variable

Mermelstein and Shulman's (1967) study dealt with the performance of Piagetian conservation tasks by children who had been without schooling for four years. Findings revealed generally no significant differences attributable to the effects of non-schooling. (Details of the study are given in Modgil, 1974, pp. 236–237.) Okonji (1971a, p. 127) argues: 'Mermelstein's evidence does not seem to be very convincing as some of his subjects have had some brief or irregular schooling experience and there was no way to show that some did not continue to get some sort of formal teaching at home when the public schools were closed'. Likewise, methodological difficulties, however, make the results uncertain: 'failure to demonstrate that the children were conservers by standard measures and the inevitable difficulty of inferring affective reaction from facial expression', Miller (1973, p. 48).

Goodnow (1969) examined three groups of 11-year-old boys on the same conservation of area (farm) task as those used by Lester and Klein (1973). The former found 80 per cent conservation performance among 'unschooled' Chinese compared to Lester and Klein's 'average' and 'dull' North American boys who demonstrated 60 per cent and 40 per cent conservation performance, respectively. In comparison, the findings of Lester and Klein suggested that conservation can be demonstrated at earlier ages if familiar stimulus materials were employed. Therefore, for the conservation of area (farm) task, the performance of the seven-year-old Guatemalan children compared favourably with the 11-year-old sample reported by Goodnow. The Harvard Centre for Cognitive Studies (Bruner, Olver and Greenfield, 1966) have gathered results from a wide variety of cultures — Boston, Senegal, Alaska, and urban and rural Mexico. 'For Bruner, development is not to be seen as structural construction. Rather, it occurs within the media by which the child represents his experience. The child constructs his world by successively representing it in an enactive, or ikonic, or a symbolic medium. Each of the three modes, and media, of representation 'places a powerful impress on the mental life of human beings at different ages, and their interplay persists as one of the major features of adult intellectual life,' Bruner *et al.* (1966, p. 1). The relations among the media give rise to conflicts, which include a constructive mobility that may push development forward: if two representational systems do not correspond, as is the case if there is a 'conflict between "appearance" and "reality"', the one being ikonic, the other symbolic', (p. 12), a disequilibrium arises that leads to the revision of the child's problem-solving method. Learning processes take place in the transition from one to another representational medium (Bruner and Kenney, 1965). Unfortunately, as Steiner (1974) has pointed out, ' . . . we are told neither which are the conditions of transition nor what remains invariant of an environmental event or of a mathematical fact when the representational medium has been changed. One must suppose that the organization of the elements of an event or the structure of the mathematical fact are the invariants of the representational constructs. Bruner scarcely considers this structural aspect of behaviour', p. 892.

Greenfield's (1966) study among the Wolof people of Senegal concluded that schooling may be the vital factor in determining whether Senegalese children ever achieve conservation of continuous quantity. A conservation task was administered to samples of rural schooled, urban schooled, and rural unschooled Wolof children from ages six through 13. The unschooled children living in rural areas demonstrated no significant gains in conservation after the age of eight. By age 13, the percentage of children in both rural and urban schools attaining conservation was nearly 100 per cent as compared with about 50 per cent among those children in rural areas who were not attending school.

The impetus behind the Greenfield study was an attempt to find the locus in environmental factors of nonstandard responses to standard measures. 'This branch of cross-cultural cognitive studies is more Brunerian than Piagetian, because it replaces Piaget's interactionism with Bruner's greater emphasis on the role of environmental factors in accounting for cognitive development', Feldman *et al.* (1974, pp. 18—19).

With respect to Greenfield's results that older, unschooled Wolof subjects depended heavily on perceptual justifications in conservation experiments. Ashton (1975) argued, 'Such cross-cultural inferences must be tempered, however, because the phenomena from which they are drawn are subject to different competing interpretations. Instead of concluding that . . . Greenfield's subjects had not achieved formal operations, we could, for example, advance the counter-hypothesis that the cultural bias in the experimental methods employed . . . precluded finding the formal operations which the subjects did in fact possess. Such a counter-hypothesis gains credence from the work of Feldman (1974), who found that when tasks were designed with culturally familiar materials, Eskimo children demonstrated formal operational thought. Since her subjects were successful on only one of two tasks designed to measure formal thought, Feldman suggested that this finding supports Inhelder's and Piaget's (1958) postulation of two substages of formal thought. She hypothesized that failure of the Eskimo children to demonstrate the second level of formal operations might be due to inadequacies in representational ability. In forwarding this hypothesis, she appealed to the Brunerian emphasis on the importance of linguistic competence for abstract thinking', p. 486. Owoc (1973) however argued that, ' . . . even by reducing conservation studies to the kind of functional equation advocated by Greenfield it seems apparent that variables like "schooling" versus ones like "native tongue used as medium of instruction" still differ only in their level of specificity and not in their explanatory power', p. 249.

In a study entitled, 'On culture and conservation once again', Owoc therefore extended the earlier work of Greenfield (*op. cit.*) 'in an effort to look again at the effects of higher order factors on the attainment of conservation', p. 250. The sample included 449 subjects of whom 127 were Efiks from the South-eastern and Rivers States, 68 who were Hausas from the North-Central and North-Western States, and 254 who were Yoruba subjects from the Western and Midwestern States. 'The design consisted of 16 partitioning contrasts. Within each of the four possible contrasts of urban versus rural and schooling versus no schooling, the four age groups of six through seven, eight through nine, 11 through 13 and over 18 (adult) were represented', p. 251. The conservation of liquid task was administered individually and all responses were recorded verbatim. Conservation attainment was related to age — as the age level increased, so did the percentage of Ss who attained conservation operativity. 'Averaging the percentages, weighted by the number of Ss across educational status and degree of urbanization, showed that 32 per cent, 94 per cent, and 85 per cent of the Ss attained conservation by the ages of six through seven, eight through nine, 11 through 13, and over 18 years of age, respectively. Perhaps more interesting than looking at age alone, was to examine conservation attainment as a function of either urban versus rural environments and school versus no schooling conditions. Again weighted by the number of Ss involved and averaged over age levels and conditions of schooling, the attainment percentages for urban versus rural subjects were 68 per cent and 60 per cent, respectively.

Statistically, this difference was not significant (t = 1.74; df = 447), nor were any of the rural—urban contrasts of any of the age levels examined. For the schooling conditions, 69 per cent of the schooled Ss, as opposed to 59 per cent of the unschooling conditions, 69 per cent of the schooled Ss, as opposed to 59 per cent of the unschooled Ss attained conservation. This overall difference was statistically significant (t = 2.44; df = 447; p < .05), as was the difference between schooled and unschooled Ss over 18 years of age (t = 4.09; df = 109, p < .001)', p. 252. (Details are given later.)

Feldman, Lee, McLean, Pillemer and Murray (1974) administered a specially devised non-verbal task to groups of children in three separate cultures, primarily to Eskimo children of Alaska's North Slope. The test consisted of a sequence of tasks using coloured blocks. These tasks represented three Piagetian stages and formed a series which began with simple perceptual matching and concluded with the abstract operations of symbolic logic. Corroborative tests were given in the mountain region of Kentucky and in Hawaii. Results demonstrated that cognitive development followed the pattern as postulated by Piaget and verified his claim that an adaptation — not unlike biological adaptation — governs cognitive acquisition. This adaptation consists of a constant interaction between the person and the environment. (Details follow.) Feldman *et al.* maintain, 'Piagetian research is often done cross-culturally, and it is often unclear just exactly what is being tested. For example, although on some level all Piagetian research is a test of aspects of Piaget's theory — usually of the universality of a particular stage — cross-cultural tests of Piaget's theory at the same time focus on the testing of subjects and vary in the interpretation of obtained differences between subject groups. Price-Williams (1961), for example, modifies the standard procedure until the between-culture differences are removed. Hence he generally blames obtained differences on the task. Greenfield (1966), on the other hand, accepts her results as, for example, indicating non-conservation in Wolof children. Here differences are attributed to the children and confidence is placed in the task. These choices are also tied up with an implicit view of Piagetian theory, and so the issues are not simple. Price-Williams, having eliminated differences, can say that he has validated Piagetian theory, at least the universality of conservation. Greenfield could argue that she has provided evidence that the theory is wrong and that culturally variable conditions affect such abilities as conservation. The present study is not any more pure a case than those of Price-Williams and Greenfield. But it reverses the order of these priorities, so that the testing of the theory is the main goal and subject ability is measured only in order to permit the testing of theory', pp. 25—26.

Ashton (1975) maintains, 'The failure to demonstrate generalizability of conservation and formal operational thought across materials and situations (Feldman, 1974) leads one to question the significance of the concept of conservation as well as the notion of generalized cognitive structures. To determine the relationship among conservation tasks and other measures of intellectual development, studies investigating interrelationships among a variety of tasks measuring different processes are required. The Campbell and Fiske (1959) multitrait—multimethod approach is appropriate here . . . ', p. 479.

Goodnow and Bethon (1966) in their study attempted to elucidate results with schooled and unschooled children in Hong Kong with respect to Piaget's conservation tasks and found that the only task on which the unschooled Chinese children operated below the 'average' American schooled child was the task of combinatorial reasoning. No differences in the American children and the unschooled Chinese subjects in the conservation operativity of the concepts of substance, weight, volume and area were observed. The strategy employed by the unschooled group did not follow any consistent pattern in a combinatorial reasoning task — a finding reported by Peluffo (1964). Peluffo's subjects found the combinatorial task harder than conservation of displacement volume for rural, but not for urban school children in Sardinia. It is interesting to point out here that full operativity in tasks requiring combinatorial strategies is regarded by Piaget as most pertinent to formal reasoning. Peluffo concluded from his results that 'low-cultural level' or an 'underdeveloped milieu' does not stimulate the development of operational thinking, though transfer to a more favourable milieu may do so. Peluffo demonstrated that there was a significant gap between children from regions of Southern Italy and those from the North. The incidence pointed out how, in children from southern families migrating north these differences progressively disappear.

Variations in the rate of conservation acquisition among several cultural groups were attributed to specific environmental differences (e.g. schooling) in a study by Goldschmid, Bentler, Kohnstamm, Modgil et al. (1973). The Conservation Assessment Kit Scale A, described more fully in Volume Four in the present series *Piagetian Research* was administered to 25 boys and 25 girls at each age level from four to eight years, comprising a total sample of 250 children in each of eight countries. Overall, the results indicated that the sequence of Piagetian conservation development in both males and females is fairly consistent from culture to culture. (Details follow.)

A study of the relationship between school experience, socio-economic status, and conservation attainment (Goldschmid and Bentler, 1968b) in first grade Orthodox Jewish children (N = 76) was undertaken by Schorr (1975). Subjects were drawn from either restricted school experience or enriched school experience. Children from the enriched school experience demonstrated higher levels of conservation operativity than children from the restricted school experience. Further, that middle SES children in the enriched school experience showed greater conservation attainment than lower SES children in the same type of school. (Details follow.)

Levels of reasoning in mapwork shown by 160 Malawian school children in four grades with an age range from 10 to 21 years were studied by Lawless (1974). 'In spite of an age range of five to seven years in each grade, results on the map reading showed greater agreement with grade than with age. It is hypothesized that this results from a complex interaction of school experience, intelligence and socioeconomic factors. In contrast to several other studies in Africa, no significant sex difference was found . . . the effect of school experience was more pronounced in map reading than it was in map drawing or in the oral questions'. (Details are given later.)

Laurendeau-Bendavid (1976) administered the tasks of seriation, conservation of area (surface) and number, as well as on a task of formal operations (quantification of probabilities) and on two tasks inspired by Piaget's earlier work on precausal beliefs. The results generally indicated a strong effect of schooling: 'the schooled Rwandese children demonstrate a significantly faster rate of development, for all of the tasks, than the partially schooled and the unschooled children'. However, 'school attendance appears to be a facilitating rather than a necessary condition for the attainment of concrete operations and objective causal representations, since some of the children without any schooling do attain these'. But schooling did not affect all the tasks to the same degree. Kelly (1976) found school experience to have 'no discernable effect on ability to conserve either quantity or length for males though there is an effect for females'.

Kiminyo (1976) hypothesized that cognitive development (as assessed by conservation tasks) would be faster in rural rather than in urban children, and in unschooled rather than in schooled children. He convincingly argued that the rural and the unschooled children have more opportunities to be active in interaction with their environment. Although the results did not fully support these hypotheses, the finding of 'no difference' between the groups is interesting in itself. However, Opper (1976) reported different results: the rate of development of Swiss children and Thai urban children was found to be almost identical, whereas a 'time-lag' appeared for the rural children.

However, Hollos and Cowan (1973, described more appropriately in Volume 5 in the present series, *Piagetian Research*) did not support Bruner's (*op. cit.*) schooling contention. Language stimulation and schooling did not play an important role in the acquisition of logical operations. The Hong Kong study of Goodnow (1962) suggested that the school's reliance on written language, book information, and learning out of context, with no foundation upon concrete experience, results in depressed conservation operativity.

That among non-Western cultures and certain Western subcultures the school's emphasis on language and out-of-context learning was contradictory to learning in everyday life was hypothesized by Scribner and Cole (1973). The linguistic out-of-context aspect of the school was related to the tendency of school children to generalize rules and operations across tasks and to use language to describe the tasks and their responses, characteristics which account for the better performance of schooled children on many cognitive tasks. If, however, the school is perceived as a hostile institution, serious learning problems may result. 'The school's knowledge base, value system, and dominant learning situations and the functional learning systems to which they give rise are all in conflict with those of the student's traditional culture . . . The antagonism the schools generate by their disrespect for the indigenous culture and by ignorance of its customs almost guarantees the production of nonlearners', (*ibid.*, p. 558). The authors suggested that the observational, nonverbal features of informal education be examined for possible benefits which could be incorporated into the formal system.

More recently, Scribner (1976) stresses the importance of schooling, 'In all cultures, populations designated as "traditional" or "nonliterate" have just somewhat better than a chance solution rate across all types of problem material . . . Within each culture there is a large discrepancy in performance between schooled and nonschooled. With schooling, there is little between-culture variation in performance for the cultures studied', pp. 5—6.

In his discussion on schooling Ghuman (1976) emphasizes that researchers ought to describe the type of education imparted to children when the factor of schooling is mentioned, otherwise it is likely to lead to erroneous conclusions regarding the role of the school in intellectual development. Ghuman considers that he has shown, what goes on in school is of crucial importance. Intent to study the effects of the European type of environment on the thinking processes of children by employing samples of British Punjabi, indigenous Punjabi and 'English' boys, he hypothesized that the thinking processes of British Punjabi boys are significantly superior to those of indigenous Punjabi boys, and that indigenous Punjabi boys perform relatively better on those tests which can be made culturally appropriate, as compared with the performance of British Punjabi boys. Further, the research was intent to discover whether the thinking processes of British Punjabi boys differed significantly from those of English boys, the ways in which the traditional milieu affects the thinking processes of boys in the Punjab and whether the cognitive style utilized by Punjabi boys is distinctive in its characteristics from the style utilized by British Punjabi boys. Results revealed that the British Punjabi boys were similar to the English boys in their responses, both quantitatively and qualitatively; 'whereas significant differences in quality as well as quantity of thinking were found between the indigenous Punjabi and the British Punjabi groups'. (Details follow.)

Pertinent here is a study by Vyas (1976) in which the relationship between the development of reading ability in the learners of English as a second language and cognitive development in Piagetian terms was explored. Fifty-five Punjabi-speaking children attending an English school in the age range of seven to 11 years, were administered the Kingston Test of Silent Reading (Hebron, 1954) together with conservation of substance tasks. No significant relationship was determined with the exception of the 10+ age group. Only three subjects of the total sample were found to be conservers. It was considered however that the study produced interesting information for further work in the bi-cultural field and that Piagetian theories could provide explanations of foreign language learning. The author discusses schooling effects. (Details follow.)

In summing the studies dealing with the effects of schooling on logical thinking, Ashton (1975) stated, ' . . . the evidence suggests that schooling does exert an influence upon cognitive development. Education that offers an opportunity for concrete, manipulative activity promotes development of logical thinking. In addition, research supports the notion that as school children are forced to talk about objects in the absence of specific referents, they learn to appreciate the process, rather than the specific product, of discriminating the relationships among objects. As they are encouraged to speak of ideas about other ideas (far removed from the sensory foundations of the abstract relationships present), they learn to use previously induced rules to develop new logical arguments. Their goals, therefore, become more far-reaching than those related to the completion of specific and clearly delineated concrete tasks. Furthermore, children within the school experience seem to attain a heightened awareness of what it is they actually "know". Because they are forced to code and re-code their information along increasingly abstract dimensions, schooled children are more conscious of the mechanisms by which they solve logical problems. In short, because children must generalize in order to survive in the milieu of the classroom, they become skilled at transferring learning from one task to another (Vygotsky, 1934 / 1962). Schooling, however, does not seem to be critical for the development of conservation, since there is evidence of conservation among the unschooled. In contrast, schooling, because of its emphasis upon symbolic thinking, may be crucial to the development of formal thought processes, at least as measured by performance on tests of combinatorial thinking. It seems most important that school activities be related to the child's developmental level if formal education is to have a positive influence on cognitive development', p. 495.

g. European 'High'/'Low' Contact in Australian Aboriginal Children

Dasen (1972) reports, 'Thus more important than schooling itself seems to be the contact with Western cognitive values and stimulation which schooling brings with it. European contact . . . is difficult to define precisely (de Lacey, 1970); it is usually linked to the urban / rural difference (Mohseni, 1966; Greenfield, 1966; Peluffo, 1967; Poole, 1968; Vernon, 1969), to linguistic difference, either in the richness of the vernacular (Greenfield, 1966), or in the fluency of the acquired European language (Vernon, 1969) or to social class (Lloyd, 1971)'.

In his 1970 study, de Lacey demonstrated that in the development of operational thinking as assessed by a battery of classification tasks, although both of the European samples were generally superior to the Aboriginal samples, a small sample of high-contact Aboriginals was found to perform as well as the low socioeconomic Europeans. However, the number of children involved was small (N = 34). (Details of the study appear in Modgil, 1974, pp. 239–240.)

In extending his above study, de Lacey (1971), alongside with two tests of Piagetian classificatory tasks, administered the Peabody Picture Vocabulary Test to 40 full-blood urban Aboriginal children and 80 white subjects. 'A trend in an earlier study for high-contact Aboriginals to perform on classification tests at about the same level as white children in a similar environment was confirmed, despite the markedly lower verbal IQ scores of Aboriginal children'. (Full details of the study appear in Modgil, 1974, pp. 243–244.)

In continuing his 1970 and 1971 studies, de Lacey (1971a) attempted to establish whether there were any differences in cognitive organization between reserve and town-dwelling part-Aboriginals, in terms of both verbal intelligence and Piagetian operational thinking.

The European subjects performed at the higher levels on the Peabody Picture Vocabulary Test and the Nixon Test (1967), than the reserve part-Aboriginals. 'Rural part-Aboriginals are, therefore, too heterogeneous to be considered as a single population in studies of cognitive development. Correlations between scores on the two tests were low'. (Full details appear in Modgil, 1974, pp. 241–242.)

De Lemos (1969) demonstrated that the conservation performance of full-blooded Australian Aboriginal children was significantly lower than for part-blooded Aboriginals. She concluded that the significant differences found may be due partly to linguistic factors and cites the work of Luria, 1961, and Bernstein, 1961, but mainly to genetic factors which could have contributed to retarded development of conservation in these children, since she found no 'apparent differences in the environment of the two groups' (p. 265). (*Cf.* recent controversial research evidence of Jensen, 1969, 1972, 1973 discussed in Section (i) of the present volume.) (De Lemos' study is described in Modgil, 1974, pp. 237–238.)

The development of conservation in Aboriginal children, was undertaken by Dasen (1972). The investigation attempted to replicate the findings of de Lemos (1966, 1969a, 1969b) (*op. cit.*) of the development of conservation in Australian Aboriginal children, particular attention being paid to de Lemos' qualitative and quantitative aspects of operational development, the quantity-weight reversal, and genetic differences. A sample of 90 Ss ranging in age from six to 16 were administered the tasks of conservation of quantity, weight, volume, length, seriation of lengths, spatial tests of topological orders, rotation of landscapes, and horizontality. Details of the tests, which followed de Lemos and Piagetian experiments, have been described elsewhere (Dasen, 1970). With respect to the qualitative and quantitative aspects of operational development, de Lemos' results were fully substantiated: 'there was an exact correspondence between the answers and explanations given by Aboriginal children and by European children, and these answers could easily be classified into the three, well-known stages', p. 77. A comparison demonstrated that the rate of acquisition of conservation with age was closely comparable in the two studies; both showed a slow and asymptotic development, with a large proportion of children failing to reach stage three. The quantity-weight reversal was not confirmed and Dasen attributed this failure to one of three causes, 'or possibly to a combination of these: (a) the change in test materials; (b) the reduction of an effect of separation of the testing sessions; (c) the elimination of systematic order effects in the present study', p. 79. With respect to genetic differences, de Lemos made a comparison between the performance of full-blood Aboriginal children with that of part-blood children living in apparently identical environmental conditions. Results demonstrated that the latter showed markedly better conservation performances than the former. However, Dasen failed to replicate such a finding and concluded, 'our results cannot, of course, be taken as conclusive until their contradiction with those obtained by de Lemos has been resolved. However, until this can be done, de Lemos' results should no longer be used to support the argument for genetic differences in mental functioning', p. 84. (Details are given later.)

In continuation, Dasen (1974) hypothesized that the Australian Aborigines, because they depend traditionally on hunting and food gathering travelling for long distances in a barren environment, would develop spatial operations relatively earlier than logico-mathematical operations. The sample comprised 145 children, aged six to 16 years, and 20 adults. The low-contact group consisted of a school population at Areyonga settlement (N = 55); the high-contact group was selected from the Hermannsburg mission school (N = 90). A reference group of 80 European children was tested in Canberra. The test battery included logico-mathematical operations: conservation of quantity, weight, volume, length, and seriation of lengths. Spatial operations included: linear, circular and reverse orders, horizontality, and rotation of two landscape models. Both in Europeans of Canberra and in Aborigines of Central Australia, Piagetian stages occurred in the same order. The reactions and responses corresponded to those of Swiss Ss reported by the Geneva school. The rate at which the concepts under investigation develop in Aboriginal Ss, however, was slow and was asymptotic at the higher ages, the reversal between quantity and weight was not observed and therefore failed to confirm de Lemos' (1966) results, as was the part-blood / full-blood comparison. The influence of European contact was more marked where concepts were concerned which were less relevant to the Aboriginal culture, in this case logico-mathematical concepts. 'This finding leads to our hypothesis based on ecological functionalism'. The relative development of logico-mathematical and spatial operations showed that in the Canberra sample, logico-mathematical operations were acquired earlier than spatial operations. In both Aboriginal samples, this relationship was reversed. (Details appear later.)

While reviewing a number of studies, including those of de Lacey, Ashton (1975) argued, 'While the studies reviewed above strongly suggest that differences in age of acquisition may indeed reflect real cognitive structural differences among cultures, it is important to note that this may be due to the impact of the environment on cognition. Dasen . . . conducted a study that dramatically illustrates the effect of life activities on the development of concrete operational thought', p. 485.

An investigation of reasoning ability in adopted and fostered Aboriginal children was undertaken by Dasen, de Lacey and Seagrim (1974). The authors state, '. . . there are clear indications that Aboriginal children profit from increased European contact in so far as their reasoning abilities are concerned when these are assessed by tests based on Piaget's work. The maximum contact is experienced by these Aboriginal children who are adopted early in infancy by European families. Such adoptions, and corresponding fosterings, occur fairly frequently but not usually with sufficient regularity and frequency in any one locality to make the collection of a useful sample possible. It has, however, been possible to locate one such sample in the vicinity of Adelaide, South Australia'. A total sample of 35 (M = 15; F = 20) was tested and ranged in age from five to 14 years. The believed ancestry of the subjects was as follows: Full-blood (N = 7); ¾ Aboriginal (N = 2); ½ Aboriginal (N = 17); ¼ Aboriginal (N = 4); ⅛ Aboriginal (N = 1); Unknown (N = 4). The mean age at adoption was 18.5 months. The tests administered were: conservation of quantity; conservation of weight; horizontality; seriation; reclassification — the Nixon test; and the Peabody Picture Vocabulary test, Form A. All testing was undertaken in the homes of the children. The authors concluded, 'Children of Aboriginal and of mixed European Aboriginal descent, raised in European families from an early age, are able to profit as much from the intellectual opportunities offered to them as are children of European descent'. (Details follow.)

Taylor, Nurcombe, and de Lacey (1973) administered the Peabody Picture Vocabulary Test (Dunn, 1965) and a Piagetian test of classification to 15 Aboriginal and 21 low SES white children attending an enrichment pre-school and to a matched sample of low SES white children, not enrolled at the pre-school. The Aboriginal children, on both tests, performed at the lower levels than the two groups of white subjects. Three dimensions of intellectual functioning in Australian Aboriginal and disadvantaged European children were investigated by Taylor and de Lacey (1974). Thirty each of Aboriginal and disadvantaged children were administered tests of verbal intelligence, operational thinking and divergent thinking. Scores obtained from the tests were correlated with each other to determine the relationship among them. The statistical techniques of t-test and analyses of variance were used to seek differences between age ranges and ethnic groups on each of the three kinds of tests. 'With the exception of the correlation between the Matrices Test and the Peabody Picture Vocabulary Test, the correlations were similar to those reported previously. The t-tests confirmed significant differences between the Aboriginal and European sample on the PPVT. However, there were no significant differences between the Aboriginal and European sample on any of the other tests', p. 49. (Details appear later.)

Concrete operational development (following Piaget) was studied by Dasen (1975) in Central Canadian Eskimo children, aged six to 14 years. The findings were compared with those of a similar study of Australian Aboriginal and European children. The structure and hierarchical ordering of the stages were identical in all populations compared. However, the rate of development was determined by ecological and socio-cultural variables. 'In Eskimo children, the developmental curves of spontaneous reasoning in the area of conservation seem to be asymptotic whereas in the area of the logic of classes and relations, and especially in the area of spatial reasoning, there is only a small or no delay in the rate of development compared to European children', p. 180. Dasen discussed some of the results in relation with the competence / performance distinction.

Flavell and Wohlwill (1969) suggested a model which introduces a distinction between competence and performance, patterned on Chomsky's theory of psycho-linguistics. More recently, Dasen (1976)* in a paper entitled, 'Cross-cultural cognitive development: the cultural aspects of Piaget's theory', asserted that according to the competence / performance model, an initial answer a child gives to a Piagetian task may not necessarily reflect his 'true' cognitive level, that is, the underlying structure or competence. 'This situation seems to occur particularly frequently in cross-cultural situations. Generally speaking the rate of development of concrete operations in rural non-Western children is reported to lag behind Western norms (Dasen, 1972), and the development curves are often asymptotic (Dasen, 1973; Dasen, 1975c). Does this mean that the rate of development of P_a (competence) is affected? There are indications that, in some cases at least, very little "help" is needed, in the form of further questioning, additional task situations or exposure to other operational tasks and training procedures, in order to "actualize" the latent structure', p. 3. As examples, Dasen cites the work of de Lemos (1969); Bovet (1974); Pinard, Morin and Lefebvre (1973) and his own works (1975b, 1976, in press). 'This is not to say that learning is always as fast as illustrated in these examples; I have picked out only those occasions in which the competence / performance distinction seems to be applicable. My interpretation of rapid learning in these examples is that the children already had a latent competence for conservation of quantity, but for some reason, were not able to demonstrate it on the pre-test; it was then activated by a minimum of operational training . . . Flavell and Wohlwill's competence / performance distinction was first introduced to cross-cultural Piagetian psychology by Heron (1974) to explain the

* Gratitude is extended to Dr P. Dasen of the University of Geneva for sending his work to be referenced.

54   *Piagetian Research Volume 8*

discrepancy in performance on tasks which ought to be characteristic of
the same stage (Heron, 1971; Heron and Dowel, 1973, 1974)', p. 5.

Dasen elaborates through his recently published study (1975a)
described elsewhere in this volume, and further cites the work of Cole
and Bruner (1971) who asserted, 'The crux of the argument, when
applied to the problem of "cultural deprivation", is that those groups
ordinarily diagnosed as culturally deprived have the same underlying
competence as those in the mainstream of the dominant culture, the
differences in performance being accounted for by the situations and
contexts in which the competence is expressed', p. 238.

Dasen concludes, ' . . . I am suggesting that future cross-cultural
Piagetian psychology should become more emic, and more process
oriented. Until that is possible, the interpretation of etic studies should
take into account more contextual aspects, such as the competence / performance distinction and ecological functionalism', p. 8.

h. African Studies

Dasen (1974) critically reviewed the literature on the psychological development of the African baby and concluded that the infant 'shows consistently a precocity in motor and general development at birth and in the first year of life. Thereafter, a slackening and even a stagnation in development seem to occur, but this phenomenon could be explained by artefacts of the techniques and the computation of results. Several suggestions as to the introduction of a more rigorous methodology are made; the author believes that research should be extended to the study of sensorimotor development (following the theory of Piaget) and to the observation of spontaneous behaviour using ethological techniques', p. 356.

Dasen (1974a) studied the development of sensorimotor intelligence in rural African children (Baoulé, Ivory Coast) aged six to 24 months, using the ordinal scale developed by Casati and Lézine (1968). 'When the results are compared to those obtained in France by Lézine, Stambak and Casati (1969), one finds a marked precocity in those situations which seem to involve a direct relationship between two objects, or between the subjects hands and an object. The results are the same in both samples for situations that seem to involve a more complex organization in space or time. Partial delays appear in two tasks that call for manipulations which are not usual in the African milieu of this study', Dasen (1974a).

A rapidly increasing number of studies within the framework of Piaget's theory of intellectual development have helped in the emergence of an outline of the pattern of cognitive development in Africa. An excellent survey reviewing the results of these studies was presented by Ohuche and Pearson (1974) at the Seminar entitled, 'The Development of Science and Mathematics Concepts in Young Children in African Countries' held in Kenya, in the University of Nairobi, 17th to 27th September. The Seminar was sponsored by the United Nations Educational, Scientific and Cultural Organisation (UNESCO) and the

United Nations International Children's Emergency Fund (UNICEF).
(Details of this survey of research in Africa are given later.)
More recently, Dasen (1976, personal communication*) stated,
' . . . the subject will receive a thorough treatment in the forthcoming
book *Concept Development in African Children* co-edited by B. Otaala
and R.O. Ohuche . . . this book (is) edited by African psychologists.
This is what the editors write about it (personal communication): "At
the UNESCO / UNICEF conference . . . it was felt that increasing
numbers of investigations were being carried out on various aspects of
the development of thought processes in African children and that
these efforts were commendable, even if there were still many issues
deserving attention. It was strongly suggested that available information
should be put together and presented in a manner that any teacher,
curriculum worker or other interested person can use. Thus, it was
expressed, should sensitize users to issues associated with concept
formation. This forthcoming book is our humble attempt to meet some
of this expressed need. In selecting the articles presented in the book
our main concerns have been: (i) Giving teachers, curriculum workers
and other persons, information, no matter how limited, on work that
has been done in Africa in the area of concept development. (ii) Giving
illustrations of work done by persons who understand the African
environment on some of the cultural activities that affect intellectual
development in order especially to inspire future researchers to explore
the use of mundane activities of our people as tools for the study of
concept formation. (iii) Sensitizing teachers and teacher educators to
the area of concept development so that they may not only be aware of
the need to match the subject matter of the curriculum to the level of
conceptual development attained by a child at a specific age, but also
that they may build on this knowledge at workshops and
seminars . . . " Section one of the book deals with theoretical issues and
has five chapters. Chapter one by Professor A. Babs Fafunwa gives a
broad coverage of the development of the African child from birth to
six years. Chapter two by Professor Ruth Beard discusses the
relationship between language and thought. Chapters three and four by
Dr Barnabas Otaala and Professor Kenneth Lovell, respectively, describe
early and later stages of conceptual development as presented in
Piagetian theory. Chapter five by Dr V. Ibikunle Johnson deals with
cognitive growth and conceptualization in science education.
The second section of the book deals with specific selected
researches conducted in Africa or with applications of knowledge
gained from research to curriculum development or the teaching—

* Gratitude is extended to Dr P.R. Dasen of Geneva University for sending the
work to be referenced.

learning situation. It contains chapters written by J. Gay, M. Cole, A.I. Kamara, R.O. Ohuche, and R.E. Pearson', pp. 30–31.

i. The Jensen Controversy

Jensen and other psychologists believe that the differences in intellectual abilities of different ethnic groups are mainly due to genetic as opposed to environmental factors. Jensen (1972, p. 124) argued from the studies of twins and related researches that 75 per cent of the variance (total difference in scores of the groups) on the IQ tests may be explained by genetic factors and 25 per cent by environmental factors. Such a finding is advanced to interpret the difference between the performance of American white and negro children — the latter scored 15 points below the former. Although this may be a sound statistical principle, Piaget (1956) asserts, 'The psychologist for his part welcomes the qualitative character of logic, since it facilitates the analysis of the actual structures underlying intellectual operations, as contrasted with the quantitative treatment of their behavioural outcome. Most "tests" of intelligence measure the latter, but our real problem is to discover the actual operational mechanisms which govern such behaviour and not simply measure it', p. 41.

Jensen (1973) while arguing whether the Piagetian tests have high heritability stated that it would be most surprising if they did not. He cites the study by de Lemos (1969) which strongly supported the idea that Piagetian tests are highly sensitive indicators of genetic factors in mental development. Commenting on de Lemos results, Jensen stated, 'The results appear almost as if the admixture of Caucasian genes, even so few as one-eighth, introduces mental structures otherwise lacking, that permit the individual to reach higher levels of mental development than normally occurs in the majority of full-Aboriginals', p. 316. In a similar vein Eysenck (1971) considered his results to be an important research which substantiates the case of geneticists. He asserted, ' . . . on the whole this study must stand as one of many props for the genetic hypothesis which environmentalists will find it difficult to dislodge', p. 101.

Voyat (1970a) claimed that 'IQ tests are simply not adequate to measure processes of thinking', p. 161. He suggested, 'Piaget's approach not only allows an understanding of how intelligence functions, but describes it. Since the interest of Piaget's tests lies in describing the mechanism of thinking, they permit an individual, personalized appraisal of further potentialities independent of the culture', p. 161. 'In contrast IQ tests, designed by whites for Western culture have value limited to the culture within which they were designed,' p. 160. Jensen (1973) maintained that Voyat 'is probably correct in his opinion that the Piagetian tests are less culture-bound than conventional IQ tests. For one thing, some groups reared under environmental conditions which are extremely different from those of Western culture have been found to show not only the same sequence of development through Piaget's stages, but are even somewhat more accelerated in this development than white middle class children. Again, Arctic Eskimos were found to excel over white urban Canadian children in the Piagetian tests, and Canadian Indians do almost as well as the Eskimos (Vernon, 1965b; MacArthur, 1968, p. 48). Obviously it is not necessary to have lived in a Western or middle class culture in order to perform up to Western middle class levels on Piagetian tests', p. 314. Jensen further commented that in rank-ordering children of the same CA in terms of their rate of mental development, the Piagetian tests are not very different from other culture-reduced tests. He further elaborated on the studies of Vernon (1965b) and Tuddenham (1970). 'Vernon . . . factor-analyzed a large number of Piagetian tests along with conventional psychometric measures of intelligence and found that the Piagetian tests were heavily loaded on "g" the general factor common to all intelligence tests. In fact, Piagetian tests measured little else than "g"; the "non-g" variance seems to be task-specific, i.e. it has nothing in common with other Piagetian tests or with conventional IQ tests. Tuddenham (1970) gave a battery of Piagetian tests, along with Raven's Matrices and the Peabody Picture Vocabulary Test (PPVT), to a large number of elementary school children, and concluded, " . . . the Raven has the higher correlations, ranging from 0.24 to 0.50, as compared with Peabody values of 0.13 to 0.37 for a similar though not identical set of Piagetian items" (p. 68). These are relatively high values for single item correlations within a restricted age range. Tuddenham notes that "Correlations with Piaget item composites of six and eight items respectively are 0.60 for the Raven *vs.* 0.21 for the Peabody". These are the kinds of correlations one should expect if Piaget's tests are culture-reduced, since among psychometric tests the Peabody and the Raven are probably further apart than any other tests on the continuum going from "culture-loaded" to "culture-free"', pp. 314–315.

Negroes did less well than whites on every item. The average percentage of children possessing the concept tested by the particular items was 32.6 for whites and 15.9 for Negroes (Tuddenham, 1969). Oriental children, on the other hand, were more advanced than white children on seven of the 10 items. The Piagetian scale also correlated substantially with SES as indexed by father's occupation, even though, as Tuddenham noted, 'these items tend to involve reasoning about matters universally available to observation, e.g., the horizontality of water levels. It is hard to see how social advantage could be a very large factor in success on some of these items. The genetic selection implicit in occupational level may well have more to do with it', p. 65.

With respect to Jensen's (1971) study in which he controlled such variables as social class, home background factors, schooling, etc. to examine achievement levels and the conceptual and associative types of abilities of Negro, 'Anglo' and Mexican-American children, Ghuman (1975) argued, 'The basic assumption of the research is that the Negro children have similar social backgrounds to the children from the other two groups. This may be the case as judged by the social inventory, but not so if we examine the historical backgrounds of the groups. American Negroes were subjected to slavery: their languages, traditions, beliefs and value systems were destroyed; family life was eliminated. It is naive to assume that all these disadvantages can be wiped out in a few generations', p. 33. ' . . . the social inventory used to assess the home background factors (Gough, 1949) of the children was constructed in 1949, when our knowledge of the social factors affecting the intellectual and educational development was rudimentary . . . the inventory includes such items: Do you have a fireplace in your home? Do you have a bathtub in your home? But there is a lack of items inquiring into (a) conceptual stimulation at home, (b) demanding home background, (c) adjustment of children, (d) perceptual and kinaesthetic experiences, (e) linguistic experiences', *(ibid.,* p. 34). Likewise, Jensen's (1971) study has been criticized by Butcher (1972) ' . . . but the difference has been one of caste rather than class and the history of the Negroes in USA, especially in the Southern States, has been one of fear and oppression. Other minority groups such as Mexicans have not suffered slavery and lynching. It would not be astonishing if the memory of such experiences should exercise a general depressive effect on the psychological development of an entire ethnic group . . . there is no reason why within a generation the mean Negro—White difference in measured ability in the USA should not shrink to a comparable degree', p. 94.

In an article entitled, 'Science, racism and ideology', Rose, Hambley and Haywood (1973) review the re-emergence of scientific racism; the historical roots of scientific racism; debate eugenics and intelligence; genetics and IQ; race and biological reductionism; heritability; genetics and population differences; and IQ and intelligence. They conclude, 'We have tried to show that the scientific basis of Eysenck and Jensen's position is not what they claim. Their "evidence" says nothing about the question of genetic differences between populations, although this is the cornerstone, the *raison d'etre,* of their analysis. We are faced with a series of questions about human propensities; questions which raise issues about man's brain and its development. This is something we can say things about... This is true not only in the sense that the correlates of the unequal distribution and control of resources (e.g. malnutrition) can include deficits in growth and performance but also in the sense that the perceptual and cognitive performance of the brain will both respond to the world view of the society in which the individual grows up, and contribute to a world view. Inevitably the critique of Jensen and Eysenck must move on from an attack on their biological determinism to the impoverished world view that underlies, promotes and is the reason for their analysis ... If their ideas are both old and scientifically discredited, why have they once again emerged from the cranky obscurity of the various eugenic and racial preservation societies, National Fronts, nordic leagues, empire loyalists and other racist or imperialist fringe groups?

The answers, interestingly, lie implicitly within the title of Arthur Jensen's original article. If we are really interested in boosting IQ and scholastic achievement, and all humans are the product of an interaction of their genotype with their environment, we can in principle do one of two things: modify genotype or modify environment. No one knows biologically how to modify genotypes, or in what direction to do so, and the only sort of society in which such modification could be achieved would be a Nazi one — or a Marcusan situation of repressive tolerance coupled with cash incentives.

On the other hand, we do not know how to modify environments. We could do quite straightforward things, like eliminate malnutrition, poverty, slum schools and the self-fulfilling prophecies of teacher labelling of children for a start. We could go on to eliminate the environment which attempts to reduce not merely children but adults from thinking, creative humans to alienated "hands" divorced from all but the most routinized thought — the life experience of the vast majority of the population of Britain or the USA. The logical consequence of being in a society whose mode of production demands cultural and material alienation is precisely the diminution of the creative potential of the great majority of its members. Thus a prerequisite to answering Arthur Jensen's question, even if we do not regard his sort of scholastic achievement as our goal, is the transformation of the society in which we live. It is because of this that, at times such as the present, of acute internal contradictions within capitalism, issues of race and IQ come to perform a twofold ideological role.

On the one hand they provide an apparent "scientific" rationale for the existing social order. If we live in an hierarchical, alienated society, a society in which some are superior, others subordinate, this is portrayed as conforming to a "biological imperative". The distribution of the IQ score conveniently parallels the social order. The ideological role of this biological imperative is as manifest — though more sophisticated — as was the use of evolutionary theory in the nineteenth century, or their contemporary equivalents such as ecology (stop the lower orders breeding and the underdeveloped nations from developing, before a resource crisis overcomes the Western world) as in for instance *Blueprint for Survival*, (Goldsmith *et al.*, 1972) or some of the cruder forms of pop-ethology typified by Morris or Ardrey.

At the same time the race / IQ issue performs another role in the service of capitalism — it is by its nature divisive; it sharpens not merely the class division of society, but also, within the working class, helps exploit the division between black and white. Where what is needed is the unity of the class in its common struggle, scientific racism, manipulated and exploited by the media, helps foster prejudice and tension within the class, sustaining racism even within the Trade Union and Labour movement. It is because their activities perform this particular ideological role that Eysenck and Jensen conform to Eldridge Cleaver's dictum, that he who is not part of the solution is part of the problem', pp. 255–256.

More recently, in an article entitled, 'Academic values and the Jensen–Shockley controversy', Kilgore and Sullivan (1975) in their concluding remarks maintained, 'Further research into the heritability of IQ has merit; the implications of such research remain open. Jensen would note that even a well-established estimate of the inheritability of a trait is not immutable. More important, ways of altering performance on IQ tests are not limited to the eugenics programme proposed by William Shockley. The phenotypic expression of a disease with an heritability as high as .9 can be altered by manipulations in the environment. The same holds for performance on IQ tests.

As a popularized interpretation of Jensen's research, Shockley's discussion of the inheritability of IQ should not be ignored. His argument as presented in the *Phi Delta Kappan* is tautological, true by definition. To provide proof that 80 per cent of the variance in IQ is attributable to genotype, . . . Shockley asks the reader to conduct a card experiment designed to determine the mix of cards that will produce the scatter diagram of the paired IQs of the monozygotic twins reported by Jensen . . . Although this exercise may be illustrative of some basic statistical operations, it is not evident that 80 per cent of IQ variation is attributable to genetic differences. Other findings, which Shockley reports as outcomes of his own research, are presented without accompanying replicability information. The tone of his writing serves to inhibit objective discussion of issues and therefore is scarcely felicitious in a scientific forum ... A "newsworthy story" has been characterized as follows: If a dog bites a man, that's not news, but if a man bites a dog, that's news. It is Jensen's unusual conclusions, and the academic community's unusual response to Shockley's attempted explanation, that attract the attention of the media.

These patterns in mass dissemination of scientific findings, and the inevitable incorporation of these findings into debates on social policy, suggest that social scientists should institutionalize some method for communicating their findings and the accompanying limitations and implications to the general public. Just as Watergate brought to the forefront the need to have legal expertise involved in the activities of the mass media, the IQ controversy has made the same need apparent for social science expertise', pp. 185–186.

In a study entitled, 'Social class differences in intellectual development: a Neo-Piagetian investigation', Case (1975, p. 257) maintained, ' ... the pattern of results obtained suggests a reinterpretation of certain data recently reported by Jensen (1968, 1970, 1973, 1974). What Jensen has found is that social class groups differ much more on certain types of mental tests (Level II) than they do on others (Level I). His interpretation of this finding is that Level II tests are measures of "conceptual" ability, whereas Level I tests are measures of "rote-learning" ability. What the present study suggests is that an equally valid interpretation might be as follows: Level II tests assess the subjects repertoire of executive structures, whereas Level I tests do not. If this interpretation is valid, it follows that it should be possible to create conditions where the performance which is measured is clearly conceptual, yet where the social class differences are relatively small (because the executive repertoire is controlled). Similarly, it should be possible to create conditions where the performance being measured is clearly rote, yet where the social class differences are relatively large (because the executive repertoire is not controlled).' (Details of the Case, 1975 study are described, more appropriately, in Volume Five of the present series *Piagetian Research*.)

More recently Haertel (1976) performed a principal components factor analysis followed by a promax rotation to oblique simple structure, following Jensen's methodology. 'Multitrait–multimethod matrices' were constructed to examine the convergent and discriminant validity of each of the constructs. The Study called 'into question the existence of the constructs of Level I and Level II intelligence as defined by Jensen. In particular, there is little support for the existence of Level I intelligence as a coherent psychological trait'. The author considered the study to be of significance given the controversy surrounding Jensen's theory of intelligence. Although the study did not examine differences between racial or SES groups, it suggested that 'Jensen's constructs do not constitute coherent psychological traits, precluding their inclusion in a working theory of intelligence.'

j. Related Studies

Noro (1961) with a group of Japanese children administered tasks from Piaget's *The Child's Conception of Number* (1952b) and results indicated identical stages to those of the Swiss Children. However, another inquiry (Fujinaga, Saiga and Hosoya, 1963) suggests that 'too much attention is paid to the natural sequence of developmental stages and not enough to the role of learning'. An investigation with completely contradictory results to those of Piaget is that of Cheng and Lee (1964), which involved Chinese children. However, the authors have not published full details of the subjects, nor of methodology or the analytic procedure of the children's behavioural responses. They state that the results of 'an experiment' are in violation of the contention of the 'bourgeois scholar Piaget' and further maintain that 'children's conception of number is completely determined by age'.

Dempsey (1971) compared children from five Indian tribes in Arizona, Mexican Americans and 'middle class' Anglos in an attempt to determine differences between the members of these different cultures in their ability to conserve certain aspects of time. Fifteen children from each age group seven, nine and eleven were involved and the population tested included Hopi Indian children from the villages of Shipaulovi, Shungopovi and Mishongnovi, Arizona; Apache Indian children from the community of Cibecue, Arizona; Pima Indian children from Scaton, Arizona; Papago Indian children from Gu Achi (Santa Rosa), Arizona; Navajo Indian children from the Tuba City, Arizona Boarding School; Mexican American children from Tucson, Arizona and Anglo children from Tucson, Arizona. The tests selected were based on Lovell and Slater's (1960) replication of Piaget's conservation of time experiments (1970). Using Piaget's criteria of three-quarters correct responses the results demonstrated that, 'No group tested was able to conserve simultaneity on any of the tests used at any of the ages tested. On the simple order of events task only Anglo children were able to conserve at age seven. By age nine all except

Navajo and Apache had conserved and by age eleven all except Apache children conserved. On the hard order of events test, none of the groups had achieved conservation by age nine and only Anglo, Mexican American and Pima achieved conservation by age eleven', p. 119. (Details are given later.)

Piagetian study with Korean and Costa Rican children dealing with judgment and imaging aspects of operations was carried out by Youniss and Dean (1974). Several of Piaget's tasks were administered for Ss to judge the meaning of actual transformations and to imagine and draw transformations or produce stimulus instances from a deductive base. Older children (11–12 years) performed at the higher levels than younger Ss (eight–9 years) with judgment procedures, and Ss from rural milieus performed like their urban age peers. However, with imaging procedures, rural Ss demonstrated impairments by comparison with Urban Ss. The results substantiated other cross-cultural studies showing the absence of milieu differences in judgment tasks of operations as well as the presence of milieu differences on imaging problems. (Details follow.)

Left–right orientation among Hausa (Nigerian) children was studied by Price-Williams and Le Vine (1974). The Ss were administered two sets of left–right orientation: (a) identification of left and right hands on the child's own body and on the body of an E facing him, and (b) subtracting from a group composed of a large middle doll with two smaller dolls each side of it, first the middle and the smaller on the right, and then the middle and the smaller on the left. The S was asked to identify which doll was the left and which was the right. The results and methods were compared with studies using a similar approach: Binet (1911), Terman (1916), Piaget (1928), Benton (1959), Galifret-Granjon (1960), Elkind (1961), Laurendeau and Pinard (1970), and Vernon (1965). Generally, the Hausa Ss performed at about the same level as the Swiss children (Piaget 1928) and children studied by Elkind (1961). 'The inclusion of the child's legs in both . . . studies (Piaget and Elkind) and our omission of them, however, reduce the comparability of the findings. We gave the children a task that is probably somewhat easier than that of the other studies . . . and all of the youngest Hausa children were able to do it. This may be due to factors other than the case of the task: e.g., the small and sex-skewed sample, and possibly early training of Hausa children in differentiating their right and left hands as part of Islamic toilet training,' p. 358. With respect to the doll questions, there was a clear increase with age in performance on both items, after age seven, but a high percentage of correct response among the four- to five-years-old was also observed. (Details appear later.)

Some comparative data on the performance in product and process in cognitive development in school age children (N = 1536) in different cultures (New South Wales, New Guinea, Sydney) was studied by Philp and Kelly (1974). The tasks were grouped as either 'product' (getting it right) or 'process' (how it was done). 'Behaviours, representative of development according to the theories of both Piaget and Bruner, were found in all three cultures. The order of difficulty of the product tasks, with some minor exceptions, was the same for all three, whether the children had been to school or not. The Bruner process tasks presented a different picture. There were material differences from culture to culture in the order of appearance of various identifiable processes. As difficulty of task increased, the process commonly used by the children of each culture changed. With the most difficult tasks the children from all cultures tended to use the same process', p. 248. (Details follow.)

The data from the 'Product and Process' study (Philp and Kelly, *op. cit.*), therefore demonstrated a high degree of uniformity across cultures for task difficulty (product) and some major differences across culture in method of solution (process) in a series of problems patterned after Piaget and Bruner. 'The data were reported in general terms for each culture group, partly because of lack of space and partly because finer analysis of the interactions between such variables as sex, subculture groups, and age had not been completed', Kelly and Philp (1975, p. 189). The latter authors therefore explored the relationships among a series of these variables. 'Analysis of results of tests of cognitive development in Papua New Guinea indicated that membership or different language / culture groups was an important source of variance. Three groups each of 48 children were selected from one language culture group and equated for age and sex. Two groups were made up of school children equated for school experience, the third group had no school experience. One group of school children was tested in English, the language of the school; the other two groups were tested in the vernacular common to all three groups'. The tasks administered included an equivalence grouping of pictures, a class-inclusion test, and conservation of length. 'All three tasks were chosen because there were language differences between English and the vernacular in labelling the components of the task. Significant differences were found between the groups in their performance on the tasks. These differences were related both to amount of school experience and language of testing but the latter was, by far, the more significant', (*ibid.*, p. 189). (Details follow.)

Three stages were found in the development of the concept of 'night', 'clouds', and 'rain', among Iraqi children (Al-Fakhri, 1975e). During the first stage (ages four to six) children's answers were *artificialistes*: 'Night takes place so that we sleep'. 'Rain to irrigate'. Some of the answers related rain to clouds, but considered clouds an aftermath to rain. During stage two (seven to nine years) night was connected to sundown. Religious reasons were given for nightfall; sometimes children connect the disappearance of the sun behind the clouds to night. A relationship of rain to clouds was established. Rain however was seen as a deed of God or human beings. Some children connected rain to vapour but the source remained manufacturered. During the third stage (10 and above) natural reasons were given for all the phenomena. (Details appear later.)

Developing Piaget's notions of egocentrism and Feffer's (1970) work on social judgment, Reich and Purbhoo (1975) hypothesized that greater cross-cultural contact would result in greater generalized cross-cultural role-taking ability and more favourable attitudes toward ethnic groups in general. 'This was tested by comparing students in schools with a high proportion of new Canadians (HiD, $\bar{\chi}$ = .65) with students in a matched group of schools having a relatively low proportion of new Canadians (LoD, $\bar{\chi}$ = .29) on tests devised to measure cross-cultural role-taking ability, tolerance for diversity in society, and on performance on the Prisoner's Dilemma Game. Both Canadian and new Canadian students in HiD schools scored higher than comparable students in LoD schools on the cross-cultural role-taking test. However, only new Canadians showed greater tolerance in HiD than in LoD schools. There was no support for the hypothesis from results of the Prisoner's Dilemma game', Reich and Purbhoo (*op. cit.*, p. 313) (Details follow.) (HiD and LoD refer to high density and low density, respectively.)

More recently in a study entitled, 'The socialization of possession and ownership among children in three cultural groups: Israeli kibbutz, Israeli city and American', Furby (1976)* explored the nature and development of possession and ownership among children living in quite different environments with respect to material possessions. An open-ended interview was designed to examine seven major topics of possession: (a) the meaning or definition of possession, (b) the nature of possessables, (c) means of acquisition, (d) motivation for possession, (e) use and sharing of personal possessions, (f) collective possession, and (g) unequal distribution. Subjects from three different cultural groups were interviewed: American, Israeli kibbutz, and Israeli city. Within each culture group there were thirty five-year-olds and thirty 10-year-olds. Subjects were interviewed individually and their responses were tape recorded, transcribed, and Hebrew interviews were translated into English. A content analysis was performed on all 180 interviews.

* Written and prepared by the author for inclusion in this volume. Gratitude is extended to Dr Lita Furby of the Oregon Research Institute.

The resulting dimensions in each of the seven topical areas are presented, and the relative saliences of these dimensions for different culture and age groups are discussed. (Details follow.)

Conclusion

The growing literature of cross-cultural Piagetian studies reflects primarily an interest in verifying the universality of Piaget's stages of cognitive development. Dasen and Seagrim's (1969–1976) inventory of such cross-cultural research is perhaps the best demonstration of this expanding concern. Levine (1970) has suggested that by testing children in different cultures, those critical of Piaget's theory have attempted to disagree with his stage formulations whereas Piagetians seek to show their universality.

Children in non-industrial societies have been found to score at the lower levels of Piagetian operativity as well as on traditional Western intelligence tests (Bruner *et al.*, 1966; Levine, 1970). Such differences have been attributed to lack of formal schooling, residence in rural areas, or linguistic handicaps (Levine, 1970; Vernon, 1965). European children perform at the higher levels of Piagetian operativity than Australian Aborigines (e.g., Dasen, 1974; De Lacey, 1970, 1971; De Lemos, 1969; Nurcombe, 1970), but again environmental differences (e.g., frequency of contact with Europeans) played a significant role. Cole and Bruner (1971) and Cole *et al.* (1971) have stressed the importance of the situation − i.e., its significance 'for the person's ability to cope with life in his own milieu,' (Cole and Bruner, 1971, p. 874).

Dasen (1972) in a summary of cross-cultural Piagetian research has classified these studies as 'descriptive' (essentially attempts to verify Piaget's stages in non-Western cultures) and 'quasi-experimental' (attempts to link cognitive performance to specific cultural factors). Dasen concluded that (i) in most cases the sequence of cognitive development (or the qualitative aspects) postulated by Piaget was substantiated, while the rate and ultimate level reached (or the quantitative aspects) are affected by cultural factors, and (ii) the quasi-experimental research has not yet advanced enough to offer convincing conclusions in respect of specific links between cognitive behaviours and cultural factors.

In elaboration, Dasen discusses the nature of research in this area. 'Following the disappointing results of the "culture-free" and "culture-fair" movements, the attention of many cross-cultural cognitive psychologist(s) has turned to the developmental psychology of Jean Piaget (often called "genetic psychology"). The Piagetian psychologist is not concerned with the score on a test, but attempts to describe the basic structures and functioning of higher mental processes. He studies how the child gets to know about the world, how he develops basic scientific concepts, and how reasoning obeys certain structural properties which can be described by models drawn from logic and mathematics. It is thus interesting for the cross-cultural psychologist to determine whether these properties of thought, which are described by Piaget as basic to any knowledge, are universal or whether they are influenced by cultural factors. Implicitly, or explicitly, most cross-cultural studies in genetic psychology ask whether cognitive development in non-Western cultures follows the same sequential succession of stages described by Piaget and by many other investigators in middle class, Western children. And, if so, do these appear at approximately the same age levels?', pp. 23, 25.

In an article entitled, 'Cross-cultural Piagetian research: an experimental perspective', Ashton (1975) maintains that, 'Piagetian research has been conducted in over one hundred cultures and subcultures from Switzerland to Senegal, from Alaska to the Amazon. This research typically has attempted to verify the basic structures and hierarchical stages of logical thinking, as well as to establish age trends for the acquisition of cognitive abilities and the transitions from lower to higher cognitive stages. The Piagetian conservation-of-quantity experiments have revealed both basic similarities and striking differences among children of different cultures. Individuals in diverse cultures seem to move through Piaget's hierarchical stages in the same invariant sequence, although some cultural groups appear never to attain the stage of formal operations. Within a given stage, groups also vary in their performance on specific cognitive tasks. An eight-year-old middle class white child growing up in the United States will respond to the "water and beaker" experiment by noting the equality of liquid in both cases, while a Wolof youngster in Senegal, West Africa, may insist that the water has changed and increased in quantity when poured into the tall, thin beaker. Piagetian experiments have also shown wide variations in performance between subgroups within the same culture. Children of pottery-making families in Jalisco, Mexico, perform better on conservation-of-substance tasks than do their peers from non-pottery-making families. These findings raise important issues concerning the validity of Piaget's theory, the nature of cultural and subcultural differences, and the general conduct of cross-cultural research', p. 476.

Ashton's paper surveys the results of cross-cultural Piagetian research under such headings as: (a) the basic assumptions of Piagetian theory, (b) stage transition in cognitive development, (c) social factors which influence cognition, (d) the effects of schooling on intellectual development, and (e) the design and methodology of cross-cultural research. 'For the present, the reader is warned that in almost all previous research these factors have been highly intertwined. Conclusions attributing cross-cultural differences to any one particular factor must generally be viewed askance', (ibid., p. 477).

She concludes, 'The application of complex research design to Piagetian questions in a cross-cultural context opens up exciting possibilities for significant contributions to developmental theory. By designing studies to investigate cognitive development in varying cultural settings, researches may produce the natural experiment that has the potential advantage of being representative of cognitive developmental processes as they actually operate in the environment', (ibid., p. 502).

Ashton maintained, 'although Labov specifically addresses himself to the plight of black children in "white" school systems, his criticisms apply to much of the cross-cultural Piagetian research', p. 491. Cole and Bruner (1971) have provided a thorough discussion of Labov's (1970) attack of the experimental method as applied to the problems of subcultural differences in cognitive capacity, and the same formulations may be applied to cross-cultural studies: '(a) formal experimental equivalence of operations does not ensure de facto equivalence of experimental treatments; (b) different subcultural groups are pre-disposed to interpret the experimental stimuli (situations) differently; (c) different subcultural groups are motivated by different concerns relevant to the experimental task; (d) in view of the inadequacies of experimentation, inferences about lack of competence among black children are unwarranted', p. 235. Dasen (1976, personal com-munication*) asserted, 'Thus the cultural or subcultural differences reported in cross-cultural Piagetian studies may simply reflect methodological problems, for example, the fact that the tasks were not "their problem". I do not personally believe that all or most of the results accumulated thus far ought to be discarded on these methodological grounds (cf Kamara and Easley's critique, [1976]). If we were to follow such an extreme position in the interpretation of the comparison of Australian Aborigines, Eskimos and Ebrié Africans

*   Gratitude is extended to Dr P.R. Dasen of Geneva University for sending the work to be referenced.

summarized (in) (Dasen, 1975a), we would have to assume that the development of spatial and conservation concepts occurs congruently in these populations, but that the conservation tasks were inadequate for the Eskimos and Aborigines but not for the Africans, and that the spatial tasks were inadequate for the African but not the Eskimo and Aboriginal children. Whereas this possibly cannot be ruled out, it is definitely not the impression I had when carrying out the study. I believe it is more appropriate to consider the differences found as a true reflection of eco-cultural demands, but restricting the conclusions at least momentarily to the performance level. This, I believe, is consistent with Cole and Bruner's position, since they caution against "inferences about lack of competence". Finding differences at the performance level is not trivial if we want to know under which circumstances basic competences are expressed in overt behaviour.

Thus, whereas I reject a "Labov effect" interpretation in its extreme form, I do not wish to minimize methodological problems. Indeed I particularly welcome Kamara and Easley's methodological critique . . . (1976)', pp. 17–18.

More recently, Buck-Morss (1975) in an article entitled, 'Socio-economic bias in Piaget's theory and its implications for cross-culture studies', maintains, 'The cross-cultural application of Piaget tests has generated a tangled controversy due to the fact that Western children appear to undergo a more rapid cognitive development than their non-Western peers (Berry and Dasen, 1974; Bruner *et al.*, 1966; Price-Williams, 1969). Participants in the controversy tend to fall into two groups: psychological universalists, who stress the subjective universality of human psychology, and cultural relativists, who emphasize the objective, cultural and environmental variables in psychological development. I spoke recently with psychologists in several African countries where Piaget tests have been administered frequently to children of the first post-independence generations (Evans, 1970, pp. 75–83), and where, with education a major issue of national policy, the controversy has an implicit political content. Yet this content is obscured by the fact that the ideological implications of the two positions are not unequivocal. The psychological universalist position – which is taken, with qualifications, by Piaget (1966) himself – assumes that a general theory of cognition is possible, and thus appears to stand squarely opposed to ideologies of biological racism; but it cannot account for the frequent chronological "lag" in test performance of non-Western samples and the fact that members of some cultures never "reach" certain levels of logical operations (Dasen, 1974) without implying another kind of ethnocentrism, the cultural superiority of the West. Cultural relativists, sensitive to this problem, point to a plethora of cultural variables both within the tests (method of testing, equipment used, language and translation) and among those tested (literacy level, child-rearing, parental occupation), and claim that the test results are therefore culturally biased. On the level of theory such relativism maintains its moral and political purity, but in practice it cannot avoid contamination: here anthropological tolerance can become a veil for paternalism. For however much respect is given to "traditional" cultures, unless the children of these new nations become capable of performing the kind of abstract thinking Piaget has identified, they will have difficulty in competing on an international level where Western "culture" controls the playing field and has already determined the rules of the game. This argument, in turn, has its problems, however, as it runs into that dilemma which structures so much of Third World intellectual debates: acknowledgement of a need to imitate the West in order to achieve "equal" cognitive skills can encourage another kind of psychological inequality by feeding the subjective sense of inferiority which "Franz Fanon" so perceptively analysed and which the cultural movement of "négritude" was designed to overcome', pp. 35—36.

Buck-Morss speculates that the existence of a 'time-lag' found in the cross-cultural application of Piaget tests may result from a socioeconomic bias in Piaget's theory. Abstract, formal cognition may reflect a particular social structure, encompassing the principles of exchange value, reification, and alienation which dominate production and exchange in the industrialized West. The objective as well as the subjective variables of conscious participation in the abstract levels of the social structure, might account for cross-cultural disparities in Piaget test performance. She concludes with the following tentative hypotheses: '1) Among certain groups, cognitive development in the skills of abstract thinking may be *a priori* impaired by these groups' exclusion from direct, conscious participation in the abstract levels of society. The child's imitation of parental models would function to perpetuate inequalities of cognitive development, whereas for the middle class Western child or the children of the Third World urban elite, identification with parents and education in formal logic are mutually reinforcing experiences in socialization, they are conflicting in the case of the out-groups, where "satellization" on parental models and the development of abstract cognitive competence lead in opposite directions. (2) Differences in cognitive style both reflect and perpetuate class distinction within industrialized countries, and reflect and perpetuate the domination of urban elites in developing countries. To count on the socialization process as a self-regulating mechanism to adjust disparities between social and cognitive structures would seem to be overly optimistic. (3) Development of abstract cognitive skills among groups who presently "lag" behind, demands socioeconomic and political reform as much as reform in educational curriculum. In regard to research, the implications of viewing Piaget's stress on abstract formalism as expressing a socioeconomic bias would suggest the importance of relating test results to the structure of the child's society and his place within it, as well as his cognitive grasp of that structure. It also suggests the need for developing theories of cognitive structures other than abstract formalism, where the content of thought determines its logic, as it does not only in the structure of myths, of oral legends, and dreams, but also in the Hegelian-Marxist tradition of dialectical thought', (*ibid.*, pp. 46—47).

More recently, Dasen (1976, personal communication) stated, 'Even though the details of Buck-Morss' reading of Piaget are partly the result of her own historical dialectics, the general criticism of a socioeconomic bias or of the ethnocentrism of Piaget's theory has to be taken seriously and will be part of the debate for some years to come', p. 8. Dasen has edited a book of readings, *Piagetian Psychology: Cross-Cultural Contributions*, with a Foreword by Jean Piaget. Questions raised in this book include: How universal are the cognitive processes described by Piaget? To what extent is cognitive development determined by cultural variables? Which aspects of Piaget's theory have to be modified to take cultural variations into account? 'Its purpose, however, is not to provide definitive answers; that would certainly be premature. Cross-cultural Piagetian psychology is a relatively recent development. It has not reached maturity, but is still at the stage of concrete data collection. This book is a reflection of this stage; at the same time its goal is to provide promising leads for future research. Contradiction is the motor of development: in presenting the sometimes conflicting viewpoints of several authors in a same volume, there is hope to increase the likelihood of a development to a next, more formal stage . . . Cross-cultural psychology enables us to test the hypotheses and theories established on limited and homogeneous populations. Too much of psychology is only the psychology of rats and first-year students. How does it apply in other cultures? A large amount of decentration is necessary to answer these questions, but until we can do so, we are in the situation of the traveller who has a map of New York to find his way through Shanghai', pp. 1—2.

Abstracts

Perceptual set induction in young children: cross-cultural support for the role of active classification
E. Abravanel, 1975

AIM / To study perceptual set induction among Indian children.

SUBJECTS / N = 120 children from the city of Mysore in India. The younger sample (N = 62) had a mean age of four years four months and the older sample (N = 58) had a mean age of five years three months.

METHOD / Each experimental child was presented with a stack of 13 pictures composed of the Human Series and the Plant Series together with the ambiguous Rat-Man. The latter was patterned after Bugelski and Alampay (1961). The S was told that each successive picture was to be named and piled together with 'those pictures which it was most like; more the same as'. 'As the subject was presented with each picture (randomly arranged), he was encouraged to name it and sort it. If the subject found the sorting task difficult, coaching was given by specifying that pictures in one pile have leaves and grow from the ground, whereas those in the other pile are alive and can move from one place to another. This kept the criterion sufficiently vague to allow for either "Rat" or "Man" to be named for the 13 critical card — the ambiguous Rat-Man. After the subject indicated how he perceived the ambiguous figure, we asked him to point to distinctive features, such as eyes, nose, mouth, ears, etc., in order to be certain of the organization he had made. This was especially important for subjects who labeled their percepts as a cat, monkey, dog, rabbit, etc. One further check on the subject's perceptual organization involved asking whether the "picture could be something else"? Our purpose for including this question was to determine whether the children could readily perceive both "Rat" and "Man" alternatives in an ambiguous figure . . . Control-group subjects were shown only the Rat-Man drawing for identification, without exposure to a set-series, in order to assess the relative likelihoods of seeing either "Rat" or "Man" at each stage. These data would provide the baseline against which to determine a set effect', pp. 160–161. (Fuller details of the experimental procedure are given in Abravanel, 1975, pp. 160–161.)

RESULTS / The evidence produced demonstrated the formation of perceptual sets in pre-school age children and provided a firmer basis for conceptualization. It also explained the failure of other studies to find evidence for susceptibility to perceptual sets among young children. The author also considered the results in relation to contemporary ideas about symbolic mediation and production deficiencies in children's memory and thinking. Piaget's (1952, 1967) results are cited in the discussion of the results.

The development of the concept of spatial co-ordinate system (Concept of perpendicular and horizontal) amongst Iraqi children *
S. Al-Fakhri, 1975

AIM / This study attempted to determine the development of the concept of spatial coordinate system, i.e. the concept of perpendicular and horizontal among Iraqi children.

SUBJECTS / N = 180 children taken from the Iraqi public schools and kindergarten, ages 4–12 years, 20 children for each level, divided equally for sex.

METHOD / The method used is a replica of Piaget's called 'Les Systèmes de Reference et Les Coordonnées; L'horizontale et La Verticele' in his book *La Representation de L'Espace Chez L'Enfant*. The orientations of the bottle were 45°, 90°, 135° and 180°.

RESULTS / Results show a gradual development of the concept. Three stages were evidenced:

A. *First stage* (four to six years): Answers of children of this stage were distinguished by topological relations. Children find it sufficient to put a point or a line or a circle inside the bottle, irrespective of its orientation.
B. *Second stage* (ages seven to eight): Children are able to determine the surface level of the water in the natural position of the bottle. They are unable however to imagine the level of the water in the different orientations of the bottle, and they use the edges of the bottle as a reference line where the remains attached to the base (bottom) of the bottle, irrespective of its orientation. When the liquid is separated from the bottle, it remains parallel to it.
As to the concept of perpendicular, the children of this stage put things perpendicular to the slope of the mountain. They become

* Written and prepared by the author for inclusion in this volume. Gratitude is extended to Dr Salima Al-Fakhri of the University of Baghdad.,

perpendicular only on the plain next to the mountain or on the peak of the mountain.

C. *Third stage* (10 and above): The child uses a reference outside the bottle itself. It is evidenced first with the 90° orientation. It was more difficult however, in regard to 45° and 135°, where only 42, five per cent for age 11—12 children, were able to accomplish the task.

The same results were found with regard to the concept of perpendicular.

DISCUSSION / It can be assumed that our children pass through the same stages designated by Piaget but with a lag of three years if compared with the Geneva sample. This lag is attributed to cultural factors.

The development of the concept of length amongst Iraqi children*
S. Al-Fakhri, 1975a

AIM / The study tries to determine the development of the concept of the conservation of length among middle class Iraqi children.

SUBJECTS / N = 180 children ages four—12 years, divided into 20 subjects for each age level, divided equally for sex. All children were taken from school and kindergarten in a generally middle class section of Baghdad.

METHOD / Each child was tested individually and the Piagetian clinical approach was used. The children's answers were recorded verbatim.

1. The child is shown two parallel and corresponding rows of match sticks. Each row is composed of six match sticks. The rows are about 5 cm apart. The child is requested to determine whether the two lines are equal in length. If he expresses their equality, we move to the next age.

The sticks in the first row are arranged so that they form an acute angle with the other row which is kept straight. The child is then requested to determine whether the two rows are still equal in length. Then, he is requested to justify his answer irrespective of whether his answer was correct or not.

In order to be sure that the child understands what we mean, we ask him if two ants walked on each of the two roads formed by the match

---

*   Written and prepared by the author for inclusion in this volume. Gratitude is extended to Dr Salima Al-Fakhri of the University of Baghdad.

sticks would both of them walk the same distance or not. Then he is requested to explain why.

2. The child is shown two strips of cardboard, 30 cm long each and 1 cm wide. The two strips are laid down parallel with the ends corresponding to each other.

The child is allowed to be sure of the equality of the two strips. One of the strips is cut into smaller parts of different lengths and arranged in a circular fashion. The child is then requested to determine whether the lengths of the strips are still equal and to justify his answers.

RESULTS / Three stages were distinguished in the development of the concept of length among Iraqi children:

1) The first stage is characterized by the non-conservation of length, which was noted among children ages four—eight years.

2) The second stage is a transitional stage where the children exhibit hesitation regarding the conservation of length in one case but not another, and even when he denies conservation, he remains hesitant and takes a different stance when compared to the younger children.

3) During the third stage, children exhibit conservation of length. This phenomena appears at the age of ten amongst 50 per cent of the sample, and it rises to 85 per cent at the age of 11. The remaining 15 per cent are in the transitional stage.

DISCUSSION / It can be safely assumed that our children pass through the same stages distinguished by Piaget. However, the onset of the formation of the concept of length seems to lag about two years when compared to the Swiss children. This difference can not be attributed to methodological differences, nor can they be attributed to biological variables. It seems that cultural factors including the educational system are responsible for the lag.

The development of the concept of class-inclusion among Iraqi children*
S. Al-Fakhri, 1975b

AIM / This study tried to determine the development of the concept of class inclusion among Iraqi children.

SUBJECTS / N = 180 children ages four—12 years, from the public

* Written and prepared by the author for inclusion in this volume. Gratitude is extended to Dr Salima Al-Fakhri of the University of Baghdad.

schools and kindergarten of a predominantly middle class section of Baghdad, equally divided among the sexes and ages.

METHOD / Is a replication of Piaget's (1964) method approximately.

RESULTS / Three stages were evidenced:

A. The first stage where the part is perceived by the child to be longer than the whole. The red beads form the longer necklace and the smaller beads form the longer necklace also. This stage is seen in children ages four—9 years.

B. A transitional stage where the child forms the concept in one element and denies it for the other. He (she) remains hesitant and contradicts himself (herself). Ages of this stage, nine—10 years.

C. The concept is formed amongst children 10 years—above.

DISCUSSION / Results indicate that the concept is formed in accordance with the stages designated by Piaget. The onset of the formation of the concept however, shows a lag of two years when compared to the Geneva children. This lag is attributed to cultural factors.

*The concept of the conservation of continuous quantity among Iraqi children**
S. Al-Fakhri, 1975c

AIM / This project attempts to determine the development of the concept of the conservation of continuous matter (liquids) amongst middle class Iraqi children.

SUBJECTS / N = 160 children, ages four—11 years. Twenty children for each age level divided equally for sex. Children were taken from Iraqi public schools and kindergarten in a predominantly middle class section of Baghdad.

METHOD / Children were tested individually using the Piagetian clinical approach. The following procedure was used:
Two identical flasks containing equal amounts of coloured water (one blue, one red) are shown to the child. He is then requested to

* Written and prepared by the author for inclusion in this volume. Gratitude is extended to Dr Salima Al-Fakhri of the University of Baghdad.

determine whether the flasks contain equal amounts of liquid. If the child denies the equality of the amounts of liquid he is allowed to change the amounts until they become equal.

The liquid is poured from one of the flasks into another bottle of a different shape, and the child is then asked if the liquid in the new bottle is equal to the liquid in the standard flask, and he is requested to give the reason.

The liquid is then returned to the original flask. The child is then given six small glasses. The liquid in the flask is poured into these glasses, and the child is asked if the liquid in the six glasses is less, more or equal to the liquid in the standard glass. He is asked also to give reasons for his answer.

Two of the small glasses are taken, then the child is requested to make sure that both of them contain an equal amount of liquid. The contents of one of the glasses is poured into a test tube. The child is asked if the liquid in the test tube is equal to the liquid in the standard glass or not and he is requested to give reasons.

RESULTS / It was possible to distinguish three different stages with regard to the development of the concept of conservation of continuous matter.

1) The first stage is characterized by non-conservation. The amount of liquid, as seen by the child, increases or decreases in accordance with the general shape of the container. This stage was found among the children between the ages of four–seven.

2) The second stage is characterized by the appearance of conservation in some of the tests but not others, or hesitation regarding the concept of conservation. The stage reaches its peak in ages seven and eight.

3) The third stage where the concept of conservation is established amongst the children. The amount of liquid is seen as constant irrespective of the shape of the flask or container. This stage was evident among children ages nine and above.

DISCUSSION / The results of this study were similar to the general studies with regard to the sequence of stages. Our results were similar to those of Za'rour (1971) in Lebanon where the concept was found to appear during the age of nine. This indicates that Iraqi children like the Lebanese children seem to lag about two years behind the Genevan children. The lag is attributed to cultural differences including education.

*The formation of the concept of measurement amongst Iraqi children.
The determination of a point on a straight line**
S. Al-Fakhri, 1975d

AIM / This study tries to determine the development of the concept
of measurement amongst Iraqi children by determining a point on a
straight line.

SUBJECTS / N = 180 children ages four-12 years, divided into 20
subjects for each age level, divided equally for sex. All children were
taken from public school children and kindergarten in a predominantly
middle class section of Baghdad.

METHOD / The method used was the replica of Piaget's study called
'La Determination d' un segment sur une Droite' in *La Geométrie
Spontanée de l'Enfant.*

RESULTS / Three stages in the development of the concept were
indicated by the data:

1) *Stage one*: The concept is not formed where the child places his
bead in front of the model bead disregarding distances. This stage
covers ages four-eight years.
2) *Second stage*: The child is in a transitional stage, and instead of an
actual measurement uses visual estimation, ages range from nine-11
years.
3) *Third stage*: The child depends on rendering correct answers by
using units, ages range 12 and above.

DISCUSSION / The result indicates the existence of consecutive
stages of development in concept formation. Results indicate a lag of
two years when compared to the Geneva sample. This lag is attributed
to the educational system particularly since such topics are included in
the curriculum.

*The development of some concepts relevant to natural phenomena
among Iraqi children**
S. Al-Fakhri, 1975e

AIM / The aim of this study is to determine the development of the

---

*   Written and prepared by the author for inclusion in this volume. Gratitude is
extended to Dr Salima Al-Fakhri of the University of Baghdad.

concept of 'night', 'clouds', and 'rain', among Iraqi children.

SUBJECTS / N = 180 children ages four-12 years, from the public schools and kindergarten of a predominantly middle class section of Baghdad, equally divided among the sexes and ages.

METHOD / The clinical Piagetian approach was used. Children were tested individually. A dialogue is started on each subject by a question 'What is night?', 'What is rain?', 'What are clouds?'. The nature of the dialogue depends on the answers of the children themselves.

A later analysis of the dialogues was conducted where the answers and explanations of the children were classified and the frequencies of these explanations were compiled.

RESULTS / Three stages were noted:

A. *First stage* (ages four-six): The children's answers are 'artificialistes'. 'Night takes place so that we sleep'. 'Rain to irrigate'. Some of the answers related rain to clouds, but considered clouds an aftermath to rain.

B. *Second Stage* (seven-nine years): Night is connected to sundown. Religious reasons are given for nightfall sometimes children connect the disappearance of the sun behind the clouds to night. A relationship of rain to clouds is established. Rain however, is seen as a deed of God or human beings. Some children connected rain to vapour but the source remained manufactured.

C. *The third stage* (10 and above): Natural reasons are given for all the phenomena.

*An experimental study of the development of the concept of quantitative conservation: substance, weight and volume in Iraqi children**
A.A. Al-Shaikh, 1973

AIM / This project attempted to test the following hypotheses:

1) The number of conservation responses varies significantly with: sex (boys and girls); type of question (prediction, judgment and explanation); type of quantity (substance, weight and volume); age level; and interaction between type of quantity and age level.

2) The onset of appearance of the concept of conservation amongst

* Written and prepared by the author for inclusion in this volume. Gratitude is extended to Dr Abdul Aziz Al-Shaikh of the University of Baghdad.

Iraqi children lags behind its appearance among Swiss children.

3) The development of the concept of conservation passes through a transitional stage.

The writer also attempted to study the cultural aspects of the mental operations.

SUBJECTS / N = 264 children, their ages ranged from about four to 14 years, were randomly selected from a kindergarten and five mixed primary schools located in a district of Baghdad inhabited mainly by middle class residents. The sample was classified into 11 age-levels (24 children at each level; 12 boys and 12 girls).

METHOD / The procedure being kept as close as possible to that of Elkind (1961). But we used an ordinary balance in order to show the children the equality of weight, and two identical glasses half-filled with water to test the volume (by displacement method), instead of Elkind's abstract questions.

RESULTS /
1) The general tendency of the results confirmed Piaget's findings with regard to the development of the concept of conservation progressively with age.

2) Results did not show any significant differences between males and females in their acquisition of the concept.

3) The F-ratio for the type of question was 8.02 and was significant beyond the .01 level. T-tests indicated that explanation was more difficult than judgment or prediction for small children.

4) The F-ratio for the type of quantity obtained in the present study was better than chance expectations ($F = 42.64$; $p > .01$). T-tests for the means of conservation responses of substance, weight and volume revealed that they were significantly different from each other ($p > .01$).

5) Differences among age-level were found to be significant beyond the .01 level ($F = 31.92$).

6) Analysis of variance for the interaction between type of quantity and age-level supported Piaget's theory concerning the development of the concept of conservation of substance, weight and volume in three stages ($F = 6.93$; $p > .01$).

7) Seventy-five per cent of the children were able to acquire the concept of conservation of substance, weight and volume at the ages nine-10, 10-11 and 13-14 respectively.

8) Transitional stages were witnessed in all three concepts.

9) Four types of explanation were found: ambiguous, perceptual, concrete and formal operational.

10) Iraqi school children exhibited mental operations similar to those stated by Piaget such as reversibility, identity and composition.

DISCUSSION / The lack of difference between the sexes may be attributed to equal opportunities given to boys and girls. Results also indicated that explanation responses were rather difficult when compared to prediction or judgment responses. So it is insufficient for research needs to obtain only a judgment or prediction response from the child. to facilitate the acquisition of the concept. The 'stages' designated by Piaget (1941) were confirmed in a general sense, although the onset of concept-formation shows a lag of two years. It may be concluded from the findings related to the arguments which were used by children to defend their judgments, that the principles of cognitive development are universal.

The development of the concept of conservation of length among Iraqi school children*
A.A. Al-Shaikh, 1974

AIM / The following hypotheses were tested:
1) The number of conservation responses varies insignificantly with sex (boys and girls).
2) The number of conservation responses varies significantly with type of question (judgment and explanation).
3) The onset of appearance of length conservation amongst Iraqi children lags behind its appearance among Swiss children.
4) The development of length conservation in Iraqi children passes through the same Piagetian 'stages'.

SUBJECTS / N = 235 children (114 boys and 121 girls) were used. The sample was randomly selected from some mixed primary schools. They were predominantly from the middle class section of Baghdad. Ages ranged between five and 13 years.

METHOD / Two experiments were conducted, as those originally designated by Piaget *et al.* (1960) and replicated by Lovell *et al.* (1962). The general procedure was the same as that of Lovell, except that in this study the child was requested to explain his judgments i.e. give reasons for his judgments irrespective of the nature of the answer. The same criteria for stages were also used. The two experiments were:

*   Written and prepared by the author for inclusion in this volume. Gratitude is extended to Dr Abdul Aziz Al-Shaikh of the University of Baghdad.

Experiment One, conservation of length, the length of lines and the coincidence of their extremities, and Experiment two, conservation of length, comparison of length and change of position.

If 50 per cent of the children exhibited conservation the concept was considered formed.

RESULTS /

1) No significant differences were noted between boys and girls in their responses of conservation in both tests.

2) The mean of the conservation responses were significantly different with regard to explanation *vs.* judgment. ($p > .01$)

3) Iraqi children lagged about three years behind Swiss and English children with regard to the acquisition of the concept.

4) Three stages were discovered. The onset of the first stage is about (five–six years), the onset of the second stage is about (seven–eight) and the onset of the third stage is about (10).

5) The first experiment was relatively easier than the second one.

6) In the second experiment, it was noted that the second question (when the rods were placed to form the letter T) was more difficult than the third question (when the rods were placed at an acute angle), but it was easier than the first one (when one rod was pushed about 1 cm. ahead of the other). The F-ratio for the type of position was significant beyond the .01 level. Individual t-tests revealed that the mean of responses of each question varied significantly from both others ($p > .01$).

7) It was found that Iraqi school children had used the same arguments which were described by Piaget to explain their judgments.

DISCUSSION / The absence of differences between the sexes with regard to concept formation may be attributed to similar life conditions. The lag indicated in this study is greater than that found in other studies conducted in Iraq (Al-Shaikh, 1973). This may be due to the difficulty of the tasks required of the child. Sticks used in this study were very small and Piaget found that longer sticks were responsible for the formation of the concept at an earlier age.

Taking these factors into consideration it may be assumed that development of this concept is not different from other concepts studied in Iraq.

Note on conservation differences for Indian and White children
A.D. Bowd, 1975

AIM / To examine the acquisition of length and volume concepts

87

among a group of Canadian Indian children and a group of Whites.

SUBJECTS / N = 68, thirty-five Indian children (mean age seven years 11 months) and 33 white children (mean age eight years one month).

METHOD / The tests administered were the Piagetian concepts of length and volume. The experimental procedures were patterned after Philp and Kelly (1975).

RESULTS / Of the Indian children 37 per cent and 58 per cent of the White children demonstrated length operativity. However, the difference was not statistically significant (χ^2 = 2.96). With respect to volume, of the Indian children 43 per cent and 67 per cent of the whites demonstrated operativity — a difference which was significant at the .05 level (χ^2 = 3.84). 'When the groups were compared for those children who conserved both length and volume, 29 per cent of the Indian sample and 55 per cent of the Whites, the difference achieved significance at the .05 level (χ^2 = 4.33). The magnitude of differences observed in the rate of acquisition of conservation in this study is small in relation to those noted for comparisons employing more traditional cultural groups (Dasen, 1972), and might tentatively be attributed to differences in the quality of English spoken in the home together with differences in socioeconomic status', Bowd (1975, p. 362).

*The development of conservation in Aboroginal children: a replication study**
P.R. Dasen, 1972

AIM / The study attempted a replication of De Lemos (1966, 1969a, 1969b) investigations.

SUBJECTS / N = 90, with an age-range from six to 16. In addition to the school sample, ten adults also participated. These Aborigines lived at the Hermannsburg missions. The subjects were either full- or part-blood.

METHOD / Each subject was seen individually on the following tests: conservation of quantity; weight; volume; length; seriation of lengths; spatial tests of topological orders; rotation of landscapes and

* Gratitude is extended to Dr P. Dasen of the University of Geneva for sending his work to be abstracted.

horizontality. These were derived from the experiments of Piaget and associates and the full details, including scoring procedures are described in Dasen (1970).

RESULTS / The Piagetian stages of development were fully evidenced as were in De Lemos' studies. The qualitative aspects of both European and Aboriginal children were substantiated. However, the rate of conservation acquisition was slower with an asymptotic development for the Aboriginal children (Hermannsburg — De Lemos, 1966 and Hermannsburg — Dasen, 1970; for percentage of subjects conserving quantity, weight and volume). Overall, both the studies produced similar quantitative and qualitative resultant patterns. However, Dasen's results did not support the quantity-weight reversal as did De Lemos' findings. Dasen attributes this disconfirmation to three causes: (a) 'the change in test materials; (b) the reduction of an effect of separation of the testing sessions; (c) the elimination of systematic order effects in the present study', p. 79. Dasen's study showed a 'weight–volume reversal' and the author admits, 'no explanation of this new reversal comes to mind, except that the concepts of weight and volume are equally irrelevant to Aboriginal culture. What the present study and that of De Lemos show, is that the particular horizontal shiftings (*décalages*) typically found in European chlidren may not apply in the same way to other cultural groups', p. 82. With respect to genetic differences, the De Lemos (1969a, p. 262) result of part Aboriginal children performing markedly better conservation performances, was not upheld. Dasen finally concludes, 'Our results cannot, of course, be taken as conclusive until their contradiction with those obtained by De Lemos has been resolved. However, until this can be done, De Lemos' results should no longer be used to support the argument for genetic differences in mental functioning', p. 84.

*Piagetian research in Central Australia**
P.R. Dasen, 1974

AIM / The author hypothesized that due to the Australian Aborigines' hunting, food gathering and travelling long distances in barren environments, their acquisition of spatial tasks would be relatively earlier than logico-mathematical operations.

SUBJECTS / N = 245. Of these 145 were aged between six to 16

* Gratitude is extended to Dr P. Dasen of the University of Geneva for sending his work to be abstracted.

years and 20 were adults. 'The low-contact group consisted of the total school population at Areyonga Settlement (N = 55); the high-contact group was selected from the Hermannsburg mission school (N = 90). A reference group of 80 European children was tested in Canberra'.

METHOD / The tests administered were: conservation of quantity; weight; volume. Length and seriation of lengths (Logico-mathematical operations). Spatial operations included: linear, circular and reverse orders; horizontality and the rotation of two landscape models. Full details of the tests including experimental procedures and scoring are described in Dasen (1970).

RESULTS / The results demonstrated that the stages occur in the same order for both the European subjects of Canberra and the Aborigines of Central Australia. However, the rate of concept development in the latter subjects, is slow and asymptotic at the higher ages. The reversal between quantity and weight was not evidenced and did not substantiate De Lemos' (1966) finding that 'the reversal in the order of development of quantity and weight from the invariant order postulated may be due to the effects of experience on the tests'. Both studies, however demonstrated that 'the particular horizontal *décalages* typically found in European children may not apply in the same way to other ethnic groups'. With respect to part- and full-blood comparison in the Hermannsburg sample, De Lemos' (1966, 1969b) evidence was not supported. (De Lemos' study has been described in Modgil, 1974, pp. 237-38). The relative development of logico-mathematical and spatial operations indicated that, 'In the Canberra sample, logico-mathematical operations are acquired earlier than spatial operations. In both Aboriginal samples, this relationship is reversed: Aboriginal children develop spatial concepts earlier than logico-mathematical concepts. A detailed analysis (Dasen, 1970) shows that the difference, again, is statistically significant only in the older age groups'.

An extension of the study involved 80 children at Hermannsburg tested with a modified test battery. Almost identical results were recorded in both studies, except for weight conservation, 'where the attainment level was situated between those reported respectively by De Lemos (1966, 1969a, b) and Dasen (1970). Thirty-six of the 80 subjects had been tested 16 months earlier, and a marked improvement was noticed in the younger age-groups in the extension study.'

*Concrete operational development in three cultures**
P.R. Dasen, 1975.

AIMS / The author was intent to extend Berry's (1971) model of ecological functionalism to Piagetian developmental psychology. '. . . if three subsistence-economy populations are placed on an ecocultural scale, with low food-accumulating, nomadic, hunting groups at one extreme (e.g., Eskimos and Australian Aborigines), and high food-accumulating, sedentary, agriculturalist groups at the other extreme (e.g., Ebrié of the Ivory Coast), the former are expected to develop spatial concepts more rapidly than the latter will . . . furthermore, it seemed reasonable to expect that the African group, under the pressure of its own ecocultural milieu, would develop other concepts more rapidly than would the Eskimo and Aboriginal groups ..... because of the agricultural production, accumulation, and exchange of food in the African group, its members are expected to attain concepts of conservation of quantity, weight, and volume . . . more rapidly than would Eskimos and Aborigines . . .' p. 158.

SUBJECTS / N = 190 children, aged six through 14 from three cultural groups: Canadian Eskimos, Australian Aborigines, and Ebrié Africans.

METHOD / Each subject was administered the following tasks: (a) Linear, reverse, and circular order; (b) Rotation of landscape models (localization of topographical positions); (c) Horizontality; (d) Conservation of quantity (liquids); (e) Conservation of weight (plasticine); and (f) Conservation of volume (water displaced by plasticine).

RESULTS / Berry's (1971) model of ecological functionalism was fully supported. The prediction that the rate of development of concrete operations might be partly determined by ecological and cultural factors, was substantiated. More specifically, that if three subsistence-economy populations were placed on an ecocultural scale, with low food-accumulating, nomadic, hunting groups at one extreme, and high food-accumulating, sedentary, agriculturalist groups at the other extreme, the former were expected to develop spatial concepts more rapidly than will the latter, whereas the sedentary group was expected to attain concepts of conservation of quantity, weight, and volume more rapidly than nomadic groups will, received full credence.

*   Gratitude is extended to Dr P. Dasen of the University of Geneva for sending
    his work to be abstracted.

Dasen concluded with a discussion on the ambiguous results obtained in the age range eight to 11 years for the conservation tasks. The structural properties of the stages and their hierarchical ordering were verified in each sample.

*An investigation of reasoning ability in adopted and fostered Aboriginal children**
P.R. Dasen, P.R. De Lacey and G.N. Seagrim

AIM / The authors hypothesized that the Aboriginal children, 'had they been reared under similar conditions, would not have performed at a superior level to Aboriginal children of comparable age reared on missions or government settlements'.

SUBJECTS / N = 35, with an age-range from five through 14 years. Other personal details such as the believed ancestry of the subjects and some early medical histories were obtained.

METHOD / Each child was tested at home on the following tests:
(a) Conservation of quantity, (b) Conservation of weight, (c) Horizontality (d) Seriation, (e) Reclassification: the Nixon Test, and (f) The Peabody Picture Vocabulary Test, Form A. (Dunn 1965). (The Nixon test was not administered beyond the age nine and the Horizontality test was not given before the age of eight).

RESULTS / The results were compared with Dasen (1970), Piaget and Inhelder (1969, p. 159), De Lacey (1969) and 'from the only Aboriginal comparison data available, from the unpublished longitudinal study . . . ' The authors conclude, ' . . . the performance of these children on four of the tests is equal to that of comparison European groups. In each case their performance is superior to that of comparison Aboriginal groups. However, in the two tests of conservation their performance is intermediate between that of the comparison European and Aboriginal groups and this finding requires some discussion. A possible explanation for their relatively poor showing on these tests is that the two conservation tests demand an advanced level of verbal competence. In one of the Conservation tests used, the European comparison sample was drawn from a population which would not be representative of the average Australian population in respect of verbal fluency and Canberra children, forming the

---

* Gratitude is extended to Dr P. Dasen of the University of Geneva for sending this work to be abstracted.

comparison group for the conservation of quantity, tended to come from relatively high socioeconomic levels of the population. The Aboriginal children, however, were living with families who would not be expected to have such an advantage in verbal fluency . . . therefore, . . . the comparison being made is not a "fair" one and that the deficit of our experimental group is being over-estimated. A second possible explanation is that the conservation tests provide a more accurate estimate of untutored intellectual ability?'

Time conservation across cultures
A.D. Dempsey, 1971

AIM / The author attempted a comparison of the conservation of the time concept among subjects of different cultures from five Indian tribes in Arizona, Mexican-Americans and 'middle class' Anglos.

SUBJECTS / N = 45. Fifteen children from each age group seven, nine and eleven. The sample included Hopi Indians; Apache Indians; Pima Indians; Papago Indians; Navajo Indians; Mexican-Americans; and Anglo children.

METHOD / Each child was administered two tests of the conservation of simultaneity and two for the conservation of order of events. These were replications of Piaget's (1970) conservation of time experiments. Questioning and the general experimental procedure followed Lovell and Slater (1960).

RESULTS / When using Piaget's criterion of three-quarters operational responses, the results were as follows: 'No group tested was able to conserve simultaneity on any of the tests used at any of the ages tested. On the simple order of events task only Anglo children were able to conserve at age seven. By age nine all except Navajo and Apache had conserved and by age eleven all except Apache children conserved. On the hard order of events test, none of the groups had achieved conservation by age nine and only Anglo, Mexican-American and Pima achieved conservation by age eleven', p. 119.

The author draws attention to the effect of culture on the conservation of time and recommends 'that the study be expanded to include a larger sample, utilize more of the tasks devised by Piaget, utilize trained interpreters where necessary and be carried out in a longitudinal fashion to determine more precisely the intellectual process involved in acquiring the time process and to determine which operations are amenable to training and which are not', p. 119.

The development of adaptive intelligence
C.F. Feldman, B. Lee, J.D. McLean, D.B. Pillemer, and J.R. Murray, 1974

AIM / To examine the Piagetian hypothesis that 'development has the same hierarchical structure in all cultures undergoing successful adaptation'.

SUBJECTS / Groups of children in three separate cultures — Eskimo children of Alaska's North Slope, and children in the mountain region of Kentucky and in Hawaii — within the age range from seven to 19 years.

METHOD / Ss were administered a specially constructed nonverbal test of logical thinking. The test consisted of a sequence of tasks using coloured blocks — The Coloured Blocks Test. The tasks represented three Piagetian stages and formed a series which began with simple perceptual matching and concluded with the abstract operations of symbolic logic. The Coloured Blocks Test was divided into five sections preceded by two training tasks. 'Each of these sections can be interpreted as testing abilities characteristic of a particular Piagetian stage. Earlier sections of the test deal with the construction of simple classifications according to colour and shape, and later sections construct propositions involving sameness or difference of colour and shape. The last sections test the child's ability to transform the relations expressed in these propositions', (*ibid.*, p. 49). Additionally, an analogue task was given where 'the first analogue section is structurally identical to Section I of the Coloured Blocks Test. The stimulus and response sets consist of drawings of walruses, seals, bears and foxes. As in Section I of the Coloured Blocks Test, the S is presented with a partial matrix. The task is to complete the matrix with a drawing from the response set', p. 62. Generally, five cognitive operations were defined: '(a) completing a matrix by attending to one set of relations between attributes (Section I of the test); (b) completing a matrix by coordinating two sets of relations between attributes (Section II); (c) identifying the operation performed on a set of relations between attributes (Section III); (d) operating on a set of relations between attributes (Section IV); and (e) operating on operations (Section V)', (*ibid.*, p. 66).

RESULTS / That the appearance of cognitive abilities follows a logically invariant sequence was confirmed. Cognitive development followed the staging pattern Piaget described and verified Piaget's claim that an adaptation — not unlike biological adaptation — governs cognitive growth. This adaptation consists of a constant interaction between the person and the environment.

With respect to the Eskimo children, the focus of the study, the percentage of correct responses for The Coloured Blocks Test, for the five sections substantiated the stage hypothesis. 'All age groups possess the ability required to perform correctly on the questions of Section I; none of the differences is significant. The ability to perform correctly on Sections II and III appears at age ten; the only significant difference between age groups in performance on Sections II and III is found between the eight- to nine-and ten-year-olds, distinguishing ten years as the age of acquisition (t = 3.04, p < .01, and t = 6.63, p < .001). The ability to perform correctly on Section IV appears at age eleven; only the difference between the ten and the 11- to 12-year-olds is significant, thereby distinguishing 11 to 12 years as the age of acquisition for the abilities tested (t = 2.29, p < .05). None of the age groups performed correctly on Section V above the average predicted by chance – that is, above 25 per cent, and none of the differences is significant', (*ibid.*, p. 76). (Results of 'mixed inputs'; the analogue test; effect of cultural factors on sequencing; effect of cultural factors on stage; and the Kentucky corroboration of Alaska results are described on pp. 78–93.)

Mixed-age grouping and performance on standard conservation tasks
R.J. Firlik, 1975

AIM / The relationship between age-grouping of Ss and performance on Piagetian conservation tasks was examined.

SUBJECTS / N = 108 aged six- and seven-year-old subjects. Half of these were selected from Britain and the remaining half from the United States. 'In each country equal numbers of children were randomly assigned to either mixed-age, same-age, or independent treatments. Six three-member mixed-age groups each consisted of one child aged five, one aged six, and one aged seven. Six three-member same-age groups were each composed of children of the same age, yielding two groups of five-year-olds, two groups of six-year-olds, and two groups of seven-year-olds. In each country 18 Ss of different ages were treated independently.'

METHOD / From a Piagetian perspective it involved a comparison of situations in which pre-operational level Ss would be expected to be confronted with different degrees of challenge to their conservation beliefs. Ss were pre-tested on the Goldschmid and Bentler (1968b) Conservation Kit. Ss were permitted to manipulate conservation-related materials as they dealt with questions posed by the experimenters. The three-member groups, both same-age and mixed-age, were asked to reach consensus in their responses. The identical questions were answered by the independently working children. This treatment lasted for one week after which all Ss were post-tested on an alternate form of the Conservation Kit.

RESULTS / A significant relationship existed between mixed-age grouping and performance on conservation tasks. The mixed-age groups performed significantly better than same-age and independent subjects. No significant relationship was computed between performance on the criterion measure and country of abode. Firlik discussed the implications of the results for the organization of classrooms and schools.

The socialization of possession and ownership among children in three cultural groups: Israeli kibbutz, Israeli city, and American*
L. Furby[1], 1976

The study reported here is part of a long-range and continuing programme of research whose purpose is to examine the nature, development, and function of possession and ownership among human beings. The general goal is a thorough understanding of the nature of possession — the nature of individual possessiveness, acquisitiveness, desire for material gain, and the social institutions of possession and ownership.

Developmental approach
The identification and understanding of developmental sequences in various aspects of behaviour is recognized as a major analytic approach in our study of human beings. Perhaps more than any other individual, Piaget (1926, 1932, 1952, 1954) has demonstrated the fruitfulness of such a method in understanding cognitive development. He has documented clear developmental differences in the way children think and reason about the world around them. Piaget's research established a trend, however, in that 'with few exceptions, psychological investigations specifically concerned with concept formation in children have shown a marked preference for the study of concepts about the physical world rather than the social world' (Danzinger, 1958, p. 231).

---

*   Written and prepared by the author for inclusion in this volume. Gratitude is extended to Dr Lita Furby of the Oregon Research Institute.
[1]   See Footnotes starting on page 126.

Notable exceptions to this trend are Kohlberg's (1969) work on moral judgment, investigations of children's cognitive understanding of interpersonal relationships by Baldwin and Baldwin and their colleagues (1969), and recent work on role-taking skills (Feffer, 1959; Flavell, 1968). There is an obvious need to turn more attention to the implications of cognitive-developmental theory for an understanding of the conceptual and attitudinal frameworks underlying social and interpersonal behaviour.

It may well be that a child's particular cognitive level is a major determinant of the way s / he both thinks about and responds to issues concerning possession and ownership. Alternatively, it may be that one's behaviour is more dependent upon specific child-rearing practices, independent of age or developmental level. A combination of these two alternatives offers still a third possibility: Whereas child-rearing variables may be critical determinants of the particular societal values and / or models presented to the child, these may also be interpreted differently by children at different cognitive levels. Thus, a major aim of the present research effort is (a) to chart the developmental course of perceptions, concepts, feelings, and behaviours related to ownership, possession, and acquisitiveness, and (b) to determine whether there are any systematic developmental patterns comparable to those demonstrated in other areas (and most notably in cognitive development by the work of Piaget).

Cross-cultural approach

The greatest obstacle to valid and significant research on possession and acquisitiveness is undoubtedly the severe difficulty one experiences in trying to step back and out of one's own conceptual framework and assumptions concerning possession and ownership. Our initial study (Furby, Harter, and John, 1975) had been limited to children and adults within a single culture, and thus it risked the possibility of missing at least some of the more fundamental dimensions and determinants of possessiveness. It seemed advisable at this point to employ a cross-cultural approach, 'a research strategy for using measurable variations among human populations (in behaviour patterns, environmental conditions, gene frequencies) to search systematically for the causes of individual behaviour and development' (LeVine, 1970, p. 559). In an unexplored area such as possession and ownership, a major purpose of cross-cultural comparisons is to first *generate hypotheses* about the nature and origins of possession, rather than to test already formulated hypotheses. The value of this strategy has been noted by others: 'From the viewpoint of the logic of discovery, it is expressly in the generation of new hypotheses that the cross-cultural method has its particular strength' (Strodtbeck, 1964, p. 228).

Given the above considerations, the most obvious research strategy is to examine several different societies which have different values, different child-rearing practices, and different legal systems with respect to ownership and possession. Although our own culture (American) was an obvious place to begin, the choice of a cross-cultural comparison group was difficult. While it seemed wise to select for study societies with very different economic, legal, and socialization practices with regard to possessions, the difficulties of adapting research methods to societies very different from our own should not be minimized. Indeed, it was doubtful that valid data from radically different cultures could be obtained at this early stage in our research.

The Israeli kibbutz seemed to offer a unique opportunity. 'The upbringing of children in the agricultural collectives in Israel is for the social scientist what an "experiment of nature" is for the natural scientist' (Rapaport, 1958, p. 587). While the values and legal system of the nation of Israel are not very different from those of the US with regard to possessions, there are important aspects of kibbutz life with respect to possession which differ from the rest of Western culture. Western culture places a strong emphasis on individualism and private ownership and acquisition of wealth, while the kibbutz is based on collective production, collective property, and collective consumption.

'Communal ownership, it is believed, prevents the development of economic classes and the inevitable social inequality that seems to characterize societies stratified by class . . . Having abolished money within the kibbutz both as a medium of exchange and a symbol of wealth, the kibbutz has also eliminated the profit motive as a stimulus for economic production. The distribution of goods is determined by the principle of "from each according to his ability, to each according to his needs."' (Spiro, 1965, p. 4)

The child-rearing environment which has resulted from the ideological tenets of the kibbutz movement is unique. Devereux and his colleagues (1974) note that:

The most distinctive feature of kibbutz upbringing lies in the fact that the children live, not with their own parents, but in special 'children's houses' nearby, with a cohort of age-mates, under the care of a trained metapelet. Typically, the kibbutz has a whole colony of such houses, divided by age level from the infants' and toddlers' houses up to those for the teenagers. (p. 270)

Given the strong socialist convictions of kibbutz adults, it is somewhat surprising that there has not yet been any systematic study of the effects of this deliberate emphasis on collective ownership for possessive behaviour in kibbutz-raised children.[2] However, the few reports in the literature which do mention possessive behaviour in the kibbutz suggest that there are significant consequences of the collective nature of ownership in kibbutz society:

> In the kibbutz all private possession is shunned, whether of property, persons, or experiences ... To the kibbutz infant, it is obvious that any private possession is undesirable, that everything is owned by the community, to be used and shared by it. He cannot possess his *metapelets* or his parents since his being with them is so strictly regulated. And he cannot possess a friend because the group will not stand for it, and the *metapelet* would try to break up such a twosome (as will the youth group later). Thus, the feeling is deeply ingrained that to wish to possess is wrong, and the guilt about even having such a wish interferes with the desire for exclusive belonging. (Bettelheim, 1969b)

Bettelheim suggests that for kibbutz-raised individuals 'community property is not an idea defensively or consciously embraced, but the only normal way to live' (1969a, p. 281).

Spiro (1955) concurs with and supplements Bettelheim's analysis: '*Kibbutz* culture would not long survive if the desire for personal acquisitions were a strong drive in the *sabras* [kibbutz-born individuals]' (p. 291). Spiro reports evidence from interviews with kibbutz children that the acquisition of material goods is rarely mentioned as a source of happiness, and that the lack of material goods is likewise rarely the source of sadness. From this and other similar data, he concludes that: 'It seems abundantly clear that "collective education" has succeeded in inculcating in the *sabras* the values of *kibbutz* culture with respect to personal acquisitions' (p. 291).

A slightly different aspect of possession has been reported in Faigin's (1958) comparison of the social behaviour of young kibbutz and American children:

> Two interesting differences may be noted. The American three-year-olds tended to use more rules about property, that is, about toys and play space, than rules of interaction, how to behave. In the *kibbutz* group, the children although younger tend to use more rules about social interaction than property. This difference would seem to follow from the fact that the *kibbutz* children live and interact with one another to a much greater extent than do nursery school children. The other interesting difference concerns the nature of the property rules. The American nursery school

children used rules referring to this being 'mine' — 'I had it first, you can't have it' — whereas the *kibbutz* children's property rules refer to sharing, 'This is ours, this belongs to all of us.' The social control methods used by these very young children thus appear to reflect the values of the society in which they grow up: one society in which private property is highly valued, the other in which there is communal ownership and no private ownership (pp. 123–124).

It should be noted that these descriptions stem from impressions and anecdotal observations rather than from any well-documented empirical evidence on these issues. We therefore decided to examine possessiveness in the kibbutz more systematically, in order to explore the possible importance of quite large differences in socialization practices with respect to this aspect of human behaviour.

The rationale for examining possession and ownership in kibbutzim was based on the desire to first document possible differences in possessive behaviour between very different societies, before attempting to explain any such differences. Nevertheless, it seemed advisable to include a 'control' group which would aid in suggesting hypotheses about the causes of any differences we might find between the American and the kibbutz sample. As others have pointed out,

If we really want to know the effects of collectivism, we cannot legitimately compare the kibbutz with the American community, because so many relevant factors are not controlled. American society differs not only in being based on private property; it is also older, technologically more advanced, drawn from a different cultural tradition, etc. How then can one know precisely which effects to attribute to collective organization and which to these other factors? When comparison is possible within the same cultural context, these problems disappear. (Schwartz, 1958, p. 574)

Such a comparison within the Israeli cultural context is indeed possible: Kibbutz members constitute only 3.6 per cent of the Israeli population. There remains 96.4 per cent of the population, the majority of whom resemble kibbutzniks in many aspects of Jewish culture and nationalism, but who participate in a much more individual-oriented, private system of ownership in their daily lives. Thus, by studying both kibbutz-raised individuals and those raised in more traditional homes, we are able to compare individuals whose environments with regard to possession differ in potentially significant ways, but whose environments and backgrounds with regard to many other factors are relatively similar (*much* more similar than the environments and backgrounds of American and kibbutz individuals).

METHOD / INSTRUMENT

Given the absence of previous empirical research on this topic (see Furby, 1976h), an initial goal was to identify the particular psychological dimensions and attributes which form the conceptual framework and related network of attitudes that children and adults have developed about possession and ownership. An open-ended interview method was chosen as the most suitable for gathering the kind of data that would enable an initial mapping of the dimensions of this unexplored domain. It has the advantage of providing a wealth of information and suggesting hypotheses about which variables and dimensions are likely to be relevant and fruitful for the examination of behaviour in more experimental and observational settings. The flexibility of the interview gives the subjects sufficient latitude to introduce and discuss topics of their own choice, as well as allowing the interviewer the freedom to probe further when necessary.

In our initial work (Furby, Harter, and John, 1975) we had identified seven general topics of inquiry which deal with the basic meaning and characteristics of possession and ownership. The interview was designed to focus on a number of specific issues, each related to one of the seven general topics. Table 1 presents a description of these specific issues, and Table 2 shows their relation to each general topic. The interview format used is presented in Table 3. In order to obtain the Hebrew version, a combination of backtranslation and decentering methods (Werner and Campbell, 1970) were used. The latter entails equal familiarity and colloquialness in both languages, and we worked extensively with our Israeli collaborators (whose native language was Hebrew, and who subsequently did all the interviewing) in developing the Hebrew instrument.[3] This involved discussions about the meaning and purpose of each sentence in the English version, backtranslation of preliminary versions, further discussion of exact meanings and purposes, etc. While there is never a perfect solution to the problems involved in translating instruments such as interview questions (Sechrest, Fay, and Zaidi, 1972), we felt that this procedure was the most satisfactory for our research purposes.

SUBJECTS / This study included two overlapping samples. The *American Developmental Sample* consisted of 150 subjects, 30 at each of five age levels: kindergarten, second, fifth, and eleventh grades, and 40- to 50-year-olds. There were 15 females and 15 males at each age level. The school-aged subjects were obtained from three local schools in the New Haven, Connecticut area. The older group of adults was obtained by soliciting volunteers from among the parents of children in the schools where we were conducting the study (this older group is subsequently referred to as the 'adult—parent' group). All subjects were white and from the middle and upper middle classes.

Table 1: Specific issues of focus [a]

A. *Meaning / definition of personal possession*

C. *Personal possessions*
    1. Specific possessions (in parents' home for kibbutz)
    2. Specific possessions in children's house for kibbutz only
    3. Collections (in parents' home for kibbutz)
    4. Collections in children's house for kibbutz only
    5. General possessables

D. *Means of acquisition*
    1. Exhaustive list   2. Sources of money   3. Principal means

N. *Implications of different aspects of means of acquisition*

		Implies / allows / ensures		Does *not* imply / allow / ensure
Holiday or special occasion	1.		2.	
Gift, other gives object to owner	3.	"	4.	"
Other buying object for owner	4.	"	6.	"
Owner buying object	7.	"	8.	"
Owner earning / working for object	9.	"	10.	"
Owner making / collecting object	11.	"	12.	"

    13. Effects of different persons as sources of possessions
    14. Reasons for no differences between means of acquisition
    15. Reasons for differentiation between possessions other than means
         of acquisition

I. *Definition-mechanics of collective possession*

Non-family (or unspecified):	1. Actual instances	2. Hypothetical instances	3. Item
Family:	4. Actual instances	5. Hypothetical instances	6. Item
	7. Generally collectively possessable items		

H. *Consequences / implications / attributes of Collective Possession Ownership*
    1. Positive evaluation of collective (or negative evaluation of personal)
    2. Negative evaluation of collective (or positive evaluation of personal)
    2. Non-evaluative, general characterization of collective
    4. Non-evaluative, general characterization of personal

E. *Decisions about use and sharing of personal possessions*
    1. Conditions when permit, positive consequences of sharing
    2. Negative consequences of not sharing
    3. Conditions / Reasons when prohibit
    4. General dimension (use / nonuse unspecified)

F. *Morality of sharing*
    1. Reasons people should share   2. Reasons given as justification
                                        for not always sharing

[a] The letters and numbers preceding each issue were used for subsequent coding purposes and data analysis

Table 1, cont'd: Specific issues of focus

V. *Definition of sharing*

G. *Reasons people possess*
    1. Motivation for / importance of personal possession
    2. Consequences of not possessing privately
    3. Most important possessions
    4. Characteristics of most important possessions
    5. Consequences of not possessing most important possessions

J. *Existence of unequal distribution of possessions*

Reasons why:	1. Some have more	2. Some have less	3. General Comment
Known instances:	4. Those with more (outside kibbutz)	5. Those with less (outside kibbutz)	
	6. Those with more (in kibbutz)	7. Those with less (in kibbutz)	

K. *Evaluation of unequal distribution of possessions*

Positive Evaluation:	IF:	1. Characterization of those with less	SINCE:	3 Characterization of those with less
		2. Characterization of those with more		4. Characterization of those with more
		5. General comment		
Negative Evaluation	IF:	6. Characterization of those with less		8. Characterization of those with less
		7. Characterization of those with more		9. Characterization of those with more
		10. General comment		
Non-evaluative Comment:		11. Characterization of those with less		
		12. Characterization of those with more		
		13. General comment		

Table 2: General topics of inquiry

The definition of possession: What does possession mean to the individual? What are its defining characteristics? (Issue A)

The nature of possessables: What kinds of things are possessed? (Issues C1—5)

Motivation for possession: What is it about human beings and / or their environment that results in possession and ownership? (Issues G1—5)

Acquisition: When and how does something become a possession, and what are the different implications of various means of acquisition? (Issues D1—3, N1—15)

Control over use: What is the relationship between possessing something and exclusive use and control of its use? (Issues E1—4, F1—2, V)

Collective vs. personal possession: To what degree is collective possession possible, and to what degree is it desirable? (Issues I1—7, H1—4)

Unequal distribution: Why do some people have more than others, and is such inequality desirable? (Issues J1—7, K1—K13)

Table 3: Possession interview format

General introduction to subject	Comments

General introduction to subject

A. *S's personal possessions*

    Purpose: (1) to get S to talk about his own possessions, (2) to determine some of his possessions, (3) set tone of a comfortable conversation (without 'pushing' S).

  ** WHAT ARE SOME THINGS THAT $^{ARE\ YOURS}_{YOU\ OWN}$, WHAT ARE SOME THINGS THAT BELONG TO YOU?

B. *S's definition of ownership re his possessions*

    Purpose: to get at the S's own definition of ownership, his concept of what ownership means to him.

  ** WHAT DOES IT MEAN THAT THESE THINGS ARE YOURS, THAT THEY BELONG TO YOU?

  * Probe about several specific possessions mentioned by S, i.e., LIKE YOUR _____ , WHAT DOES IT MEAN THAT IT'S YOUR _____ ?

C. *Means of acquiring possessions*

    Purpose: (1) to get at S's notions of different means; (2) to determine the major means for him; (3) to see if any difference between possessions acquired through different means.

  ** HOW DO THINGS GET TO BE YOURS?

  * Probe to get at several origins, if possible, i.e., ask: IS THERE ANY OTHER WAY YOU GET THINGS?

  ** WHAT'S THE WAY YOU GET MOST OF YOUR THINGS?

  ** DO YOU FEEL ANY DIFFERENTLY ABOUT THE THINGS YOU GOT BY (means A) and (means B)?

  (Probe, if S mentions parental ownership and / or control over child's possessions, i.e., ask S to elaborate.)

D. *Instances of collective ownership in S's experience*

    Purpose: to get at (1) whether collective ownership is feasible in S's experience, (2) how it works, and (3) how S feels about it.

  ** CAN SOMETHING BELONG TO BOTH YOU AND SOMEONE ELSE, CAN YOU OWN SOMETHING TOGETHER? (Additional probe: CAN ONE THING BELONG TO MORE THAN ONE PERSON?)

  * Probe for *several* instances of collective ownership, e.g., ARE THERE OTHER THINGS WHICH BELONG TO YOU AND SOMEONE ELSE?; THAT YOU OWN TOGETHER WITH OTHER PEOPLE?

  * Probe for a detailed description of how the collective ownership works.

  * Probe about how S *feels* about the collective ownership he describes.

  ** HOW ARE THESE THINGS DIFFERENT FROM THE OTHER THINGS YOU TOLD ME ABOUT – THE THINGS THAT BELONG JUST TO YOU LIKE _____ AND _____ ?

Comments

—If need additional questions to get S talking, try to go to B, rather than probing about origins

—With younger Ss who may have difficulty answering, possible probe: TELL ME SOME MORE ABOUT HOW YOUR _____ IS YOURS

—If S needs help, ask about things he wants, and how he would get them.

—If S mentions *money* (anywhere) ask how he gets his money, and if he had to do anything to get it.

—Ask about *each* means, e.g., "and how' about things you get by _____ ?"

—If S answers in the abstract, ask about specific examples in his life, e.g., 'do you have some things like that?'

—If S mentions difference between family and others, probe. If only mentions family, ask if there are other places where that happens.

Table 3 cont'd: Possession Interview format

Introduce section E with: LET'S TALK SOME MORE ABOUT THE THINGS THAT BELONG *JUST TO YOU*, LIKE YOUR _____(name several of S's possessions).

E. *Basis of decisions about use of personal possessions*

    Purpose: In general, how S makes decisions, including (1) characteristics of people with whom he shares, (2) specific conditions under which he shares, and (3) if bases of decisions are object-dependent.

    ** WHO IS ALLOWED TO USE YOUR THINGS?

       (who can't use your things?)

      * Probe to get at the characteristics of the people who can use S's things, why, and when they can use them.

    —E.g., get at whether S *always* lets person use things.

    ** HOW DO YOU DECIDE IF SOMEONE CAN USE YOUR THINGS?

       (when can't other people use your things?)

    —Ask whether *anyone* can use things in these cases.

      * Probe to get at whether decision rules are object dependent, e.g., IS THAT THE WAY YOU DECIDE FOR EVERYTHING YOU HAVE?

    ** DO YOU ALWAYS GET TO DECIDE WHEN OTHER PEOPLE CAN USE YOUR THINGS?

F. *Feelings about sharing*

    Purpose: to get at (1) S's reasoning re why people share, and (2) his views about the 'morality' of sharing, i.e., why people should or shouldn't share; (3) consequences of not sharing.

    —Additional: 'If you had children, what would you tell them about sharing?'

    ** WHAT IS SHARING, WHAT DOES IT MEAN TO SHARE SOMETHING?

    ** WHY DO YOU THINK PEOPLE SHARE?

    ** DO YOU THINK PEOPLE *SHOULD* SHARE?

    ** WHAT ABOUT A PERSON WHO NEVER WANTS TO SHARE ANYTHING, WHAT DO YOU THINK ABOUT THAT?

    ** WHAT HAPPENS WHEN PEOPLE DON'T SHARE – LIKE WHAT HAPPENS WHEN *YOU* DON'T SHARE?

G. *Importance of and reasons for personal possessions*

    Purpose: to get at (1) S's view of the reasons for individual ownership, (2) people's feelings about individual ownership, (3) importance of ownership, including S's own possessions.

Table 3 Cont'd: Possession interview format

** WHY DO YOU THINK PEOPLE HAVE THINGS THAT BELONG TO JUST THEM — WHY DO PEOPLE *OWN* THINGS?

* Probe about how people *feel* about owning their own things.

* Probe about how *important* it is to people to own things.

** OF ALL THE THINGS THAT YOU OWN, WHICH ARE THE MOST IMPORTANT TO YOU?

** DO YOU THINK IT WOULD MATTER IF YOU DIDN'T HAVE THEM?

H. *S's feelings about inequalities in possessions*

Purpose: to get at (1) reasons why unequal distribution exists and (2) how he feels about it.

** WHY DO YOU THINK SOME PEOPLE HAVE A LOT MORE THINGS THAN OTHER PEOPLE?

(Probe to get at why S thinks inequality exists; if S mentions a particular instance, get him to expand on the reasons.)

** HOW DO YOU FEEL ABOUT SOME PEOPLE HAVING A LOT MORE THINGS THAN OTHER PEOPLE?

—Additional Q: 'Why do people want things that are their very own?'

—Get at characteristics of S's most important possessions, and their value to S.

—If S answers this question in the abstract, talking about what other people think in general, ask specifically about what he thinks.

The *Comparative Cross-Cultural Sample* consisted of three cultural groups: American, Israeli kibbutz, and Israeli nonkibbutz. There were approximately sixty subjects in each cultural group, 30 at each of two age levels: kindergarteners and fifth graders, and their Israeli age equivalents. Ideally, we would have obtained five different age levels for the Israeli groups, just as we did for the Americans, but limited resources prohibited that possibility. Characteristics of each of these two samples are summarized in Tables 4 and 5. While this number of subjects does not permit separate analyses by birth order, it might be noted that the cultural groups were remarkably similar with respect to birth order of subjects: 30—36 per cent of the subjects in each group were first-born, 36—39 per cent were second-born, and 25—34 per cent were third- or later-born.

Table 4: Developmental[a] and cross-cultural[b] samples[c]

Culture

Israeli

		American		Kibbutz		Non-Kibbutz		
		M	F	M	F	M	F	All
Age	1	15	15	14	17	14	15	90
	2	15	15					
	3	15	15	12	17	16	16	91
	4	15	15					
	5	15	15					
Total		150		60		61		

[a] Broken line indicates cross-cultural sample

[b] Heavy solid line indicates developmental sample

[c] Each cell indicates the number of subjects in that culture—age—sex group.

Table 5: Mean ages in years for each culture-age group

		Culture					
		American		Kibbutz		Non-Kibbutz	
		Mean	sd	Mean	sd	Mean	sd
	1	6.14	(.35)	5.61	(.32)	5.85	(.29)
	2	7.60	(.35)				
Age Group	3	10.74	(.41)	10.82	(.37)	10.69	(.24)
	4	16.45	(.39)				
	5	48.27	(6.23)				

For the kibbutz subjects, the following criteria were important: (a) Kibbutzim were avoided in which there were strong familistic trends (emphasis on the nuclear family, e.g., children now sleeping with parents), and we tried to choose kibbutzim where the emphasis on collectivism in both social and economic affairs remains strong. Since most kibbutzim have fewer than the required number of subjects at each age level, three different kibbutzim were selected. All were of medium size (400–600 individuals), and each belonged to a different one of the three kibbutz federations.[4] (b) In order to examine the effects of the kibbutz environment on the development of possessive behaviour, we only included individuals who were born and raised on the kibbutz. (c) The success of the interview technique required that Hebrew be the mother tongue of all subjects. This requirement was easily met, since all persons born and raised in a kibbutz speak Hebrew as their first language.

Several factors were considered in assuring comparability of the comparison nonkibbutz sample. One of the variables upon which the kibbutz and nonkibbutz samples should be matched is cultural background of parents. This is particularly important given the extreme difficulty of establishing socioeconomic indices for kibbutz subjects. It was, of course, impossible to completely control for this variable ahead of time. However, since a majority of kibbutzniks come from Central and Eastern European backgrounds, an attempt was made to obtain the nonkibbutz subjects from schools where parents seemed to be predominantly of Central and Eastern European origin. During the course of the study, information was obtained on the country of origin of both the mother and father of every subject. A majority of the parents of both the kibbutz and nonkibbutz samples were born in Israel. The only significant difference between the two groups was that a sizeable minority of kibbutz subjects had parents from Brazil, whereas such was not the case for nonkibbutz subjects. This was due to the fact that one of three kibbutzim participating in the study had been founded by Brazilian immigrants. While this discrepancy between parental origin for the two groups should be kept in mind, it would appear to have little consequence for this study in terms of the kinds of conclusions we will draw from the kibbutz *vs.* nonkibbutz comparison. Rather than permitting strong statements about the effects of collective living *per se*, the nonkibbutz group will mainly be used as an aid in interpreting differences between the American and the kibbutz samples, and it will offer yet another cultural group in our search for cultural variation.

It should be pointed out that the kibbutz sample is basically rural, while the nonkibbutz sample is urban. It seemed impossible to avoid this situation, as it is very difficult to find individuals of European origin living in a rural setting in Israel, other than those in kibbutzim. The one possible exception to this is European Jews who live in Moshavim (collective farm communities). Moshavim have served in the past as control groups for studies of the effects of collective child-rearing, since they have maintained the nuclear family as their basic living unit. However, they are inappropriate for our purposes because economically both their production and consumption system is organized cooperatively, and their farm machinery is owned collectively. Thus, they do not differ sufficiently from kibbutzim on the environmental variables which we suspect may be important in determining possessive behaviour.

The nonkibbutz sample came from three different schools in the cities of Jerusalem and Akko. We applied the same criteria as for our kibbutz sample with regard to (a) individuals born and raised in Israel and (b) individuals whose mother tongue is Hebrew.

PROCEDURE / Each subject was interviewed individually by one of five trained interviewers,[5] and the entire interview was tape recorded. The interview lasted between one and two hours, and in the latter cases it was broken into two one-hour sessions.

Written transcriptions were made of all interviews, and Israeli transcriptions were translated into English. Although certain advantages might be obtained from analyzing the Israeli interviews in the original

Hebrew, the comparative goals of this project necessitated the construction of a single content analysis for all cultures, and therefore all interviews had to be in the same language for analysis.

System of analysis

A method of data analysis was required which would allow us: (a) In the short run, to discover and describe existing age and culture differences in concepts, attitudes, and reasoning about possession and ownership; (b) In the long run, to map out as completely as possible the dimensions and concepts which make up the overall conceptual-attitudinal framework with regard to possession for any given culture and any given age group (or other subgroup) within a culture.

Such a task is particularly difficult when there are no pre-established categorization systems which the researcher can utilize. Thus, the first step was to establish the categories to be used for systematizing the data. Since we did not want to make any *a priori* assumptions about possible categories subjects might employ in their structuring of this domain, our strategy consisted of a search for those categories which emerged from the data themselves. The resulting set of categories from such a content analysis constitutes a partial accomplishment of the long-range goal — they aid in mapping the dimensions of the cognitive-attitudinal domain. A comparison of the use and the interrelationships of given categories by different culture and age groups contributes to our short-range goal — the establishment of cultural and developmental differences and similarities with regard to various possession-related topics.

The *content analysis* we employed involved two phases: (a) the determination of the specific categories for coding subjects' statements, and (b) a coding of every statement in each interview with regard to both the issue and the category it represented. The first process resulted in the establishment of 290 substantive categories.

Although a given subject sometimes mentioned the same issue-category combination more than once, multiple occurrence information was not retained in the analysis, since our previous study had demonstrated that little is gained by analyzing frequency rather than simple occurrence data. Thus, for each subject, for a given issue, we used a list of all categories s / he mentioned at least once as our basic data for analysis.

Reliability measures between the two coders were obtained at regular intervals throughout the coding process. Coders were unaware of which interviews were designated for reliability comparisons. Those designated included an equal number from each culture, age, and sex. Reid (1970) has shown that reliability of observational data may vary depending on when it is assessed during the coding process, and also on whether the coders are aware it is being assessed. It seems quite possible that reliability of content analysis coding may be subject to the same effects, and thus these precautions were taken. Reliability was based on the final codings, omitting all duplicate codes for each subject as described above. Calculation of reliability was the per cent of agreed-upon categories divided by the total number of codes (agrees plus disagrees).

Reliabilities between the two coders ranged between 58.3 per cent and 89.8 per cent with a mean of 74.2 per cent. Given that a total of 1930 different codes were used (since a given coding decision included both which issue *and* which category to code), the high reliability is strong support for the viability of this categorization and analysis procedure. Furthermore, all interviews were reviewed a second time by both coders, thus minimizing the number of oversights and errors.

RESULTS / Given the extremely large amount of data this study has yielded, only a portion of it can be presented in any one article. The following discussion will focus on those results dealing with the *nature of possessables*, this area being particularly interesting with respect to the comparative cross-cultural data. Presentation and discussion of the other six topics investigated in this study may be found elsewhere (Furby, 1976a, 1976b, 1976d, 1976e, 1976f, 1976g, 1976i).

A basic aspect of possession and ownership is certainly the possessions themselves — what kinds of things do people consider to belong to them? While we attempted to obtain a relatively complete list of personal possessions from each subject, we did limit the focus of this study to tangible, material possessions, in order to restrict the domain of our inquiry to a manageable size. Table 6 presents the categories used in coding personal possessions, and Tables 7 and 8 present the rank orders of the most frequently mentioned categories of possessions by age and culture group. Note that a distinction was maintained for kibbutz subjects between those possessions they keep in the parents' home and those possessions they keep in the children's house.

American developmental sample

Toys and games[6] was the most frequently reported type of possession for the two youngest age groups. By late elementary school, it was somewhat less frequent, and then rarely reported at older ages. Female-stereotyped toys were mentioned almost solely by girls, and male-stereotyped toys were reported mainly by boys.[7] These results strongly confirm those of our previous study (Furby, Harter, and John, 1975). The fact that sex-stereotyped toys were rarely reported by the sex for which they are not considered appropriate is consistent with earlier work on preferences for appropriately sex-typed activities and

Table 6: Coding categories for personal possessions [a]

1. Food
2. Medicine
3. Clothing (including purse, umbrella)
4. Glasses
5. Beauty and grooming aids (cosmetics, shaving things, hair dryer, towel, handkerchief)
6. Jewelry (including watch)
7. Housing and shelter
8. Parts of house or yard (kitchen, laundry, bedroom, swimming pool, barn)
9. Furniture and furnishings (bed, desk, heater, rug, lamp, toybox, blanket, pillow, mailbox, shower, closet)
260. Tah, cubby hole
10. Small appliance-machines (camera, typewriter, TV console, projector, telephone, clock)
11. Decorative items (vase, wallpaper, paintings, knick-knacks, posters)
12. Plants (including garden)
13. Adult male stereotype items (home maintenance, hardward, tools, knives, weapons)
14. Adult female stereotype items (laundry, cleaning things, sewing, silverware, dishes)
15. Land
16. Motor vehicles (car, cycle, boat, airplane)
17. Business and job-related material
18. Money
19. Money containers
20. Temporary money substitutes (credit card, master charge, checks and checking account)
21. Sound equipment (records, record player, tape recorder, radio)
22. Musical instruments
23. Communications media (newspaper, magazine, movie, TV)
24. Arts and crafts materials (including crayons, scissors)
25. Stationery supplies and materials
26. Books and educational materials
259. Scientific instruments
27. Nature items
28. Toys and games (not clearly sex-stereotyped)
29. Play animals and fantasy figures
30. Male stereotype toys (trucks, cars, models, weapons, soldiers)
31. Female stereotype toys (dolls, sewing kit)
32. Sports and outdoor equipment (including bicycle)
33. Awards (trophies, badges, ribbons, diploma)

a   The number preceding each category is the number used to represent that category for coding and data analysis purposes.

34. Luggage (bookbag)
35. Pets and accoutrements
36. Souvenirs (pennants, cards, pamphlets, matches)
37. 'Personal things' (no further specification)
38. Letters, diary
39. Smoking things
40. Non-material, non-tangibles (persons, memberships, subscriptions)
272. Children's house, classroom
289. Parts of body

Table 7: Rank order of most frequently used categories of personal possessions for American developmental sample[a]

Rank	Age 1	2	3	4	5	6	7	8	9	10	11	12	13	14	15
1	9 (70%)	28 (66%)	32 (60%)	31 (50%)	30 (40%)	29 (40%)	26 (40%)	3 (40%)	18 (33%)	35 (23%)	21 (23%)	8 (20%)			
2	28 (66%)	9 (63%)	32 (43%)	30 (40%)	31 (36%)	29 (36%)	3 (33%)	18 (23%)	26 (20%)	24 (20%)					
3	32 (80%)	8 (73%)	28 (66%)	9 (66%)	3 (50%)	26 (46%)	35 (36%)	21 (36%)	30 (33%)	31 (26%)	29 (26%)	25 (23%)	10 (23%)	11 (20%)	6 (20%)
4	3 (86%)	21 (73%)	32 (66%)	26 (60%)	9 (46%)	8 (46%)	10 (43%)	6 (40%)	11 (36%)	35 (26%)	22 (26%)	18 (23%)	25 (20%)		
5	3 (80%)	6 (53%)	16 (50%)	26 (40%)	11 (40%)	32 (30%)	18 (30%)	17 (30%)	13 (30%)	14 (26%)	10 (26%)	9 (26%)	40 (23%)	12 (23%)	

[a] For each age group, category numbers (see Table 6) are indicated on the top line, and the percent of subjects at that age who mentioned a given category is indicated immediately below. Only those categories used by at least 20 per cent of the subjects at a given age level are included. Collections as possessions have been excluded here.

Table 8: Rank order of most frequently used categories of personal possessions for Israeli subjects[a]

Rank	1	2	3	4	5	6	7	8	9	10	11
Age											
					Kibbutz — Children's House						
1	11 (25%)										
3	3 (44%)	11 (34%)	25 (31%)	9 (31%)	5 (27%)	36 (20%)	26 (20%)				
					Kibbutz — Parents' Home						
1	28 (61%)	31 (45%)	30 (41%)	11 (41%)	26 (38%)	24 (35%)	32 (25%)	29 (25%)	3 (25%)		
3	28 (69%)	26 (48%)	32 (31%)	25 (31%)	11 (31%)	3 (24%)	6 (20%)				
					Nonkibbutz						
1	28 (69%)	31 (55%)	32 (44%)	30 (37%)	24 (37%)	3 (37%)	9 (27%)	29 (24%)	26 (24%)	25 (20%)	11 (20%)
3	9 (84%)	26 (81%)	28 (75%)	3 (56%)	25 (43%)	32 (31%)	8 (31%)	34 (25%)	11 (21%)		

a   For each age group, category numbers (see Table 6) are indicated on the top line, and the per cent of subjects at that age who mentioned a given category is indicated immediately below. Only those categories used by at least 20 per cent of the subjects at a given age level are included. Collections as possessions have been excluded here.

objects (Brown, 1956; Goodman and Lever, 1972; Hartley, 1960; Kagan and Moss, 1962; Rheingold and Cook, 1975).

Furniture and furnishings (e.g., bed, blanket, toycase) were also very frequently mentioned by the two youngest ages, and then slowly declined in frequency with increasing age. The salience of furnishings at the younger ages was also found in our previous work — somewhat to our surprise. That led us to speculate that the young child is perhaps being encouraged by adults to 'straighten up *her toycase*,' 'put *her blanket* on *her bed* where it belongs', etc., and this may increase the salience of these items as possessions.

Also frequently mentioned by the youngest ages was *sports and outdoor equipment*. This became the most frequently mentioned type of possession by late elementary school, and then declined slightly for the older age groups. This is exactly the same age pattern found in our previous work, and it seems that this may simply reflect a developmental shift in activity from playing with what adults call 'toys,' to playing with what adults call 'equipment' — the nature and instruments of the game may have changed somewhat, but it is still a game. This developmental pattern may also reflect an important increase during elementary school in the activities which involve close peer interaction. It should also be noted that sports equipment was mentioned by more males than females.

For elementary school ages *play animals and fantasy figures* were moderately frequent possessions, being mentioned by more females than males. *Books and educational materials* were also reported fairly frequently, and they became very frequent for high school and adult-parent ages.

Clothing was of moderate frequency for the younger ages, and was mentioned increasingly with age, being the most frequently mentioned possession for both high school and adult-parent subjects. Exactly the same developmental pattern was found in our previous study, and it would seem to reflect the shifting role of clothing from an assumed given (the young child has always had clothing provided) to something which is no longer automatically provided. The young adolescent begins to participate in selecting his or her clothing, and this may be an important means of developing and expressing one's identity. Clothing, more than most other items, is quite literally an extension of the self — an appendage to the person — and, hence, a natural vehicle for both establishing and expressing one's individuality. The fact that more females mentioned clothing than did males may reflect a sex difference in the socially-approved and encouraged activities for establishing one's identity (Goodman and Lever, 1972). A girl's role is perceived to be one requiring her to be passive and concerned with the appearance of things — hence her investment in clothes. A boy's role is perceived to be one requiring him to be active and to achieve — hence his investment in sports equipment.

For fifth graders, *parts of the house and yard* (principally 'my room') was a very frequently mentioned possession, and it was also moderately frequent for high school age, but other ages rarely mentioned it. Again, this replicates a developmental pattern found in our previous study, and it suggests that one's room (or other locations of the house) is particularly salient as a possession during early adolescence. This may simply reflect the fact that many children at this age have their own rooms, while younger children, as well as the married adults in our sample, are more likely to share a room. On the other hand, the salience of this possession at early adolescence may also reflect the importance to the individual at this age of having a place where s / he can be alone. Indeed, a moderately frequent definition of ownership for this age level only was that it permits privacy and being alone (see Furby, 1976d). The importance of privacy at this age may be related to the early adolescent's search for identity and self-definition. 'Privacy facilitates personal autonomy, vital to individuality. Privacy is basically an instrument for achieving goals of self realization; by providing a context for emotional release, self-evaluation, and psychological protection, it allows the individual a sense of control (Pastelan, 1970)', (Edney, 1974).

Sound equipment was also a moderately frequent possession among fifth graders, and then very frequent as a possession for high school subjects. Clothing, sports equipment and books were the other most frequently mentioned possessions among high school subjects. In addition, both *decorative items* and *small appliances* became of moderate importance during high school.

Sound equipment, as well as furnishings and sports equipment, all declined considerably in frequency between the high school and the adult-parent subjects. For the latter, in addition to clothing it was *jewelry* (mentioned more by females) and *motor vehicles* (mentioned more by males) which were the most frequently mentioned possessions. Decorative items and books were also frequently mentioned at this age.

As can be seen in Table 9, the average number of different types of possessions mentioned was greatest at fifth grade. It decreased between kindergarten and second grade, increased to its peak at fifth grade, then declined slightly for high school and again for adult-parent subjects.

Females mentioned more possessions overall than did males, suggesting that they have a greater variety of possessions, or at least are likely to mention a greater variety than are males when specifically asked about them.

Table 9: **Average number of different categories of personal possessions[a]
mentioned by age and sex for American developmental sample**

		1	2	3	4	5	Combined
Sex	F	6.20	6.00	8.33	8.40	7.47	7.28
	M	6.60	4.33	6.93	6.00	5.93	5.96
Combined		6.40	5.17	7.63	7.20	6.70	6.62

Age: $F (4, 140) = 4.10$, $p < .01$

Sex: $F (1, 140) = 10.12$, $p < .01$

Age x Sex: n.s.

[a] Excluding collections as personal possessions

Comparative cross-cultural sample

As was the case for the Americans, *toys* were the most frequently mentioned possession for the youngest Israeli children of both groups (see Table 8). However, the general pattern of results for most other categories was quite different for the three cultural groups at this age.

For the nonkibbutz children, *sports equipment* was very frequent, as it was for Americans, but it was somewhat less frequent for kibbutz subjects. On the other hand, *books and educational materials* were quite frequent possessions for American and kibbutz children, but less so for nonkibbutz children. *Arts and crafts materials* were more frequent for both Israeli groups than for Americans, while *play animals and fantasy figures* were somewhat less frequent for Israeli than for American subjects at this age.

For the 10- to 11-year-olds, the general pattern of results was also quite different for the three cultural groups. While *toys* were frequent for all three groups, *books and educational materials* and *stationery* were more frequent for the two Israeli groups than for Americans. On the other hand, *parts of the house or yard* was very frequent for Americans, but much less so for both Israeli groups.

Both *furniture* and *clothing* were relatively frequent for all three groups, and for kibbutz subjects these items were most often located in the children's house. *Sports equipment* was frequent for all groups, but relatively more so for Americans.

Pets were moderately frequent for American children at this age, but not for Israeli subjects. One might speculate that play animals and fantasy figures, which were frequent for the youngest age in all three cultural groups, are generally replaced at older ages by real pets which serve the same companionship function. While this may hold for American subjects, it clearly is not the case for either kibbutz or nonkibbutz children. Although play animals decline as possessions after the youngest age for both Israeli groups, there was no simultaneous increase in pets as there was for the American subjects. Of course, personal pets are very rare on the kibbutz, although a children's animal farm seems to be a frequent institution. Children do most of the work involved in caring for the animals, and often they even earn some money by selling eggs from the farm. Thus, animals are certainly a part of their environment, but rarely as personal possessions.

Perhaps the most striking cultural difference is the high frequency of *decorative items* mentioned as possessions by kibbutz subjects of both ages, in contrast to their low frequency among nonkibbutz and American children. Decorative items rank high among kibbutz subjects both at their parents' home and at the children's house. It seems possible that this may reflect the importance of establishing and identifying one's individuality with possessions. In general, the kibbutz child has one corner of a bedroom in the children's house which s / he uses exclusively, and the very few items that are privately owned in the children's house are kept there. Similarly, the child typically has his or her own corner in the parents' home — a place where the child's possessions are kept. Apparently, in both cases decorative items are very frequent, and they may serve the function of identifying what is distinctively 'mine' as compared to most everything else in the children's house which is collectively used, and to most everything else in the parents' home, which belongs to the mother and father. Decorative items serve as territorial 'markers' in Goffman's (1972) terms — they mark the space that belongs to an individual. The importance of the opportunity for individualization which private possessions provide has been discussed at some length by kibbutz educators (Neubauer, 1965). There has clearly been a shift in their thinking on this matter over the years. 'If you had come to the kibbutz ten years ago [1953] you would have seen that our children all wore the same clothes . . . Today, we think about this question in a different way . . . There should be the possibility of individuality in how one dresses, as well as in how one does other things' (Alon, in Neubauer, 1965, p. 190). Our discussions with kibbutz adults confirmed the current prevalence of a belief in the important role personal possessions can play in establishing one's individuality.

A related cultural difference is the absence of *parts of the house or yard* ever being mentioned by kibbutz subjects, while it was moderately frequent for the older nonkibbutz, and very frequent for the older American, children. This, of course, reflects the fact that kibbutz children do not have their own rooms, and probably fewer nonkibbutz Israelis have their own rooms than does this sample of upper-middle class Americans.

It should also be noted that the American children mentioned more possessions on the average than did either nonkibbutz subjects or kibbutz subjects for possessions in their parents' home (see Table 10). However, when both children's house and parents' home possessions are combined (see Table 11), American and kibbutz subjects mentioned approximately equal numbers of personal possessions, while non-kibbutz children mentioned fewer. This result is particularly interesting in light of the history and ideology of the kibbutz movement. In the early days of kibbutzim, 40 and 50 years ago, there were very few personal possessions of any kind, for adults and children alike. This was due to quite pragmatic reasons: The economic situation was tenuous and material comfort was minimal. As many resources as possible were directed toward the economic development of the kibbutz. Thus, money was spent on farm machinery rather than on elaborate wardrobes. Instead of each person having a number of shirts which s / he used exclusively, an individual obtained any shirt from the laundry which was the right size, wore it, and turned it back in to the laundry for cleaning. It was unmarked, and it was unknown who might use that same shirt the next time around. This practice seems to have been the result of pragmatic considerations, but it was also harmonious with the general economic and social philosophy of the kibbutz movement. This philosophy includes a strong belief in the value of collective ownership of the means of production, the absence of exploitation of some individuals by others, and the general equal worth of all individuals. Since private ownership is a means of both creating and maintaining exploitation and inequalities in much of Western society, this secular asceticism was quite congenial with the overall values of the kibbutz.

However, there has clearly been a trend away from asceticism and toward more material comsumption on the kibbutz (see Barkai, 1971, and Maron, 1971 for interesting discussions of the effects of this trend on the goal of equality). Our results here are a confirmation of this trend as it affects children, and these results indicate that kibbutz children report even more personal possessions than do their nonkibbutz Israeli counterparts. In a fascinating article, Talmon (1972) has analyzed in great detail this trend away from secular asceticism, and one of her suggestions is particularly interesting in light of our results.

Table 10: Average number of different categories of personal possessions kept at home[a] mentioned by culture, age, and sex for cross-cultural sample

		American			Kibbutz[b]			Non-Kibbutz			Combined		
		F	M	Comb.	F	M	Comb.	F	M	Comb.	F	M	Comb.
Age	1	6.20	6.60	6.40	5.41	5.43	5.42	6.00	4.00	5.03	5.85	5.37	5.62
	3	8.33	6.93	7.63	3.53	5.33	4.28	6.13	6.50	6.31	5.90	6.33	6.10
Combined		7.27	6.77	7.02	4.47	5.38	4.87	6.06	5.33	5.70	5.87	5.85	5.86

Culture: F $(2,169)$ = 10.85, p < .001
Age: ns
Sex: ns
Age X Sex: ns
Age X Culture: F $(2,169)$ = 4.15, p < .05
Sex X Culture: ns
Age X Sex X Culture: F $(2,169)$ = 2.96, p < .10

[a] Collections as personal possessions have been excluded here.
[b] Those possessions kept in the children's house have been excluded here.

Table 11: Average number of different categories of personal possessions[a] mentioned by culture, age, and sex for cross-cultural sample

		American			Kibbutz[b]			Non-Kibbutz			Combined	
		F	M	Comb.	F	M	Comb.	F	M	Comb.	F	M	Comb.
Age	1	6.20	6.60	6.40	7.18	6.79	7.00	6.00	4.00	5.03	6.49	5.81	6.17
	3	8.80	7.27	8.03	7.65	9.33	8.34	6.63	6.81	6.72	7.65	7.67	7.67
Combined		7.50	6.93	7.22	7.41	7.96	7.65	6.32	5.50	5.92	7.08	6.74	6.92

Culture: F $(2,169)$ = 6.22, p < .01
Age: F $(1,169)$ = 13.04, p < .001
Sex: ns
Age X Sex: ns
Age X Culture: ns
Sex X Culture: ns
Age X Sex X Culture: F $(2,169)$ = 2.47, p < .10

a Including collections as personal possessions.
b For the kibbutz sample this includes possessions kept at the parents' home as well as those kept at the children's house.

She argues that 'the continued postponement of fundamental
satisfactions inadvertently enhances their value. Consumer satisfactions
are no longer disparaged. On the contrary, every advantage or presumed
advantage that may be gained in this field assumes an exaggerated
importance' (p. 211). I think that such an analysis suggests the
possibility that kibbutz adults, who spent many years practicing
considerable asceticism, have now turned to a much more consumerism
ideology and / or life style (see Talmon's documentation on this), and
in so doing they have placed increasing emphasis on the number of
objects available to their children, both as toys in the children's house
and as personal possessions at home. This attitude might be reminiscent
of the oft-mentioned desire of parents for their children to have what
they did not have. In any case, it must be recalled that much of the
founding generation of kibbutzim was raised in middle class, European
families, then went off to Israel and practiced a high degree of
asceticism which, given their backgrounds, must have been experienced
as relative material deprivation. If Talmon is correct, such a situation
may well have led to an 'exaggerated importance' of material
possessions in recent years. There is recent experimental evidence
consistent with this analysis. Worchel, Lee, and Adewole (1975) found
that an object is valued more when it is scarce, and furthermore that a
change from abundance to scarcity enhances its value more than does a
constant state of scarcity. These investigators hypothesized that the
critical variable may be one of control. 'One possible mechanism is that
scarcity arouses reactance in the individual. The individual sees that as
the item becomes less plentiful, his freedom to have that item
decreases' (p. 911). This reactance to a loss of freedom leads the
individual to want the item even more. Although intriguing, this
analysis must be applied with caution to the kibbutz situation, where it
was *voluntary* scarcity that was experienced, rather than externally
imposed scarcity, as was studied by Worchel *et al.*

    It should also be noted that kibbutz subjects mentioned as personal
possessions far more items that are kept in their parents' home than
items that are kept in the children's house. This would seem to reflect
the fact that there are indeed very few items in the children's house
which they consider to be personal possessions (mainly clothes and
decorative items). There is a general rule that most items in the
children's house are to be shared, and this is enforced by the metapelet.
The child's *tab* — a cupboard near his or her bed — contains a few
personal items, but otherwise most everything is for collective use. If
children bring things from home, they must share them, and they are
encouraged not to bring anything that they don't want to share. Thus,
it would seem that they certainly learn a distinction between things
located in the children's house and those located in their parents' home.

They have much less control over the use of items in the children's house — everyone has a right to use them. On the other hand, items which they keep at home are much more under their control — they can decide whether or not to share them. This distinction is not an absolute one, and in recent years kibbutz educators have increasingly allowed a child to control a particularly favourite toy in the children's house. However, the general distinction between objects in the children's house and objects in the parents' home is still very applicable.

Most of the sex differences found for the American sample with respect to types of possessions were also found for the Israeli groups.[7]

Collections

Collections represent a peculiar type of possession, since they consist of a conglomerate of individual items. Children's collecting activities were a subject of early research in child psychology (Burke, 1900; Lehman and Witty, 1927; Wiltse and Hall, 1891). Unfortunately, these studies were contradictory in their results. For example, Burke reported that 90 per cent of her school-age subjects had at least one collection, while Lehman and Witty found that only 10 per cent had collections.

Our results indicate that collections are clearly most freqent for 10- to 11-year-olds (see Tables 12, 13 and 14). A few adult-parents also mentioned collections, but they were very rare at all other age levels.

Table 12: Average number of different categories of collections as personal possessions mentioned by age and sex for American sample

		Age Group					
		1	2	3	4	5	Combined
Sex	F	0.00	0.00	0.47	0.07	0.20	0.15
	M	0.00	0.07	0.33	0.07	0.27	0.15
Combined		0.00	0.03	0.04	0.07	0.23	0.15

Age: $F_{(4,140)} = 5.09$, $p < .001$
Sex: ns
Age X Sex: ns

Table 13: Average number of different categories of collections as personal possessions kept at home mentioned by culture, age, and sex for cross-cultural sample

		American			Kibbutz[a]			Non-Kibbutz			Combined		
		F	M	Comb.	F	M	Comb.	F	M	Comb.	F	M	Comb
Age	1	0.00	0.00	0.00	0.00	0.07	0.03	0.00	0.00	0.00	0.00	0.02	0.01
	3	0.47	0.33	0.40	0.53	0.42	0.48	0.50	0.31	0.41	0.50	0.35	0.43
Combined		0.23	0.17	0.20	0.26	0.23	0.25	0.26	0.17	0.21	0.25	0.19	0.22

Culture: ns
Age: $F (1,169) = 24.50$, $p < .001$
Sex: ns
Age X Sex: ns
Age X Culture: ns
Sex X Culture: ns
Age X Sex X Culture: ns

[a] Collections kept in the children's house are excluded here (see Table 14).

Table 14: Average number of different categories of collections as personal possessions kept in the children's house for kibbutz subjects by age and sex

		Sex	
	F	M	Comb.
Age 1	0.00	0.00	0.00
3	0.18	0.17	0.17
Combined	0.09	0.08	0.08

The total number of collections mentioned was too small to make any reliable comparisons of the types of items collected, but the data do suggest that Israelis tend to collect souvenir items (post cards, pennants, etc.) more than do Americans, while the latter collect coins more than do the former. It is not surprising that the types of items collected might be heavily influenced by cultural factors.

General possessables

In addition to items explicitly identified as possessions, we examined the types of items which were referred to as 'my_____' but were never explicitly named as possessions. We suspected that such items might actually be considered personal possessions, but for some reason would not be elicited when the subject was asked for a list of possessions. The results of this analysis revealed a remarkable similarity for all cultural groups and all age levels. *Furniture and furnishings*, along with *parts of the house or yard*, were the most frequently mentioned items of this type. It is possible that these results reflect the fact that items such as one's room and one's bed are so taken for granted that they are overlooked when listing one's possessions. This interpretation would be supported by the fact that the youngest subjects in all culture groups mentioned significantly more items of this type as general possessables than did other age levels, and there are other indications in the data that they tend to take possession and ownership for granted (see Furby, 1976d).

On the other hand, it may be that the central relation in referring to 'my bed' or 'my room' is a purely associational one: The object is associated with me in that I am the one who uses it. Such an association may not meet the qualifications for being a possessive relation for the subject. This seems particularly likely to be the case for kibbutz subjects who indeed do not have their own rooms, and yet some of them refer to 'my room', apparently in this associational sense. One might argue, of course, that this is simply a linguistic ambiguity — we use the possessive form for two different meanings. However, the problem cannot be that simple, because we then must ask *why* we use the same form to express what may appear to be two different meanings (see Cellard, 1975). There is room here for valuable research on the evolution and function of possessive linguistic forms in various languages, and the results would certainly add to our knowledge of the nature of possession itself.

Our examination of the nature of personal possessions has been limited to tangible, material objects. This restriction was imposed on the present study solely in the interest of delimiting a research problem of manageable proportions. However, I want to emphasize the fact that the possession of tangible goods represents only one aspect of the entire domain of interest. Clearly, studies of the possession of nontangibles will also be needed in the course of the overall research effort.

CONCLUSION / The purpose of this article has been twofold: (a) to describe a developmental, cross-cultural research project designed to study the nature and funtion of possession and ownership in human beings, and (b) to present a portion of the results from this project. The focus of the present discussion has been on cross-cultural aspects of methodology and results related to the nature of possessables. A more general theoretical formulation of the psychological foundations of possession and ownership has been treated elsewhere (Furby, 1976c). It should also be noted that the study reported here is limited to one method of data collection and analysis. A multi-method approach to nomothetic research questions such as this one is clearly desirable, and is currently being pursued (see Furby, 1974, 1975).

Footnotes

1. I have enjoyed close collaboration with Susan Harter during the initial design and data collection phases of this project, and with Karen John for both data collection and analysis. In addition to this general collaboration, a number of individuals have contributed to various portions of this project: Jerry Eagle provided invaluable computer programming assistance; Mary Wilke transcribed many of the interviews; and Larry Moran participated in final preparation of the manuscript. This research was made possible by the generous support of the Grant Foundation, Inc., by a National Institutes of Mental Health Postdoctoral Research Fellowship, by National Institutes of Health General Research Support Grant No. RR 05612-07, and by the material and intellectual support of my colleagues at Oregon Research Institute.

2. Until now, the psychological studies of kibbutz children and adults have tended to focus on the consequences of communal child-rearing for personality development, and on the emotional effects of the absence of a traditional one-to-one mother-infant relationship.

3. The data collection for the Israeli portion of this project was made possible by the invaluable collaboration we enjoyed with Gavriel Salomon of the Hebrew

University in Jerusalem, and from students working under his supervision: Geula Zaltz, Shoshanah Fleischer, Diana Daniel, and Leora Wellner. Without their hard work, ingenuity, patience with the demands of such compulsive researchers, and remarkable persistence despite the disruptions of war, this study would never have seen the printed page. Equally invaluable to the Israeli portion of this project was the assistance, advice, hospitality, and friendship of Menachem Gerson of the Oranim Institute. He devoted considerable time and effort to educating us about kibbutz life, to administrative arrangements for preliminary visits and later data collection, and to thoughtful discussions of our research topic. Our kibbutz experience would never have been the same without his contributions and stimulation.

4. Most kibbutzim belong to one of three kibbutz federations, which differ mainly in political ideology. All three adhere to a basically collective economic and social structure, and thus they were all appropriate for our research purposes.

5. All of the American interviews were carried out by a single interviewer, who was American born and whose native language was English. The Israeli interviews were conducted by four interviewers, who were Israeli born and whose native language was Hebrew. While having different interviewers for American and Israeli subjects was essential to our method, it also necessarily results in a confounding of interviewer with cultural group. For that reason, the interview contained a number of basic questions asked verbatim by all interviewers, and a number of standard probes, in an attempt to minimize the possibility for interviewer effects.

6. Most dimensions or factors discussed throughout this report correspond to specific categories whose labels are quite straightforward. In those cases where I have combined several related categories in a dimension, that will be so indicated in a footnote. This dimension includes 'toys and games (not clearly sex-steroetyped)' (#28), 'female-stereotyped toys' (#31), and 'male-stereotyped toys' (#30).

7. All of the data with respect to sex differences and similarities in personal possessions are presented and discussed in detail elsewhere (Furby, 1976e). The most salient results from that analysis are only briefly mentioned in this discussion.

A cross-cultural study of the basic thinking processes of English 'British' Punjabi and Indigenous Punjabi boys*
P.A.S. Ghuman, 1976

INTRODUCTION / The use of psychometric tests, which have been constructed and standardized in European settings, has been seriously questioned by researchers (Cole *et al.*, 1971; Berry, 1969) working in the field of cross-cultural studies. The main objection against the use of such tests is that content, format, and the procedures of administration are not appropriate to testees who are not Westernized. Attempts to produce culture-free or fair tests have met with but little success.

* Written and prepared by the author for inclusion in this volume. Gratitude is extended to Dr Paul A.S. Ghuman of the University College of Wales, Aberystwyth.

Piaget's theoretical system to some extent, is free from these limitations in that the procedures, content and format can be varied to suit the cultural setting. The clinical method used by Piaget in his researches, also helps the investigator to analyse the strategies and processes of thinking of his subjects. Hence the increasing use of Piaget's conceptual model to study the processes of thinking, cross-culturally, has appealed to many investigators. These researches have been undertaken to study the effects of social and cultural milieux on the logical operations (thinking) of children, and to test the validity of Piaget's claim that the nature of logical operations is both sequential and universal. Hyde (1959) using a cross-cultural sample in Aden, confirmed Piaget's model, but found Asian children some 2–3 years behind the European children in her sample. This she attributed to the lack of educational facilities. Goodnow's (1969 / 70) research in Hong Kong with Chinese and European children substantiated Piaget's model, but found that illiterate Chinese children were poorer on tests which involved advance mental planning. Price-Williams *et al.* (1969) studied the conservation of amount among Tiv children in Nigeria and confirmed Piaget's views on the universality of the thinking processes involved. In another study Price-Williams *et al.* have underlined the importance of previous experience with the test material. Peluffo's (1967) researches on children who emigrated from under-developed areas of Sicily to Italy, showed the significance of urban-cultural factors on the thinking processes. He found no significant differences between the immigrant children of long-stay and native children on Piaget's tests of causality, time and conservation.

It seems to be that Piaget's theoretical model has a considerable pragmatic value in the study of thinking, but there would appear to be a number of shortcomings. Piaget (1966), though recognizing the importance of social and cultural factors on logical thinking, does not characterize them in sufficient detail to be of value to research workers. Furthermore, in his theoretical system, psychological factors such as apperception, strategies of processing information, and learning sets, are of less significance than logical factors such as schemata and structures.

Bruner (1966) in order to overcome these shortcomings has developed a model of intellectual development called 'Instrumental Conceptualism'. The main principles of his model are two-fold. First, Bruner postulates that the human species has acquired three distinct but related modes of cognizing, and that each style places its own constraints on the knower. The development of these three modes – namely, the enactive, the iconic and the symbolic – depends on the amplifiers which cultures provide through their artefacts, as well as on the extent to which the children are encouraged to explore the concordance or discordance between each of the three modes.

According to Greenfield and Bruner (1966) the development of these three modes of representation are mainly related to the constituent elements of cultures, namely: type of environment (urban / rural), language system, and belief and value systems.

The model offers an explanation of the processes of cognitive development by postulating three styles of experiental representation rather than by logical constructs such as schemata and structures. Such a model also goes somewhat further than Piaget's in identifying factors which form the core of social milieux. This carefully worked out model provides a framework within which researches, probing the field of intellectual development, can be conceptually embedded. Furthermore such a system can be of pragmatic value in predicting and explaining the influences of a Western-type environment on the cognitive processes of children who have emigrated from traditional cultures.

During the sixties, the influx of immigrants from Commonwealth countries — especially Asia — has provided an excellent opportunity for research workers to study the effects of the European type of environment on the thinking processes of children. These children are mainly from the traditional cultures of India and the West Indies with different religions, languages and social values from those of the British.

RESEARCH HYPOTHESES /
1. The thinking processes of British Punjabi boys (9—9 to 11—10 years) are significantly superior to those of indigenous Punjabi boys of this age range.
2. Indigenous Punjabi boys (9—9 to 11—10 years) perform relatively better on those tests which can be made culturally appropriate, as compared with the performance of British Punjabi boys.
3. Senior age boys (11+ years) are significantly superior to the junior age boys (9—9+ years) in their thinking processes.

The following research questions were formulated:
1. Do the thinking processes of British Punjabi boys (9—9 to 11—10 years) differ significantly from those of English boys of the same age group and similar social class backgrounds?
2. In what ways does the traditional milieu affect the thinking processes of boys in Punjab? What type of tests and testing procedures are most apposite for studying the thinking processes of such boys?
3. Is the cognitive style utilized by Punjabi boys distinctive in its characteristics from the style utilized by British Punjabi boys?

EXPERIMENTAL DESIGN: DESCRIPTION OF THE SAMPLES AND TESTS / In order to test the hypotheses and to probe into the research questions posed therein, the problems of research design had to be met. According to the strict canons of scientific research as elucidated by, amongst others, Campbell and Stanley (1966) the subjects for the experiment should be selected randomly and assigned randomly to treatment groups and control groups to ascertain the effects of independent variable(s) on the dependent variable(s). These desiderata are most difficult, if not impossible, to fulfil in cross-cultural studies. The researches of Vernon, Bruner *et al.* and of other scholars, would have been impossible had they abided by these principles. The researcher in the cross-cultural field, more often than not, has to rely on *ex post facto* research designs. The present investigation is no exception, and the following diagram shows the design of the experiment:

Diagram 1
Research Design

Independent variable   Dependent variable(s)
Western-type environment   Basic thinking processes
Experimental group (British Punjabi)   Control group in Punjab (I)
(Experienced Western-type environment)(Not experienced Western-type environment)

Control group of indigenous 'English' boys (II)

The independent variable in this research is exposure to a 'Western-type environment' and the dependent variables are the thinking processes as measured by the various tests (to be described later). The Punjabi group in this country, which was selected for the investigation, served as an experimental group and a similar group (in age, socioeconomic background, ethnicity and subculture) acted as a control group in Punjab. Another control group of indigenous (English) boys was considered necessary to assess fully the impact of environmental variables on the abilities of British Punjabi children.

Control of variables
Since randomization is not practicable in *ex post facto* research designs, it is desirable to match the subjects in experimental group and control groups on as many variables as possible (Kerlinger, 1969, p. 297). Hence the following variables were controlled: age, sex, ethnicity and sub-cultural variations and social class.

Selection of the samples
The headmasters of six primary schools in Birmingham (UK) were approached, five of whom kindly agreed to provide facilities for this research. The boys were selected from the five schools according to the

desired criteria. Boys in Punjab were selected from two village schools. Two age groups were selected to study the developmental trends in thinking and concept formation and to relate these trends to socio-cultural and educational factors. The boys were also matched on social class in England, i.e. Punjabi's and the English; but it was not possible to match the Punjabi boys now living in Punjab on this variable as the structure of the society is different from that of England. The sons of small farmers were taken from Punjab as they approximate to the social strata of the Punjabi's and the English chosen for this study. The Punjabi boys both in England and Punjab belong to Jat Sikh group which has a distinct *cultural* and *ethnic* identity. The variable of 'length of schooling' is important in making viable comparisons, hence this factor was also controlled.

Choice of tests

As the major purpose of the research was to look closely at the thinking processes of boys (in different social milieux) rather than the product of these processes, it was considered prudent to use as many individual tests as practicable. All the tests except the Coloured Raven Matrices and Draw-a-Man were given individually and details of the boys' reasonings were taken down for later analyses.

Two types of tests were included: the first category consists of tests which can be easily adapted to different cultural settings (Conservation problems; Equivalence test) and the second category includes tests of a more formal nature (e.g. WISC Block Design, Vygotsky Blocks), the content, format, and procedures of administration of which cannot be changed.

This choice was based on the hypothesis that the Punjabi boys would do relatively well, as compared with the boys in England, on the tests which are presented to them in materials with which they have previous experiences; but not so well on the tests which are basically developed and standardized in the European context. Hence it was hoped to assess both the influences of familiar material and of different social milieux on their thinking processes. Here is a summary of the tests administered to the boys:

Summary of the Tests

Test	British Punjabi Boys	English Boys	Punjabi Boys
Conservation of Weight	√	√	√
Conservation of Area	√	√	√
Conservation of Volume	√	√	*
Equivalence Test	√	√	√
Vygotsky Blocks	√	√	√
Raven Matrices (Coloured Set)	√	√	√
Draw-a-Man Test (Good-enough Harris)	√	√	*

* Due to shortage of time, these were not given to Punjabi boys.

With the exception of Vygotsky test (1962), and the equivalence test (Olver and Hornsby, 1966) all other tests have been widely used in cross-cultural researches. The Conservation tasks and other tests were given according to the standard instructions. In England tests were administered through the medium of English, but Punjabi (an Indian language) was used with the Punjabi boys.

Size of samples

By and large it is considered desirable to take fairly large samples for researches; though, according to Burroughs (1971) the exact size should be determined by statistical and practical considerations. The numbers in the samples in the present study, however, were primarily based on pragmatic rather than statistical grounds.

The size of the samples, to a degree, depends on the type of tests to be used. For instance it is possible to test a fairly large number of pupils on group tests, whereas in the case of individual tests (because they are time consuming) samples necessarily have to be smaller.

Table 1: Mean age and 'range' of the samples

	Mean Age	Range	Number	Abbreviations used
1. English Junior	10 years 4.3 months	12 months	25	E_J
2. English Senior	11 years 3.2 months	10 months	25	E_S
3. British Punjabi Junior	10 years 3.5 months	13 months	25	BP_J
4. British Punjabi Senior	11 years 5 months	10 months	25	BP_S
5. Punjabi Junior	10 years 3 months	12 months	20	P_J
6. Punjabi Senior	11 years 6.6 months	8 months	20	P_S

Analysis of the results

Appropriate statistical techniques for evaluating the hypothesis were considered. After deliberation it was decided first to test whether the samples (English, British Punjabi and Punjabi) belong to the same population or come from different populations with respect to the means of the tests used. Multivariate analysis of variance was considered to be the most appropriate technique, as it processes several dependent variables simultaneously, unlike univariate analysis of variance. If it were to be established that the samples differed with respect to means and came from different populations then multiple discriminant analysis would be carried out. This analysis enables us to examine the spatial distribution of the groups in discriminant(s) space(s) and also to assess the relative importance of each variable to the dimension which maximizes the difference between the samples. Subsequent univariate analysis of variance and chi-square test were used, on the quantitative and qualitative data respectively, to further tease out the variable(s) which contribute to the multivariate differences in means.

The test on equivalence was excluded as it yields a number of conceptual categories which are distinctly qualitative in nature and are difficult to quantify. The rest of the tests are included in the analyses. The rationales for marking all the tests, except for the Piagetian tests, are fairly well established. There is, as yet, no sound rationale for quantifying Piagetian battery of tests; hence it was decided to mark the tests qualitatively on a dichotomous scale 'O' and 'I'. These variables pose a problem, as they are not normally distributed and are qualitative in nature. However, Blacketh and Reymont (1971) and Seal (1964) argue that such variables may be used in certain multivariate analyses, including discriminant analysis and canonical analysis for heuristic purposes. This practice was followed to gain maximum information from the test battery utilized. The means and standard deviation of the samples on five tests are given on the following page:

Table 2: Means and standard deviations of groups on four tests

	WISC Blocks		Raven Matrices		Vygotsky Blocks		Draw-a-Man Test	
	M	SD	M	SD	M*	SD	M	SD
EJ	10.880	2.619	28.680	5.367	91.200	28.624	91.440	14.829
ES	9.520	2.931	28.400	6.076	82.000	27.763	90.200	15.489
EJ+S	10.200	2.835	28.540	5.675	86.600	28.292	90.820	15.020
BPJ	10.840	3.050	26.280	6.496	95.400	34.123	95.920	13.874
BPS	10.480	2.551	27.680	6.388	83.800	28.660	102.160	13.496
BPJ+S	10.660	2.789	26.980	6.415	89.600	31.733	99.04	13.907
PJ	4.550	3.561	12.000	4.230	119.750	27.790	—	—
PS	5.750	2.425	15.700	4.130	116.000	24.952	—	—
PJ+S	5.150	3.068	13.850	4.532	117.875	26.137	—	—

* = High scores imply low performance

Table 3: Result of conservation tests

	Weight Successful	Un-successful	Area Successful	Un-successful	Volume Successful	Un-successful
E_J	14	11	15	10	12	13
E_S	16	9	15	10	12	13
E_{J+S}	30	20	30	20	24	26
BP_J	16	9	11	14	10	15
BP_S	18	7	16	9	11	14
BP_{J+S}	34	16	27	23	21	29
P_J	7	13	2	18	–	–
P_S	15	5	7	13	–	–
P_{J+S}	22	18	9	31	–	–

The multivariate analysis of variance was carried out with a library programme from Reading (CG DISCRI) at the computer centre of the University College of Wales, Aberystwyth. The results of the analyses follow.

The inference drawn from analysis (a) of Table 4 is that the six samples come from different populations with respect to their means; but from analysis (b) it can be deduced that four British groups (E_J; E_S; BP_J; BP_S) do not differ significantly and may be regarded as samples from the same population. The analyses (c, d, e, f) on composite groups (when age factor is not considered) point to a similar conclusion as that of (a) and (b). However, the addition of two variables (Conservation of Volume and Draw-a-Man Test) produced interesting results. We now find that British Punjabi and English groups are significantly different both when treated as four groups and two composite groups. Inspection of the group means suggests that the Draw-a-Man Test (e.g. A.M. of E_{J+S} = 90.82; A.M. of BP_{J+S} = 99.04) is contributing heavily to the significant differences. The summary of the results of multivariate analysis of variance is presented in Table 4. A number of these results, which reached significant levels, was further analysed by the technique of multiple discriminant analysis. The results are rather technical and the interested readers are referred to the original work (Ghuman, 1974). Briefly the two discriminant functions are given on page 138.

Table 4: Multivariate analyses of variance on six groups

	Groups	No. of Variables	DF	Wilks' Lambda	F	P
*a)	E_J v E_S v BP_J v BP_S v P_J v P_S	5	F1 = 25.00 F2 = 484.43	0.328	6.78	0.001
b)	E_J v E_S v BP_J v BP_S	5	F1 = 15 F2 = 254.37	0.816	1.30	NS
*c)	E_{J+S} v BP_{J+S} v P_{J+S}	5	F1 = 10.0 F2 = 266.00	0.389	16.06	.001
d)	E_{J+S} v BP_{J+S}	5	F1 = 5.00 F2 = 94.00	0.928	1.46	NS
e)	E_{J+S} v P_{J+S}	5	F1 = 5.00 F2 = 84.00	0.284	42.30	.001
*f)	BP_{J+S} v P_{J+S}	5	F1 = 5.00 F2 = 84.00	0.393	25.95	.001
*g)	E_J v E_S v BP_J v BP_S	7	F1 = 21.50 F2 = 258.98	0.703	1.61	.05
*h)	E_{J+S} v BP_{J+S}	7	F1 = 7.00 F2 = 92.00	0.829	2.71	.05

Figure 1: Positions of centroids of six samples on the first variate

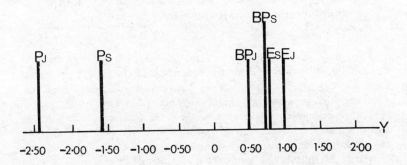

Figure 2: Positions of centroids of six samples on the two variates

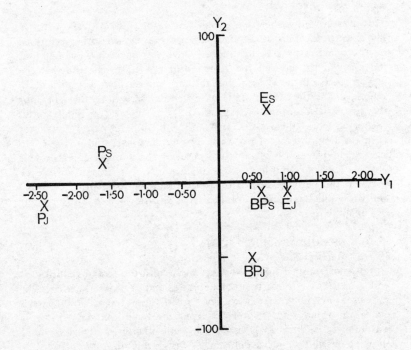

$$Y_1 = .091\ X_1 + .151\ X_2 + -.444\ X_3 + .490\ X_4 + .0023\ X_5$$
$$Y_2 = -.373\ X_1 + .0797\ X_2 + .152\ X_3 + 1.012\ X_4 - .014\ X_5$$

Y_1 = WISC Blocks; X_2 = Raven Matrices; X_3 = Weight;
X_4 = Area; X_5 = Vygotsky Blocks

The position of the group centroids are plotted on the first discriminant function to show the separation of the groups. It is clear from the Figure No. 1 that the Punjabi groups are clearly separated from the other groups on this highly significant function.

The second graph was drawn to show the positions of samples on two discriminant functions. The examination of the Figure (2) suggests that the second function, which is not related to the first, mainly separates the four British groups (E_J, E_S, BP_J, BP_S). However, we have to treat the result of this function cautiously as its discriminatory power is very low (6.05 per cent), and because of the fact that the root associated with this function did not reach the desired level of significance (.05).

It was argued earlier that should the results of 'MANOVA' prove significant, univariate analysis of variance and X_2 would be performed on the quantitative and qualitative variables respectively, to pinpoint the differences between the groups. These analyses showed that the performance of the British Punjabi and English boys is significantly superior on all the tests at .01 level (except conservation of weight); but the two British groups (BP_{J+S} and E_{J+S} do not differ significantly, except on Draw-a-Man test in which the Punjabi boys performed better than the English boys. Thus we accept hypotheses 1 and partly 2. No significant differences were found between the younger and the older boys — hence hypothesis 3 is rejected. No significant difference between the performance of the British Punjabi boys (BP_{J+S} v E_{J+S}) and the English boys were found except on Draw-a-Man test (in favour of Punjabi boys).

DISCUSSION OF THE RESULTS /
Raven's Matrices Test

It is not claimed here that this test is culture free and valid for all children, irrespective of their backgrounds and previous experiences; it was used in this research to investigate the influence of Western education on boys who belong to a traditional culture. Furthermore, it was hoped that the analyses of the Punjabi boys' responses would show-up possible cognitive deficiencies within this group.

The Punjabi junior boys found the test interesting, but difficult [Mean = 12.0, SD = 4.23] : five boys [25 per cent] of this group scored less than ten; their scores mainly consisted of correct responses given to the first eight items of set A and / or first three items of set Ab.

According to the test manual such performances indicate 'that these children are only capable of answering items which are either composed of simple continuous pattern completion or discrete pattern completion, and are unable to respond correctly to items requiring completion of a pattern showing progressive changes and other designs involving the apprehension of the three figure as a related "whole" to be completed by the fourth part' [Raven, 1963, p. 32]. The high scorers [16+] attempted successfully most of the items from set A, approximately the first half of items from set Ab and the first three or four items from set B. None of the boys responded correctly to the second half of set Ab. For example, the typical answer to Ab9 was either 1, 3 or 5. Response number [1] shows the whole pattern when completed and [3] and [5] are repetitions of the parts of the given pattern. Thus we find, even the best in this group cannot analyse the perceived pattern into its constituent elements and distinguish between what is given and what he himself has to contribute. The senior Punjabi boys are significantly better than the junior [Mean = 15.7, SD = 4.13], and show some progress, though their performance falls far short of even the junior Punjabi boys in this country, none scoring less than 10 and eight boys scoring more than 15 marks.

WISC Block Design Test

The performance of the Punjabi boys on this test was very poor, with the senior boys only marginally better than the junior boys [P_J = 4.55, SD = 3.56, P_S = 5.75, SD = 2.42]. Seven junior boys and one senior boy failed to do even pattern C of the test. The major difficulty of the Punjabi boys seemed to lie in grasping the relation between two-dimensional designs and three-dimensional blocks. Furthermore, even the best subjects in this sample made errors of orientation: for instance design number three was rotated through 180°. These boys had never handled cubes or other similar material in schools or at home and consequently had great difficulty in manipulating them. A number of the subjects when making a design insisted on looking at the vertical side of the pattern they were making, despite the instructions that they should look on the top surface. None of the boys was successful in completing design four or any of the subsequent designs. [It is interesting to note that when this test was given to the son of a village carpenter, who was not included in our sample, he showed a quick grasp of the problems and successfully completed designs up to six].

McFie (1961) also observed the orientation difficulties of African students in this type of test, and suggests that they are due to the lack of relevant background experiences. He provided such experiences to his subjects and there was an improvement in their performance. Lloyd and Pidgeon (1961) have also shown that coaching children in this type of task improves their performance. Vernon (1969) similarly comments on the low spatial ability of his testees who had little relevant experience with the material. Witkin has argued (1966) that the WISC Block Design test provides an excellent measure of Field-dependence, but as far as this sample is concerned, this test seems to be of little value in assessing this factor as it is very difficult to say whether the low-scores of our Punjabi samples are indicative of Field-dependence or due to lack of appropriate perceptual experiences which leads to a low spatial ability. We cannot but surmise how far the researchers [Dawson, 1967; Berry, 1965] who have used this type of material to assess the bipolar dimension of Field-independence and Field-dependence are correct in deriving conclusions regarding child-rearing practices and the like, without first investigating the background experiences of their samples [perceptual experiences, spatial training, etc.].

Conservation of Weight

The results of this test are interesting as no significant differences were found between the Punjabi, the British Punjabi and the English groups. The senior Punjabi boys are the best performers [C = 75 per cent, NC = 25 per cent]. It is important to discuss the results of this test in detail as they are different from the results of all the other tests.

The Punjabi boys come from families which are engaged in traditional farming, where boys usually help their fathers in looking after the cattle and doing other chores, such as measuring, storing and weighing farm produce for sale. Thus these boys have considerable experience in measuring and weighing things at their homes and farms. It is reasonable to suggest that this previous experience helped these subjects, especially the older ones, to develop a pragmatic model to deal with such types of problems. Needless to say, older boys perform better partly due to sheer maturational factors, but also, I think, largely due to the fact that they are generally given more responsibility in the tasks described earlier.

Price-Williams *et al.'s* (1969) research with pottery-making children in Mexico showed that his testees were better conservers of amount than the control group children. Vernon (1969) has also shown, with Indian and Eskimo boys, the importance of specific experiences on performance in spatial and perceptual tests. Goodnow (1969 / 70) also stressing the importance of previous experiences, of specific types on performance, quotes the remarks of a Chinese boy, who was successful in the Conservation of Weight test, as evidence to support her contention that previous experiences possibly provide 'a pragmatic model that serves as a landmark, a reference point or mnemonic device for pinning down a relationship and holding it in mind' [p. 259]. However, it is arguable whether the good performance of our Punjabi boys was due to overlearning or whether they had genuinely internalized the measuring and weighing actions to form schemata, which are related to overall structures and are transferable to other tests of conservation. This point has to be considered again at a later stage.

It is apposite now to look at the behaviour and responses of the boys in some detail. The Punjabi boys were initially very nervous as they were not used to answering questions about subject-matter on which they had not been given previous instructions by persons in authority. They were assured that their teachers would not be told the results of the test and that I was primarily interested in their individual responses, right or wrong. Even after these reassurances most of the boys were rather puzzled with the questions and looked for guidance. It was considered important not to give any facial perceptual cues [smiling, frowning and the like] during the testing sessions as they would have construed these expressions as marks of approval or disapproval. It is also interesting to note that the boys tended to pay more attention to the experimenter and his colleagues than the task in hand, considerable tact and skill was needed to draw their attention to the problem in hand to elicit unprejudiced responses.

Their responses reflect similar processes of thinking to those found with the Western-European children on conservation tests. Thus in response to the question: 'If I place this flat piece [a small chappati] on the scales, is it going to weigh the same more or less than the ball'? Some typical successful responses would be as given below:

1. 'The same as the ball [pointing] as you have weighed them before.'
2. 'The same as the ball as you have rolled the ball, having the same weight as this ball[pointing] into this shape.' Typical wrong responses included:
   1. 'Ball weighs more as it is round and the other one is flat.'
   2. 'Ball weighs more — this is round and big [pointing] and this is flat.'
   3. 'This [pointing to flat piece] weighs more.'

The successful answers were based on 'identity' [same as before type] rather than on reversibility [roll back into a ball — will weigh the same] or compensation [coordination of two dimensions]. Thus our results confirm the stance taken by Bruner (1966, p. 185) who states:

'. . . our argument is in sharp contrast to Piaget's. On purely logical grounds, we believe he has missed the heart of conservation. Both inversion and compensation to be effective must rest upon an appreciation of the original equality of quantities involved'.

He further argues (1966, p. 201):

' . . . Reversibility and compensation could not by themselves be producing conservation — they are often encountered in instances in which the child has not achieved conservation'.

This debate between the Genevan and the Harvard school springs mainly from their different theoretical viewpoints; Piaget's model is embedded in logic and genetics whereas Bruner's theoretical system is firmly rooted in psychological discourse. Consequently the results are interpreted through the respective conceptual frameworks.

The scores of the British Punjabi junior and senior boys are comparable to those of the English boys of their respective age groups, and furthermore the responses of the British Punjabi boys and the English boys are also very similar.

Conservation of Area

Here the performance of the Punjabi boys was poorer than their performance on the conservation of weight test. There were only two conservers [10 per cent] in the junior group; the number conserving in the senior group was higher (35 per cent], but not significantly different from the junior group.

Our result is similar in some ways to one of the studies of Price-Williams and his colleagues (1969). In this study they found that potter's children, who had considerable experience with shaping and moulding materials, performed significantly better on conservation of amount, but not on conservation of weight and volume tests as compared with the control group children. Inhelder (1971) reported the results of a study with Algerian children, in which they were found to be relatively more successful on the conservation of amount than of length. The explanation offered is related to their previous experiences in measuring and storing quantities at home, which is analogous to our Punjabi sample. Inhelder (1971) argues that:

' . . . these children lack the kind of stimulation which results in more developed perceptual strategies . . . they are not, as our Genevan children, made aware at a very early age of differences in height nor are they taught to compare length.' [p. 163]

The Punjabi boys of our sample whilst having a considerable experience in weighing things, do not have experiences in measuring and assessing lengths and areas. Cultivation is on traditional lines and farmers do not bother to measure or assess before cultivation. The boundaries of the fields are fixed and seldom change, consequently there is little need to measure area. However, the other possible explanation is that the test of Conservation of Area is more difficult than the Conservation of Weight test. In this test children are expected to do 'mental and arithmetic' that four houses of the same size occupy the same area, no matter how they are arranged in the field, and such a type of thinking requires a greater degree of detachment from the perceptual field. Goodnow (1969 / 70) in her survey of cross-cultural researches concludes that children from less developed social milieux find it difficult to solve those cognitive problems which require some form of mental shuffling or transformation. Our results tend to support this contention.

Lastly, it is quite probable that the Punjabi boys were being influenced more by the practical rather than the logical considerations of the problem. From their everyday experience they might have formed the opinion that the 'spread-out houses' occupy more room as each of them needs a separate compound for the families, unlike the 'terraced houses' which usually have a communal compound. This was, to some extent, revealed by questions such as these: 'How much is the area to play?' 'Are they [animals] allowed to go near the doors and walls?'

Conservation of Volume

This test was given only to the British samples. The British Punjabi group is not significantly different from the English groups. Furthermore, senior boys are not significantly different from the junior boys. The number conserving on this test is slightly lower than on the other Piagetian tests of conservation used in this research; which is in line with the often found sequential progress in Conservation tests: Amount—Weight—Volume.

Goodenough-Harris Draw-a-Man Test

The results of this test shows that the British Punjabi composite group is significantly superior [at 0.01 level] to the English composite group. This is the only test on which significant difference was found between the composite cultural groups. On further analysis of the results, it became clear that, though the junior British Punjabi boys are better [but not significantly] than the junior English boys, the real differences are between the senior boys of the two cultural groups; British Punjabi boys being superior to the English boys. Our results do not support the findings of Ashby *et al.* (1970), who found even the long-stay immigrant children performing less well than the Scottish

Figure 3: Perceptible / non-perceptible attributes used by six samples

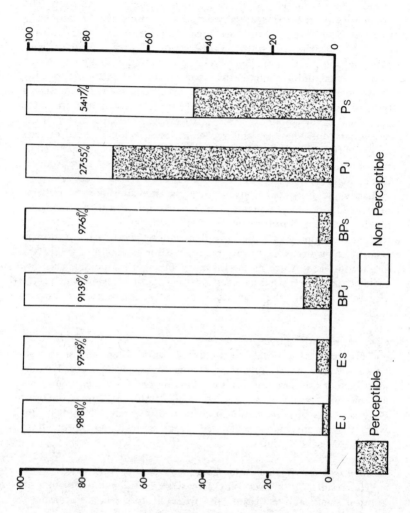

children. However, in their study the difference did not reach the significant level of .05. Haynes' (1970) Punjabi sample was significantly inferior to the English sample on a battery of tests, but not so on the Draw-a-Man test.

Equivalence Test

The analysis of the responses and behaviour patterns of the Punjabi boys suggest that they were well motivated and enjoyed during the test.

The examination of the responses showed that colour has been used predominantly by the Punjabi boys, whereas the boys from the other samples hardly used this attribute for grouping. However, we may note here that the Punjabi senior boys use this attribute less often than the Punjabi junior. All the British samples preferred to form their groupings either on function or by using an existing linguistic category, i.e. common name. But the Punjabi boys, especially the junior ones, used these attributes far less frequently to form their groupings. Again, we find the Punjabi senior group to be better than the junior in the use of nominal and functional categories.

We have graphed (Figure 3) the perceptible (colour, shape) and non-perceptible (functional and nominal) attributes of the six groups to compare and contrast their performance. It is clear from this graph that the dominant mode of grouping used by the Punjabi senior boys is perceptible. They tend to rely on surface qualities of the objects to form equivalence, whereas the senior boys show progress and look for the functional relationship between / among objects or existing lexicons in the language. All the British boys seem to rely on non-perceptible attributes with few exceptions. This finding is in agreement with the researches of Evans and Segall (1969), Serpell (1969a) and Maccoby and Modiano (1969).

Vygotsky Blocks

The analysis of the quantitative data on this test supports our major hypothesis that the British Punjabi group is significantly superior to the Punjabi group. We found no significant differences between the composite British Punjabi and the composite English samples. This test was found difficult by most of the boys in our sample. There were no solutions of grade one in Punjabi groups; the British Punjabi and English groups had only 2 and 4 solutions respectively in this category.

The performance of the Punjabi junior boys was the poorest. Three boys did not even complete the test satisfactorily when all the blocks were upturned. However, even when we include these boys with others who did sort out the blocks correctly, but were not successful in re-sorting [grade 5 solutions], the proportion giving a poor solution is still very high indeed [70 per cent]; only six boys [30 per cent] re-sorted correctly. Thus we may conclude that these boys were perceptually orientated and found it difficult to abstract attributes for correct grouping, even when cues were provided for doing so. This result is in line with the equivalence test, in which we found a large proportion of the boys using colour as an attribute of grouping and employing complexive and thematic strategies for structuring their sorting procedures. The Punjabi senior boys performed relatively better on this test: only one of the boys did not complete the test, showing a distinct improvement on this test. Forty per cent of the boys, however, could not re-sort the blocks correctly, and there was only one boy whose solution fell in grade two. Thus their performance shows a distinct improvement on this test: again in line with the results of the equivalence test. The performance of the British Punjabi boys was superior to that of the Punjabi boys. There were only five senior and eight junior boys who could not re-sort the blocks correctly. The modal location of the correct solution fell in grade three, i.e. the one based on interrelationships of the groups, e.g. these are the largest — smallest and so on. The English groups show a similar pattern of solution except that the junior boys produced fewer grade three solutions. We can deduce from this that the Punjabi groups needed far more cues than the other groups to do correct sorting. The British Punjabi and the English junior boys needed slightly more cues than the senior boys of these respective groups.

In sum, then, we have found the British Punjabi boys to be remarkably similar to the English boys in their responses, both quantitatively and qualitatively; whereas significant differences in quality as well as quantity of thinking were found between the indigenous Punjabi and the British Punjabi groups. Both the junior and the senior Punjabi boys are poorer in their performance on all the tests except on the test of Conservation of Weight. Their performance on the Raven Matrices test showed that they were global in their perception and were unable to analyse the problems objectively. They could not analyse the perceived whole into its component parts and distinguish between what is given and what is required. These characteristics according to Bruner (1966) reflect the iconic style of representation and are also to some extent an indication of Field-dependence. Their other common error was of orientation; they were unable to locate a figure's orientation with respect to themselves and other objects in the field. This was confirmed in our analysis of the Block Design test. Their poor performance on this test is also an indication of poorly developed spatial-ability, which is an important predictor of technical-mechanical aptitude. However, from their poor performance we cannot conclude that they also lack the ability to 'induce' as they have had no experience with this type of material either at home or in school. Their responses on the Conservation test of Area showed their excessive reliance on perceptual rather than conceptual aspects of the problem. They were unable to distinguish between the real and the apparent change and consequently made illogical judgments. This heavy perceptual bias in the orientation of the boys is further reflected in their responses to the test of Equivalence and Vygotsky Blocks. In forming equivalence groups, they predominantly used colour as an attribute of objects. The choice of functional and nominal categories, on the other hand, is an indication of the ability to go beyond the surface qualities of the objects and search for deeper relationships between / among objects. In other words, sorting by non-perceptible attributes involves the use of the higher mental processes [abstraction and generalization, etc.] which these boys did not use. In the concept-formation test a high proportion of the subjects could not re-sort the blocks correctly, despite the cues provided. This suggests that they were unable to abstract the relevant attributes from the blocks to form the concept, and their first successful sorting was based on perceptual rather than conceptual considerations. Thus to conclude, we have found the Punjabi boys to be perceptually orientated, rigid in their thinking and operating at lower levels of abstraction.

It is now appropriate to look for a possible explanation of their poor performance. The genetic explanation is not tenable as the Punjabi boys in this country who belong to the same ethnic group perform just as well as the indigenous English boys. So we focus our attention on socio-cultural and educational factors for possible explanation.

These boys live in rural environments which are simple — the social system is based on face to face interaction, the network of relationships is limited and the communication is mostly direct. As a consequence, there are relatively fewer demands placed on them to use abstract style of thinking. It would also be correct to say that physical identification of objects and persons is important for effective role playing in a close-knit traditional community. A child adopting a symbolic mode of interpretation of reality would be considerably handicapped in his social adjustment. Khulman argues:

'... that a conceptual child gains the ability to abstract and analyse, but loses his ability to preserve the distinctive quality of perceptual experience as such.' [Bruner, 1966, p.27]

A major value-orientation of this community is collective as opposed to individualistic. It nurtures a strong belief in corporate life; social conformity is prized and deviants are rigidly controlled through social sanctions. Elders, expecially those in authority, are held in great respect, and their judgments, pronouncements and views on nature, society, religion and social events are sacrosanct. These values are reflected in the child-rearing practices. There is very little of what Bruner calls Contingent dialogue between the child and the adults in the family. The children are treated as receptacles which are to be filled with the social and elementary technical know-how of the community. Such a type of training is not conducive, according to Witkin (1966), to analytical and independent thinking. Thus we found our boys to be subdued in their attitudes and concrete, global and synthetic in their cognitive style.

The technical know-how of this community is limited. There are very few scientific concepts used in every day social exchanges and the possession of technological objects is confined to only a handful of people. Because of the rigid system of stratification [castes] and division of labour, the members of this community do not engage in woodwork, metal work, painting and designing activities which are considered to provide spatial and perceptual experiences. In summary we can state that the amplifiers, to use Bruner's term, provided by the community for these boys are not adequate to push the cognitive development from the iconic to the symbolic mode of representation.

Lastly, we evaluate the impact of formal schooling on the intellectual development of these indigenous Punjabi boys. Formal schooling, according to Greenfield and Bruner (1966) can provide children with the opportunity to learn about the world in a non-action context, and such learning promotes good structuring of experiences. For instance the use of written language in schools forces the children to plan and structure their thoughts prior to writing, as the written communication has to be understood without concrete cues. Furthermore, there is a contingent dialogue between the teacher and the pupils which helps the children to see contradictions between 'what things look like and what they really are'. This stance is supported by the findings of an empirical study done with the Wolof school-going and illiterate children.

However, in our research the performance of the senior Punjabi boys, who have been in schools for at least three and a half years, falls far short of the performance of even the junior British Punjabi boys. This leads us to conclude that the education which these children receive must be of a very poor quality in terms of the objectives of our inquiry. Our description of schools confirms our view. We found the teaching in these schools to be entirely mechanistic. Teachers are obliged to handle large classes and consequently use drill method for teaching the basic skills. The authority of the teachers is supreme in school; no child ever dares to question the views and interpretations given by the teachers. There is no opportunity for children to explore, manipulate and make things for themselves. As a consequence, schools fail to provide the necessary experiences and intellectual stimulation which are necessary for the development of higher mental processes. One wonders whether the intellectual development of these boys is in any way enhanced by this type of schooling. What emerges from our discussion on schooling is that researchers ought to describe the type of education imparted to children when the factor of schooling is mentioned, otherwise it is likely to lead to erroneous conclusions regarding the role of the school in intellectual development. As we have shown, what goes on in the schools is of crucial importance. Thus to summarize, the boys in our sample are poor in their performance owing to lack of perceptual — kinesthetic experiences, poor use of the language, stultified curiosity and imagination, as well as rigid inflexible attitudes which are acquired from their elders.

A cross-cultural investigation of conservation
M. Goldschmid, P. Bentler, R. Debus, R. Rawlinson, D. Kohnstamm, S. Modgil, J. Nicholls, J. Reykowski, B. Strupczewska, and N. Warren, 1973

AIMS / To assess the sequence and rate of conservation acquisition in several different cultures and to assess the cross-cultural reliability of the Concept Assessment Kit-Conservation.

SUBJECTS / N = 1500. Twenty-five boys and 25 girls from each of five age groups from four to eight years in each of the following countries: Australia, England, Holland, New Zealand, Poland and Uganda.

METHOD / Form A of the Concept Assessment Kit-Conservation (Goldschmid and Bentler, 1968b) was administered in its original version in English-speaking countries or in the native language of particular samples. The Kit includes the Piagetian tasks of: conservation of two-dimensional space; number; substance; quantity and weight; and discontinuous quantity.

RESULTS / Age trends in conservation development for both males and females were fairly consistent from culture to culture. The rate of conservation acquisition differed somewhat across the samples studied. These variations were most likely due to specific environmental differences among the groups compared. The Concept Assessment Kit appeared to be a reliable indicator of conservation across several cultural groups.

*Comparing dimensional categorization in natural and artificial contexts:
a developmental study among the Zinacantecos of Mexico
P. M. Greenfield, 1974*

The author refers to the studies such as those of Fjellman (1971),
Irwin and McLaughlin (1970), Kellaghan (1968) and Okonji (1971)
which employed both familiar and unfamiliar materials in the development of concept formation. However, 'none has held other features of
the task constant while varying familiarity', and the one study which
appears close to fulfilling this criterion was that of Irwin and
McLaughlin (1970).

AIM / The role of familiarity and cultural relevance in the acquisition of categorization behaviours was investigated among the Zinacantecos of Southern Mexico.

SUBJECTS / N = 36. The sample comprised 12 unschooled four- and
five-year-olds; 12 unschooled eight-, nine-, and 10-year-olds; and 12
unschooled ranged in age from 13 to 18 years. Some Ss in the eight to
10 group had experience in selling flowers and in the 13 to 18 years
group, six boys had attended schools. Ages of the subjects were
provided by mothers. 'The participants ... were constituted into
groups along the dimensions of age, sex, work (whether or not they
sold flowers), and schooling', p. 164.

METHOD / The first test involved sorting and resorting a set of eight
flowers. These varied in colour, length and species. The second task,
likewise, involved sorting and resorting a set of eight wooden rods, also
varying in colour, length and circumference. The task was a modification of Nixon's reclassification task and described by de Lacey
(1970). Each subject was requested to sort each array three different
ways.

(Fuller details of the experimental procedure and diagrammatical
representation of the tasks are described in Greenfield, 1974, pp.
163–165.)

RESULTS / Three major results are reported by Greenfield as
follows:
(a) 'The ability to use verbal concepts in sorting and resorting an array
    of objects developed with age in both schooled and unschooled
    Zinacantecos.
(b) No aspect of sorting behaviour showed a positive effect of
    familiarity of object domain. On the contrary, grouping and
    regrouping familiar objects (flowers) by colour sometimes was

done more poorly than grouping and regrouping unfamiliar objects (rods) because of the irrelevance of the colour dimension to flower bouquets in the context of Zinacanteco culture. Flower sellers . . . did not sort flowers better than other subjects.

(c) Although the species dimension is relevant to categorizing the culturally familiar flowers, its use as a basis for grouping developed after all other dimensions used in the experiment — colour, length, and circumference — probably because of its multidimensional perceptual qualities', pp. 157–158.

Piaget's concept of conservation: a comparative study of Libyan and American children's conservation status
A. Y. Hamza, 1976

AIM / To compare the conservation status of different age groups of Libyan children with that of similar American age groups. The study also considered the judgment of selected Libyan teachers of the Libyan child's cognitive status.

SUBJECTS / N = 111, a sample of 86 Libyan children and 25 first, second, and third grade teachers assigned to teach in these schools.

METHOD / Children's conservation status was tested by 'a test of conservation designed to measure the child's ability to conserve eight different tasks on two different test forms.' The teachers were interviewed by the investigator and their responses to the teacher questionnaire were recorded and descriptively analyzed.

RESULTS / Libyan boys' and girls' status of conservation was equivalent, and American normative scores were higher than the scores of Libyan children. The Libyan teachers advanced accurate descriptions as to the age at which Libyan children demonstrated conservation operativity. The author concluded with a strong support for Piaget's theory of cognitive development.

*Weight conservation and matrix-solving ability in Papuan children**
A. Heron and W. Dowel, 1973

AIM / To obtain data in a different cultural setting from that of

* Written and prepared by the authors for inclusion in this volume. Gratitude is extended to Professor Alastair Heron of the Centre for Educational Research and Innovation, Paris, and Dr W. Dowel. (Professor Heron is now at Sheffield University.)

Zambia (Heron, 1971) concerning the ability of children to conserve weight, at the point of transition from primary to secondary education, and to explore the relationship between this conservation performance and that on reasoning tasks of the kind used in non-verbal psychometric tests.

SAMPLE / 55 boys and 54 girls (Papuan) in Form 1 classes of an urban high school in Port Moresby, capital of Papua / New Guinea. Stated ages ranged from 10–16, median 13 years.

METHOD / Conservation of weight tested by non-verbal method (Heron and Simonsson, 1969); reasoning by three sets of six matrix tasks, demanding respectively perceptual, simple counting, and fully operational solutions, preceded by practice items.

RESULTS / No sex differences; 50 per cent of sample demonstrated weight conservation (as in Zambian sample); substantial support for the *a priori* types of solution, in expected difficulty order; little relationship between weight conservation and matrix-reasoning performance. Five non-conservers solved all the reasoning tasks, and non-conservers in general showed evidence of reasoning ability almost equivalent to that of conservers.

DISCUSSION / The authors suggest that these results and those reported previously from Zambia are probably best explained in terms of the 'competence–performance' model (Flavell and Wohlwill,, 1969) and a prolongation of the period during which 'transitional' performance can be expected, for a variety of cultural reasons.

The questionable unity of the concrete operations stage*
A. Heron and W. Dowel, 1974

AIM / To investigate further (in the light of results from Zambia and Papua) the capacity of some non-conservers of weight to achieve operational solutions to tasks involving multiple classification ability.

SAMPLE / The entire population (N = 49) of Yugoslav children (ages nine to 12.5, median 10.5 years) in the Melbourne school system who had arrived in Australia during the previous 24 months (range

---

*   Written and prepared by the authors for inclusion in this volume. Gratitude is
     extended to Professor Alastair Heron of Centre for Educational Research and
     Innovation, Paris, and Dr W. Dowel. (Professor Heron is now at Sheffield
     University.)

12—24 months).

METHOD / The tasks used were Piagetian tests of conservation (number, quantity, weight, volume); seriation; class inclusion; and multiple classification. All tests were administered in Serbo-Croat by an interpreter trained by the second author and working under her direction during all testing.

RESULTS / The sample was retarded on several aspects of concrete operational performance by about two years compared with Genevan results. Although an association was found between performance on quantity and weight conservation and that on multiple classification, one-third of the non-conservers of weight could provide operational solutions to seven of the eight multiple classification tasks. In respect of the non-conserving group as a whole, no differences could be found (in terms of success / non-success on multiple classification) in relation to age, sex, urban *vs* rural domicile of origin, more *vs* less recent arrival in Australia, or Macedonian *vs* Serbian ethnicity; nor did they differ systematically in approach strategy to the multiple classification tasks, as evaluated by errors made. On six of the eight tasks, those in the whole sample immigrated longer (12—14 months) did significantly better than the more recent arrivals (three—11 months).

DISCUSSION / The authors suggest that these and previous results are compatible with the position of Flavell and Wohlwill (1969) that conservation is but one of a number of structures which, in certain conditions of interaction between biological development and environmental influences, tend to appear concomitantly with one another and with age. The relevant environmental influences are probably mediated from the earliest days of childhood by the 'ambiance' (Heron and Simonsson, 1969) surrounding the child. It is argued that the concrete operational stage should not be seen as a formal unity, but rather as a set of structures without *necessary* interdependence.

The effects of training on uneven concrete operational development in Yugoslav migrant children *
A. Heron and E. Kroeger, 1974

AIM / To extend the investigation of uneven concrete operational

---

* Written and prepared by the authors for inclusion in this volume. Gratitude is extended to Professor Alastair Heron of Centre for Educational Research and Innovation, Paris, and Dr E. Kroeger. (Professor Heron is now at Sheffield University.)

development among children, of an age by which they should be fully operational, through the use of training procedures. This study arose directly from the findings of Heron and Dowel (1974).

SAMPLE / 109 children of Yugoslav migrant-workers (age range nine—13, median 11.6 years) who had been in West Berlin between 6 months and five years (median 3.4 years).

METHOD / The sample was pre-tested in Piagetian tasks of conservation (quantity, weight, volume); class inclusion; dichotomous and multiple classification. Experimental and control groups were formed for training and post-testing (nine weeks) on conservation and multiple classification, as required.

RESULTS / On conservation training no training effect claimed, as gains by experimental and control groups were not significantly different; on multiple classification a highly significant training effect was evident at nine weeks, with significant generalization to selected items from Raven's Progressive Matrices. At the conclusion of the experiment the presence or absence of weight conservation performance was 'both unaccounted for, and essentially independent of cognitive performance in other domains (including school mathematics grades)'. Previous findings by Heron and Dowel (1974) were confirmed in respect of length of residence in the host country on performance in multiple classification.

DISCUSSION / The authors attribute the failure of conservation training to the brevity of the procedure, and suggest that the success with training in multiple classification indicates a 'latent competence'. If so, uneven concrete operational development is probably remediable. The overall results are seen as consistent with the view advocated by Flavell and Wohlwill (1969) that the *structures d'ensemble* are best regarded as a *family of separate structures*.

Topological and Euclidean spatial features noted by children: a cross-cultural study
G. Jahoda, J. B. Deregowski and D. Sinha, 1974

AIMS / The authors formulated three hypotheses for verification: (a) That Ss in industrial (IC) setting would show a decline in the proportion of topological responses with increasing age; this trend would be less marked in non-industrial setting; (b) That the overall proportion of topological responses would tend to be at a higher level in non-industrial setting (NIC); (c) 'In ICs stimuli consisting of irregular forms will induce a higher proportion of topological responses than regular forms, but no such difference is expected in NICs'.

SUBJECTS / N = 415 children drawn from Glasgow, Hong Kong, India and Zambia, with an age range from four to twelve years. '. . . the Hong Kong CM (Chinese Medium) and EM (English Medium) subgroups as well as the Glasgow children are clearly "high" in terms of both industrialization and socioeconomic background; Hong Kong boat and Indian NSC (Non-scheduled castes) children may be regarded as intermediate, and the Indian SC (scheduled castes) and Zambian ones as "low"', p. 165.

METHOD / The general design was patterned after Cousins and Abravanel (1971) with some modifications: 'first . . . the reliance on verbal instructions had to be minimized and the children's understanding of the task had to be evident from the nature of their responses; second, it had to be possible to identify random response patterns. These requirements were met by devising an oddity choice task such that on each trial there were three possible responses, namely topological (T), Euclidean (E) and unrelated (U)', p. 161. Full details of the structural characteristics of the stimulus materials and experimental procedures are given in Jahoda, Deregowski, and Sinha (1974, pp. 161–165).

RESULTS / Highly significant cultural and subcultural differences were computed. However few significant age trends were observed. 'Contrary to expectation, T responses were roughly constant while the proportion of both E and U responses showed systematic cross-cultural variations. There was evidence that it is U responses rather than the proportion of E responses which directly reflect spatial ability', p. 159. The authors conclude with a discussion of the findings which have a bearing on general developmental theory.

The effect of language on concept acquisition in bilingual children
D. M. Keats and J. A. Keats, 1974

AIM / The authors were intent to determine whether logical concepts acquired in one language could be transferred to another language.

SUBJECTS / N = 100 children aged four to seven years. This sample comprised 35 Polish and English bilinguals, 31 German and English bilinguals, and 34 who spoke only English. 'All subjects were selected on their inability to conserve weight (in one of their languages) and ability to count to ten (in one of their languages). Each bilingual subject was matched with an Australian control subject on age, sex, socioeconomic status, school or pre-school attended, school grade, and location of home', p. 84.

METHODS / Testing was carried out by three testers, one bilingual in German and English, one bilingual in Polish and English, and an English speaking research assistant. The overall testing procedure involved four stages: Pre-testing, training, immediate post-test, and delayed post-tests. Each subject in the pre-test was administered the Peabody Picture Vocabulary Test Form A (Dunn, 1965), (in German or Polish for the Experimental subjects) or Form B (always in English). The Counting Test (from Binet Test) (translated or in English) was administered to check that subjects were able to use the numbers required. Pre-tests comprised tests of the concepts of conservation of number, discontinuous quantity, weight and volume and the concept of class-inclusion. Peabody test and the Counting test were administered again in the other form and language. The training was carried out in the language other than that used for the pre-tests and was restricted to the concept of weight. The immediate post-test was identical to the pre-test and conducted in the same language. The delayed post-tests were the same as the pre-tests in content, were administered in both languages after a four week interval after the immediate post-test. Interviews with parents helped in obtaining information about the use of the two languages in the home, parental background, and reference groups. The first five phases of training procedure followed that of Bearison (1969) with slight modifications. The sixth training phase was adapted from Sheppard (1971). In sum, after pre-testing in one language, they were trained in the acquisition of the concept of weight using the other, then post-tested in the previous language. Four weeks later, delayed post-tests were administered in both languages.

RESULTS / The resultant patterns demonstrated 'that the concept was acquired in either language, and there was some generalization to other concepts . . . gave some support to the Piagetian standpoint that a concept may be considered independently from the language by which it is acquired. Interference between languages was indicated in the German group in that the earlier they had learned English, the poorer was their final performance in both languages', p. 80.

'*Concept acquisition in Malaysian bilingual children*'
D.M. Keats, J.A. Keats and W. Rafaei, 1976

AIM / The aim of the study stemmed 'from previous work (Keats and Keats, 1974) with Polish-speaking and German-speaking bilingual children in Australia which examined the role of language medium in concept acquisition using a manipulative approach'. The study was designed 'to see if concepts acquired in one language could be transferred to the children's other language'.

SUBJECTS / N = 108 five-year-old children bilingual in Malay and English, and Chinese (Cantonese dialect) and English. The criterion for selecting subjects was their inability to conserve weight in either of their languages.

METHOD / 'Subjects in the two bilingual groups were randomly allocated to one of four groups comprising two experimental and two control groups, maintaining matching between the groups on age, sex, socioeconomic status and kindergarten attended.' The procedure for the experimental groups involved four main stages — pre-tests in both languages, training in one language on the conservation of weight only, immediate post-tests in the language other than the one used for training and delayed post-tests in both languages. The control groups received no training and the experimental groups differed on the language of training and immediate post-test.

Tests, presented in random order, included the Piagetian conservation tasks of number, discontinuous quantity (rice), weight, volume and class inclusion. Training in weight followed the procedures adopted in the previous study. 'When the child reached criterion on the training task he was tested again on the same tasks as the pre-tests but in his other language.' The Peabody Picture Vocabulary Test (Dunn, 1965) was given in both languages and a questionnaire to the child about his use of English and his other language.

RESULTS / The authors concluded that for children of this age: '(1) language plays at best a minor part in the acquisition of cognitive concepts, and (2) children will perform at a slightly higher level on these tasks if tested in their native language, but this effect may be due to the tester or some other artifact.' (Full discussion of the results can be found in Keats, Keats and Rafaei, pp. 94–98.)

Vernacular test instructions in relation to cognitive task behaviour among highland children of Papua New Guinea
M. Kelly and H. Philp, 1975

AIMS / To test the hypotheses that children tested in their own vernacular language would perform similarly on Piaget–Bruner type tasks involving language whether or not they had been to school. And that children at school would perform differently when tested in the language of school instruction (English) than when tested in the vernacular.

SUBJECTS / N = 144 divided into three groups. Two groups were drawn from the school population and one from the non-school population. All three subsamples were matched for age and sex and, in addition, the two school samples were matched for school experience, both in terms of years of schooling and classes.

METHOD / One school subsample and the non-school (village) subsample were tested in the vernacular, Melpa. The other school subsample was tested in English. The tests administered included: an equivalence grouping of pictures; a class inclusion test, and conservation of length. 'All three tests were chosen because there were language differences between English and the vernacular in labelling the components of the task', p. 189.

RESULTS / Significant differences were computed between the groups in their performance on the tasks administered. Such differences were related both to amount of school experience and language of testing but the latter was, by far, the more significant.

Some unusual conservation behaviour in children exposed to two cultures
M. Kelly, M. Tenezakis and R. Huntsman, 1973

AIM / To investigate the conservation performance of Greek migrant children attending Australian schools, with English as the medium of instruction.

SUBJECTS / N = 183, with an age-range from six to 11 years.

METHOD / Each child was individually tested in both Greek and English on the conservation tasks of length and number. The Ss were drawn from communities which maintained 'Greek culture', and in a pre-test demonstrated full comprehension of the terms 'same length'; 'shorter than'; 'longer than'; 'same number'; 'more' and 'less'.

RESULTS / The authors conclude, 'children who passed the language pre-tests and failed to conserve in English, did show conservation when subsequently tested in Greek but again failed to conserve in a post-test in English . . . 25 per cent of the effective samples displayed fail—pass—fail behaviour in the conservation tasks after demonstrating a behaviourally acceptable grasp of the terms used. This is difficult to explain in terms of translation difficulties, and difficult to explain in Piagetian terms if translation difficulties are not the problem. It may well be that there is a much closer relationship of language and cognition to that hitherto supposed by Piaget', p. 182.

A cross-ethnic study of language and cognitive ability*
M.D. Klippel, 1976

The relationship between language and cognitive ability is given different emphases by various theorists. The present study has been evolved from Piaget's theory that classification and seriation are prerequisites for the development of logical thinking and from Bruner's emphasis on the categorical and hierarchical properties of language.

In New Zealand the school year is divided into three terms and children may commence their formal schooling on the day of their fifth birthday. As children generally attend schools close to their homes, school populations tend to reflect the characteristics of the community in which they are sited.

Two ethnic groups are being studied, Maori (Polynesian, native of New Zealand) and European. These have been sampled from two types of schools, those having a high proportion of Maori children and those with a low percentage of Maoris. It is believed that by sampling in this way, a possible socioeconomic variable will be controlled without the application of criteria which may not be appropriate for different ethnic groups.

The sample selected in this manner comprises 120 children in four groups (2 ethnic x 2 school density) with 30 children per group. Each child will be assessed on his (her) ability to classify and seriate and analyses will be carried out on the recorded language related to these tasks.

The research is designed to follow each child through his first sixteen

* Published with the kind permission of the author. Gratitude is extended to Dr Margot D. Klippel of the University of Auckland, New Zealand.

months of primary schooling. All children will first be tested within one month of their fifth birthday and of commencing school, thus providing control of age as well as school experience. Thereafter each child will be tested every eight months (equivalent to alternate school terms) to provide a longitudinal record of their development in the cognitive areas being studied.

Because research indicates some syntactic differences between 'Maori' English and Standard English, it is anticipated that the data will reveal qualitative differences between the ethnic groups and quantitative differences between the children attending the two types of schools having different densities of Maori pupils.

Both direct and indirect relationships have been postulated between physical health and psychological abilities, and as a disproportionate number of Maori children with respiratory disorders have been noted, provision has been made for the gathering of evidence concerning possible correlations between medical conditions and any observed psychological differences.

At present, collection of data for the five-year-old phase is proceeding. These results will be analysed by early 1976.

Levels of reasoning in mapwork shown by school children in Malawi*
S.R. Lawless, 1974

The aims of this study are, firstly, to establish at what age or grade school children in Malawi acquire concepts necessary for proficient map interpretation and secondly, to identify the problem areas in mapwork for Malawian school children.

A map reading exercise, scored on a Piagetian reasoning scale, and a map drawing task were given to 160 Malawian school children in four grades with an age range from 10 years to 21 years. One-third of the sample was asked oral questions about the local area.

In spite of an age range of five to seven years in each grade, results on the map reading showed greater agreement with grade than with age. It is hypothesized that this results from a complex interaction of school experience, intelligence and socioeconomic factors. In contrast to several other studies in Africa, no significant sex difference was found in the present inquiry. The effect of school experience was more pronounced in map reading than it was in map drawing or in the oral questions.

Map drawing skill is well developed by mid-primary school, with

*   Published with the kind permission of the author. Gratitude is extended to
     Sheila R. Lawless.

most subjects showing some appreciation of perspective.

Scores in the multiple-choice section of the map reading exercise were assigned to one of four levels: (4) Upper-Concrete; (3) Concrete; (2) Perceptual / Associative; (1) Imaginary / Tautological. To these four categories, is added category (5) Formal Reasoning, for the oral questions and the interpretative section of the map reading exercise.

Reasoning levels on the multiple-choice items was variable. This was largely due to certain strong distractors. In the interpretative items, reasoning levels 1 and 2 predominated at primary school and levels 2 and 3 at secondary school. The oral scores were generally slightly lower. This may indicate different approaches to reasoning in school and in everyday life.

The paucity of reasoning levels 4 and 5 in the oral task and the interpretative section of the map reading exercise, may indicate reasoning is limited to the concrete level. However, it may be an artifact of the situation, for the type of question and the type of geography taught in schools would not encourage hypothetico-deductive type of reasoning.

The effect of stimulus familiarity on the conservation performance of rural Guatemalan children
B.M. Lester and R.E. Klein, 1973

The authors review some of the pertinent studies and cite the work of Greenfield (1966); Lloyd (1971); Price-Williams (1969); Lovell, Healey and Rowland (1962); and Calhoun (1971) to formulate their hypotheses. (The majority of these studies have been described in Modgil, 1974.)

AIM / The authors were intent to verify the effect of stimulus familiarity on Piagetian tasks of conservation.

SUBJECTS / N = 80, within an age-range of five to seven years. Children normally attended school when seven or eight years of age.

METHOD / Each child was tested twice on each test, with the testing sessions being one month apart. The four Piagetian conservation tasks included continuous quantity, conservation of matter, and two conservation of area tasks — one with familiar and the other with unfamiliar stimulus materials. 'As a metric for the determination of stimulus familiarity has not been reported in previous conservation research, the present study included a sample of adults who were asked to judge the familiarity of the two conservation of area tasks. Twenty mothers of the subjects were shown the two sets of stimulus materials after the children were tested. None of the mothers witnessed the testing procedure. The materials were described to the mother as two different toys, and the mother was asked to judge which of the toys was more familiar to her child. Ninety-five per cent of the mothers reported that the area (farm) materials were more familiar to their children than the area (cubes) materials', p. 200. Fuller details of the experimental procedure including scoring techniques are described elsewhere (Lester and Klein, 1973, pp. 199–201).

RESULTS / For both first and second testing, area performance (farm) was superior to performance on each of the other conservation tasks, while performance levels did not differ among the remaining three tasks. This finding substantiated the results reported by Calhoun (1971); Lovell, Healey and Rowland (1962) and Uzgiris (1964). In these studies conservation operativity was found to vary positively with stimulus familiarity. The results in respect to the age at which conservation develops supported other studies which have reported 75 per cent conservation behaviour between seven and nine years of age on tasks identical to the ones used in the Lester and Klein Study (Flavell, 1963, pp. 357–402; Greenfield, 1966, pp. 225–256; Lloyd, 1971; and Price-Williams, 1969). Piaget and Inhelder (1969) and Goldschmid (1967) demonstrated that conservation of continuous quantity and substance develop earlier than conservation of area, weight, and volume. No such resultant patterns emerged in Lester and Klein's study. The authors conclude, 'Rather, performance for the conservation of area (farm) task was clearly superior to the other conservation tasks, at both five and seven years of age and for both testing sessions . . . it may be argued that the sequence of development of conservation is both a function of the stimulus materials used and the general familiarity of the problem. In an agriculturally based community, such as Canalitos, conservation of area may be demonstrated earlier than conservation of continuous quantity or conservation of matter when familiar stimuli are used in the context of a "real" problem', p. 204.

The cognitive development of Kenya African children as shown by their performance on selected Piagetian tasks of conservation
R.J.W. Mwangangi, 1975

AIM / The author was intent to examine the effects of environment (rural *vs.* city), sex, and age upon the cognitive development of Kenya African children.

SUBJECTS / N = 160 between the ages from six to 10 years six months. Children were drawn from rural and city schools and were matched in both age and sex.

METHOD / Piagetian tasks of the conservation of clay, water, number, and area were individually administered and all responses recorded verbatim.

RESULTS / The variables of parents earning wages, type of house, number of siblings, chores done before and after school, and news media in the home were not good predictors of children's performance on conservation tasks. Rural Ss performed at the higher levels of clay conservation than city school children. No such trends were computed for the tasks of conservation of water, number, and area. Likewise, no sex differences were noted. Conservation operativity increased as a function of age and the ages of acquisition of conservation were found to closely parallel those of children from Western cultures. Implications of these findings for education and research in Kenya were discussed.

*Piaget and Africa: a survey of research involving conservation and classification in Africa**
R.O. Obuche and R.E. Pearson, 1974

1. Introduction

Everywhere in Africa the search is on for an educational model that will effectively serve the needs of the society. Such a model, it is hoped, will be built upon the best aspects of the traditions of the people as well as any good qualities which have arisen from contacts with Europe and other parts of the world. The model will also have to take account of the cognitive styles and strategies which people have developed to deal with problems of relevance to them. Many studies in Africa have investigated various aspects of the thinking of its peoples, but a rapidly increasing number have been undertaken within the framework of Jean Piaget's theory of intellectual development. From these studies based on Piaget's work, and other investigations, is emerging an outline of the pattern of intellectual development in Africa. This survey reviews the results of these studies.

2. Purposes of Piagetian research in Africa

Most of the early studies, and some of the more recent ones as well,

* Published by the kind permission of the authors. Gratitude is extended to Dr Ogbonna Ohuche of the University of Liberia and Dr Robert E. Pearson of the University of Ghana.

have mainly replicated Piaget's work, for the purpose of testing the generality of his ideas across different cultures. Investigators have been particularly interested to test in different populations his proposal that children's thought develops through a definite sequence of stages, each of which has its own unique characteristics. Also, possible differences in performance between ethnic groups as well as among subgroups of various cultures have been explored. Increasing numbers of studies have been designed to investigate other variables which may be responsible for differences in performance.

3. Results of Piagetian research in Africa

Most Piagetian research in Africa has utilized tasks relevant to the stage of concrete operations. Within this stage, most studies have concentrated on tasks dealing with concrete conservations. Our survey reflects this emphasis.

3.1 *Concrete Conservation*

Table 1 summarizes the information gleaned from published studies and from major theses. The *Inventory of Cross-Cultural Piagetian Research** provides a source of information about unpublished research, including work in progress. Despite the large number of studies of concrete conservations that have been published, the making of comparisons and of generalizations is rendered difficult by the great variety of experimental methods that have been used, often with little or no justification for the particular elements of procedure chosen. Thus, before tentative conclusions can be drawn from these studies, it is wise to refer to some procedural problems that have been associated with many of these researches. Information relevant to the first five of these are listed in Table 1. Of the seven types of procedural problems touched on below, those under (a), (b) and (g) have been discussed in detail by Kamara and Easley (1973).

(a) Language presents a problem where the local language is not the medium of instruction. A choice has to be made as to whether children should be tested in the vernacular, or in the language in which they are undergoing formal education. The latter will often be less familiar to the children, particularly the younger ones, but it will be more convenient for the non-indigenous tester.

---

* Published approximately yearly, and available from either Dr Pierre R. Dasen, Ecole de Psychologie, Universite de Geneva, Switzerland, or from Professor Gavin N. Seagrim, Department of Psychology, Australian National University, P.O. Box 4, Canberra, A.C.T. 2600, Australia.

The translation of questions and instructions from one language to another presents great difficulties in establishing functional equivalence. Only Vernon (1969) tested entirely in English. Heron and Simonsson (1969) avoided the problem by using a non-verbal method. The effect of language on performance is not known, although Margaret Earle (personal communication) found that twelve-year-old Ghanaian boys performed equally well in both vernacular and English on Vernon's (1965) battery.

(b) The use of a tester from another culture raises problems, some of which are also connected with language. Unfavourable interactions between subjects and testers have been found in societies where interracial tensions exist, but no conclusions can be drawn from these studies which would be valid for work in most parts of Africa. In many studies, foreign researchers have trained members of the target culture to administer the tests.

(c) While most studies have used individual testing, two have made use of paper and pencil tests administered to groups: Beard, 1968; Poole, 1968. The effect on performance of this variation is not known.

(d) Too little overlap in choice of tasks presents yet another problem for comparison. About eight different conservation tasks have been used, but over half of the studies employed no more than two at a time, and few of these used any other Piagetian task. The choices are fairly well distributed, with conservation of liquid quantity being most popular. This presents problems of interpretation, since success on tasks presumably related to the same cognitive structures are not achieved at the same time, and may be attained in different orders in different cultures.

(e) Problems due to lack of standardized procedures for administering tasks appear in a number of ways. In some studies the procedure, or materials used, have been modified to such an extent from the original tasks used by Piaget's workers, as to raise the possibility that the very nature of the task itself has been altered. In many others, slighter modifications, the effects of which are unknown, have been made. Performance may be enhanced by use of familiar materials, but this proposition has not yet been tested adequately. It is known that in western societies, performance on various Piagetian tasks may be affected by the nature of the task, even though identical basic problems are involved (Lovell and Slater, 1960; Szeminska, 1965), by the use of different materials (Uzgiris, 1964; Szeminska, 1965; Guyler, 1969), and by the type of response required (Pratoomraj and Johnson, 1966). On the other hand, some workers in non-Western societies have specifically stated that performance was unaffected by the materials used (de Lemos, 1969; Roll, 1970; Lloyd, 1971b). In the fifth column of Table 1, a 'Yes' indicates what we consider to be a significant modification of the task or of materials used.

(f) Great ranges in the criteria by which successful conservation is judged can also be found. Many researchers have not required explanations for conservation answers, and those that have, exhibited great variation in the degree of consistency that they required in order to judge subjects as conservers.

(g) The determination of the age of the subjects has presented serious problems to many researchers who have for the most part resorted to rough estimates or have accepted the subjects' own statements of age. Kamara's work (1971; Kamara and Easley, 1973) suggests that one way to solve this problem is to make use of indigenous methods of telling age.

These problems notwithstanding, we give in Table 1 some characteristics of the samples used by various researchers, as well as notes on the results of comparisons made. From the table can be extracted results for more detailed consideration.

3.1.1 Nature of children's responses

Responses can usually be analysed in terms of Piaget's main stages, and these stages always appear in the same order, for each task, with increasing age of subjects. From this it is usually inferred that the subjects themselves pass through the same sequence of stages, although no longitudinal study has been carried out to confirm this.

3.1.2 Intercultural comparisons

Many of the studies have included comparative studies across or within cultures. Direct intercultural comparisons have been made by Beard (1968), Poole (1968), Heron and Simonsson (1969), Vernon (1969), Hendrikz (1966) and Goldschmid et al. (1973). All showed that African children were behind Europeans in their performance on the operatory tasks, but in no case were efforts made to check on the subjects' understanding of the problem.

Indirect comparisons, that is, comparisons with results obtained in other studies, have been made by Price-Williams (1961), Lloyd (1971a, b), Ohuche (1971), Kamara (1971) and Nyiti (1973), who found little or no difference between African and European performance. Indirect comparisons, however, have limited value in this respect, since results of different researchers in Europe and America show considerable variation of performance on the same task. Particular attention, however, should be given to the work of Kamara (1971) and Nyiti (1973), who both reduced intercultural differences by using refined methods of determining age, and by taking precautions within a flexible interview technique to ensure that the subject understood the problem in a relevant cultural context and had adequate opportunity to display his competence.

The results suggest that intercultural differences are least when the research involves:

(a) subjects from the elite classes;
(b) simpler tasks;
(c) a flexible clinical method, rather than standardized interviews, and
(d) an accomplished interviewer from the same culture as the third-world sample.

3.1.3 *Intracultural comparisons*

Intracultural comparisons have employed several different dimensions: Etuk (1967) and Lloyd (1971a, b) both found that children from 'modern' homes were superior to those from 'traditional' backgrounds. Both used the mother's education as the criterion for determining the modern / traditional classification.

The urban / rural dimension has been employed by Greenfield (1966), Poole (1968), Fitzgerald (1970), and Owoc (1973). No consistent results emerge from these studies, but only Fitzgerald described her sample in any detail. She found that, overall, elite children were superior to village children, who in turn performed better than those from crowded urban areas.

Schooling has provided some advantage to children in the studies of Greenfield (1966), Kamara (1971), Okonji (1971a) and Owoc (1973), and this difference often increases with age. Several of these researchers, using older subjects, have reported evidence that in the absence of schooling, a substantial proportion of the population may never succeed on the tasks used.

Kiminyo (1973) and Nyiti (1973), on the other hand, found no differences between their schooled and unschooled samples. It may be, as in intercultural comparisons, that able testers, suffering no linguistic or cultural handicaps, are able to elicit better performance from unschooled children, who otherwise may respond more slowly and in unexpected ways when compared to their schooled counterparts.

Several studies have attempted to correlate environmental variables with performance on Piagetian tasks. Vernon (1969) in Uganda found that economic status and cultural stimulus had significant loadings in a factor analysis. Fitzgerald (1970) and Adjei (1973), both working in Ghana, found that some aspects of maternal behaviour in a teaching situation correlated with the child's performance on an operative task, although Adjei's relations were weak and inconsistent. Adjei also found that both children and adults with pottery-making experience tended to perform better on conservation tasks than subjects without that experience.

3.2 Classification tasks

A second type of task from the period of concrete operations which has been widely used in Africa is classification. Inhelder and Piaget (1964) used a variety of classification tasks to investigate the development of structures of mental operations in children. Most later studies in Africa, unlike those in which conservation tasks were used, were not conducted for the purpose of investigating any aspect of Piaget's theory, but mainly to assess children's abilities to abstract as judged by such criteria as flexibility in shifting bases of classification, use of super-ordinate concepts, and type of basis (colour, form, function, etc.) preferred for classification. These classification tasks, by themselves, have limited use in diagnosing the developmental stage achieved, according to Inhelder and Piaget (1964), since the concrete operational structure of classification is attained only' when class-inclusion is also mastered. Only Hendrikz (1966), Etuk (1967) and Otaala (1971a) have included a test of this ability. A summary of the studies of classification, probably much less complete than that of conservation, is given in Table 2.

The classification tasks which have been used in Africa, and are comparable to those used by Inhelder and Piaget, can themselves be categorized into three different types:

(a) Free sorting of an array of objects, with little or no constraint on the number or type of bases of classification available;
(b) Sorting with constraints, where the objects presented possess only a limited number, often three or four, dimensions available as bases for grouping;
(c) Oddity problems, where one item must be excluded from a larger group, to which it is dissimilar.

Again, drawing general conclusions from these studies is made difficult by the differences in methodology, the variety of purposes for which the studies were undertaken, and the variation in performance resulting from the use of different materials. Only two conclusions can be stated with reasonable conviction:

(a) Performance depends to a great extent on familiarity with the material to be classified and the bases of classification;
(b) The use of abstraction increases with increasing age.

In studies where constraints have been imposed, colour seems to have been preferred to other attributes as the basis for sorting, but this finding may not be generally valid since these cases usually involved test materials with which the subjects were unfamiliar. In the case of Gay and his collaborators (Gay and Cole, 1967; Cole *et al*., 1971), the discovery of the problems which Kpelle persons encountered with classifying unfamiliar objects led to the investigation of culturally relevant methods of classification. A similarly fruitful line of investigation was adopted by Fjellman (1969) who, after discussions with adults, selected wild animals as a semantic domain with which rural Akamba children of Kenya were familiar, and developed appropriate tests to examine the formal characteristics of the childrens' sorting. In both cases colour was not used as an important criterion in the childrens' classification, and children were able to form classes on the basis of more abstract characteristics.

4. A necessary orientation

Over a period of more than 10 years, Gay and Cole and their collaborators have carried out a sustained and valuable series of investigations among the Kpelle of Liberia. Their major tool has been ethnographic analysis through which daily activities of the Kpelle can be related to such cognitive activities as problem-solving, memorization and rule learning. The researchers now hold the view that cultural differences in thinking indicate differing uses of general cognitive skills in specific situations. This is a position with which we are in complete agreement.

Traditional mathematical concepts have also been investigated in Nigeria (Taiwo, 1968), Sierra Leone (Ohuche, 1972, 1973) and Tanzania (Mmari, 1974). These should be of great value in investigating the types of mathematical and scientific concepts with which rural and urban children in Africa are equipped before they start school, since they should reveal the foundations upon which initial school activities in mathematics and science should be built. They would also enable teachers to determine how to extend the social and physical experiences of children in directions which will help them cope with the demands of formal thought.

5. Some unresolved issues

(1) To what extent do the materials used for a particular task, and the procedures adopted, affect performance? How can the basic competence of the child be determined, rather than just his performance in a specific situation?

(2) Very few studies have investigated the order in which operations are attained within the period of concrete operations. No study has investigated the transition to and attainment of formal operations, a change of utmost importance in second-cycle education.

(3) Is the levelling effect found in several studies in the absence of schooling a general phenomenon? Does it have any practical effect

on the lives of those with little or no schooling?

(4) In the absence of schooling, does intellectual development nevertheless continue in areas which are not probed by the tests currently in use? Is it possible to develop methods to explore development in such areas as kinship relations and games?

(5) We have almost no specific information about the factors which influence the pace of intellectual growth. Although performance may vary with such gross variables as schooling, this does not reveal what specific influences operate.

(6) Heron (1971) found that results on his non-verbal tests of conservation did not correlate well with either academic achievement or with general reasoning. How does performance on Piagetian tasks relate to school performance in other situations? To what extent does either measure indicate desirable outcomes of science and mathematics education?

(7) The need for studies involving classroom applications of Piagetian theory is urgent in this period of active curriculum development and adaptation.

(8) The Geneva school holds the view that from the study of the stages in cognitive development will eventually emerge an explanation of the form, quality and character of the linguistic structures which children can cope with. Work needs to be done on the association between the stages of development and language acquisition and use.

6 Value of Piagetian research

For those concerned to relate the intellectual development of children to the content, pace and method of the curriculum, especially science and mathematics education, it seems likely that Piagetian theory and the growing body of knowledge related to it, at present, provides the most useful framework within which to undertake empirical research and to apply research findings to curriculum design. This is adduced from the following considerations:

(a) Piaget's theory can be used to specify which types of intellectual abilities are required by the content and objectives of various topics in a curriculum (Ingle and Shayer 1971; Shayer, 1972). If the stage of intellectual development attained by the child can be diagnosed by the use of appropriate tasks, it may be possible to estimate the chances of his being able to deal with the topic. This link between the curriculum and the child's performance on psychological tests is not possible for any other theory.

(b) At the final stage of mental growth proposed by Piaget, and probably attained by school children during the years of adolescence, the diagnostic tasks derived from Piaget's work involve situations and problems very similar to those which might appear in a modern secondary school science or mathematics curriculum. Many of the tasks connected with the earlier stage of development also have obvious links with the curriculum, especially mathematics curricula. Those which are less clearly connected to the curriculum can be related by means of theory. Although other problem-solving tasks of relevance to science and mathematics education appear in the psychological literature, they are not explicitly linked to any comprehensive theory of mental processes or growth.

(c) Studies in a variety of cultures give support to the proposition that at least the major aspects of Piaget's theory can be applied to all human societies. This degree of generalizability has not been established for any other theory of human intelligence. The types of operative tasks which have been developed by Piaget and his colleagues can be adapted and extended for use in different cultures.

(d) Within the framework of Piaget's views, group differences in performance can be accounted for, without imputing inferiority or deficiency. Piaget (1966) distinguishes four factors which influence the development of cognitive functions:

(i) biological factors, which account for the invariant sequence of stages;

(ii) equilibration factors, which arise through interaction with the environment and determine the development of mental operations;

(iii) general socialization factors, or social interactions between individuals, which are identical for all societies, and

(iv) social factors which differ from one society to another, and include particularly factors of educational and cultural transmission.

These factors do not operate independently, but the second and fourth do vary from one society to another, and may be used as a basis for investigating differences in performance in cultural subgroups.

Finally, we should state that some studies have not been included in this survey. They include a number of theses upon which bachelor's degrees or postgraduate diplomas have been awarded, and other unpublished work.

Table 1: Conservation tasks

Country	Authors	Testing + Situation	Tasks ++	Modified	N	Age Range	Background Of Ss	Comments (+ indicates positive effect)
Senegal	Greenfield (1966)	1	Q(1)	No	187	6–13	Urban / rural	+age; +schooling; rural > urban
Sierra Leone	Kamara (1971)	4	Q(s), W, V	No	55	6–12	Schooled / unschooled	+schooling (slight); +age
Sierra Leone	Ohuche (1971)	5	N, W	Yes	231	5–8	Town / village	+age; independent of location
Ghana	Beard (1968)	5	Q(s)	No	240	7–14	Urban	individual scores not reported
Ghana	Fitzgerald (1970)	5	Q(s), L	Yes	413	5–11	Urban / suburban / rural	+age; +schooling; +suburban (except Q(s))
Ghana	Ayisi (1972)	4	Q(1,s), N, A	No	74	5–12	Univ. primary school	+age; no sex difference
Ghana	Adjei (1973)	4	Q(1,s), N, W, V	No	76	7–9	Rural / elite	+specific experiences; +maternal behaviour
Nigeria	Price-Williams (1961)	1	Q(s), N	Yes	45	5–8	Rural, unschooled	+age

continued on page 173

Table 1 continued

Country	Authors	Testing + situation	Tasks ++	Modified	N	Age Range	Background Of Ss	Comments (+ indicates positive effect)
Nigeria	Poole (1968)	5	Q(1,s), W	Yes	150	10–11	Urban / village / rural	English > urban > village > rural
Nigeria	Etuk (1967)	4	N	No	110	6–8	Traditional / modern	male > female; modern > traditional
Nigeria	Lloyd (1971 a, b)	5	Q(1), N	No	80	3.5–8	Urban	+age; elite > traditional
Nigeria	Owoc (1973)	5	Q(1)	Yes	449	6–over 18	Varied	urban > rural; schooled > unschooled
Rwanda	Pinard et al. (1973)	5	Q(1, s)	No	64	6–8	Rural; schooled / not	training effective; no group differences
Uganda	Vernon (1969)	2	Q(1, s), L, A, V	Yes	50	11	Urban boys	below Jamaican, British
Uganda	Almy et al. (1970)	5	Q(1), N	No	64	5–11	Urban	some improvement with years in school
Uganda	Okonji (1971a)	5	L	Yes	300	6–16	Not urban	+age; +schooling
Uganda	Otaala (1971a, b)	4	Q(1, s) N	No	160	6–12	Rural	+age

continued on page 174

Table 1 continued

Country	Authors	Testing + Situation	Tasks ++	Modified	N	Age Range	Background Of Ss	Comments (+ indicates positive effect)
Uganda	Otaala (1971c)	5	Q(1, s) N	No	91	Adults	Unschooled	lower than children
Uganda	Otaala (1972)	5	Q(1, s), N	No	678	6–13	5 ethnic groups	+age
Uganda	Goldschmid et al. (1973)	5	Q(1, s), N, W, A	No	198	5–8	Rural	+age
Kenya	Kiminyo (1973)	4	Q(s), W, V	No	120	7–12	Urban /,rural	no difference for schooling, urbanization, sex
Tanzania	Nyiti (1973)	4	Q(s), W, V	No	139	8–14	Schooled / unschooled	+age; no difference for schooling
Zambia	Heron and Simonsson (1969)	3	W	Yes	336	5–17	Urban	+age; European > African after 10 years
Zambia	MacArthur (1973)	?	Q(1, s), L, A, V	?	192	9–40	Varied	results not reported
Rhodesia	Hendrikz (1966)	1a	Q(s), N	?	304	5	Urban	+nursery school; European > African

continued on page 175

Key to table 1:

+	Key to testing situation
1.	Foreign tester in local language
1a.	Foreign tester with interpreter
2.	Foreign tester in English
3.	Foreign tester, non-verbal method
4.	Originator of experiment tested in local language
5.	Originator of experiment trained indigenous testers
++	Key to conservation tasks
Q(1)	= liquid quantity
Q(s)	= solid substance (continuous and discontinuous)
W	= weight
V	= volume by displacement
N	= number
L	= length
A	= area

Table 2: Classification

Country	Authors	Tasks	Comments
Senegal	Greenfield et al. (1966)	Free sorting; constrained sorting	+schooling; colour > form or function
Sierra Leone	Kamara (1971)	Free sorting	both schooled and unschooled Ss can abstract
Liberia	Irwin and McLaughlin (1970)	Constrained sorting	+age; colour > form
Liberia	Cole et al. (1971)	Free, constrained; oddity problem	+schooling; different factors determine classificatory behaviour
Nigeria	Price-Williams (1962)	Free sorting; oddity problem	+age
Nigeria	Etuk (1967)	Free sorting; class inclusion	+age; class inclusion more difficult than conservation
Nigeria	Kellaghan (1968)	Free sorting; constrained sorting	modern > traditional on many; colour > form
Nigeria	Okonji (1970)	Free sorting	+ training
Nigeria	Okonji (1971b)	Free sorting	+age; European = African
Nigeria	Lloyd (1971a)	Oddity problem	modern > traditional
Uganda	Vernon (1969)	Free sorting	below Jamaican, British
Uganda	Almy et al. (1970)	Free sorting; constrained sorting	colour > form; abstraction increases with age

continued on page 177

Table 2 continued

Country	Authors	Tasks	Comments
Uganda	Otaala (1971a, b)	Free sorting; class inclusion	class inclusion more difficult than conservation
Kenya	Fjellman (1969)	Free sorting	abstraction aided by locally relevant system
Zambia	Serpell (1969a, b)	Oddity problem	colour > form; form choice increases with age
Zambia	Deregowski and Serpell (1971)	Constrained sorting	European > African; pictures not equivalent to objects
Rhodesia	Hendrikz (1966)	Class inclusion	more difficult than conservation, easier than seriation

Developmental order of spatial concepts among school-children in Tanzania
I.M. Omari, 1975

AIM / To study the developmental order of spatial concepts among schoolchildren in Tanzania.

SUBJECTS / N = 240, sixty from each of grades one, three, five and seven. The distribution of children by sex was nearly balanced.

METHOD / The tasks administered were: conservation of distance; conservation of area; and the concept of horizontality in the coordinate system. These were adaptations of the Piaget and Inhelder (1956); Piaget, Inhelder and Szeminska (1960). (Fuller details of the experimental procedures including scoring techniques are described elsewhere, Omari, 1972, and Omari, 1975, pp. 446–449.)

RESULTS / The data was subjected to chi-square analyses and demonstrated that the developmental sequence was: conservation of distance, conservation of area, and operativity of the concept of horizontality in the coordinate reference system. A stagewise progression was evident, but each stage was achieved at a later age when compared to the Geneva norms. Omari argued that, 'the acquisition of these concepts in children is a function of the spatial dimensions involved in each concept, and that environmental factors retard the developmental tempo of spatial concepts among the African children', p. 444. The author elaborates, 'While in all tasks progression toward higher levels of performance was evident, the rate of acquisition was relatively slow compared to that of children from technological industrial cultures. This relative retardation or developmental gap has been observed by various researchers using Piagetian materials across cultures (e.g., Dasen, 1974; de Lemos, 1968 among Australian Aborigines; Otaala, 1973 among Ugandans; and Vernon, 1965 among West Indians). This observation has been quite intriguing since the tasks under microscope (i.e., area, distance, and coordinate system) seem to demand abilities based on experiences familiar to any human population. It seems, however, that this phenomenon in part could be attributed to motivational variables that include the possibly low face validity of the tasks: in populations where such tasks do not form part of the play materials researchers may need more time to familiarize their subjects with the nature of the materials and the logic inherent in these tasks developed within a framework of an industrial culture rationality. These tasks demand scientific inferences available to a highly literate culture. In Tanzania, this observed slow rate of acquisition of these conservation concepts can be attributed to a multiplicity of factors. They include lack of technological industrial influence, poor schooling facilities, different cultural stimulation, and general motivational factors. All these dwarf equilibration processes essential for rapid cognitive growth', Omari (1975, pp. 452–453).

Some pictorial artifacts in studies of African children's pictorial depth perception
I.M. Omari and W.H. MacGinitie, 1974

The authors cite the work of Carothers (1971), Deregowski (1972), Poole (1968), Jahoda (1971) and Vernon (1968) which demonstrated that African subjects experience difficulties in perception of depth cues in pictures and in manipulation of spatial relations. Further they state an example of Omari and Cook's (1972) study where children responding to Hudson's (1960) picture three, responded that 'the antelope was nearer to the man because the elephant was on a hill, and climbing there would be more tiring and consequently take more time – responses reminiscent of Piaget, Inhelder and Szeminska's (1960) symmetry experiment'.

AIM / The authors were intent to investigate 'the effect of eliminating two possible sources of errors in depth perception in Hudson's pictures:
  (i) the unfamiliarity of the principal depicted objects; and
  (ii) the basis for confusing motivational inferences relating to the depicted scene'.

SUBJECTS / N = 20 in grades one, three, five, and seven, from three schools in Tanzania, East Africa.

METHODS / Two groups of 10 children each were involved. One group was administered four of Hudson's (1960) pictures (p. 186), pictures one, three, four, and six. The second group was tested using an experimental revision in which a cow and a goat were substituted for the elephant and antelope, and the man's spear was not aligned with either animal. Sample questions included: 'What do you see in the picture'? 'Which is farther away from the man: the elephant (cow) or the antelope (goat)'? 'How do you know'? 'Would the man have to travel a longer distance to the elephant (cow) or to the antelope (goat)'? Fuller details of the experimental procedure, including scoring techniques and examples of Hudson's (1960) pictures are given elsewhere (Omari and MacGinitie, 1974, pp. 536–537).

RESULTS / The results demonstrated that revised-version scores were higher and increased with age. The original-version scores were low in all grades. The urban subjects performed at higher levels than the remote area subjects. The authors caution in interpreting the generality of Hudson's (1960, 1962) findings.

Conservation, seriation and classification as factors in the acquisition of mathematics in Nigerian children
H.M. Omotoso, 1975

AIM / The author was intent to investigate the relationship between the acquisition of mathematics achievement and the abilities of conservation, seriation and classification among Nigerian children.

SUBJECTS / N = 120 within the age range from four to eight years.

METHOD / The mathematics test I was administered to age groups five, six, and seven years. Piagetian tasks of length, volume, number, seriation and classification were individually given to all the subjects. Following this, a second mathematics test was administered to the five-, six- and seven-year-olds.

RESULTS / A strong relationship was computed between mathematics achievement and all the Piagetian tasks − seriation yielded the strongest individual relationship across all groups. The Piagetian tasks predicted mathematics achievement better for boys than for girls. No sex differences were noted in either the mathematics test or the Piaget tasks on seriation, classification and the conservation of number. Nigerian children demonstrated operativity around CA eight years. However the number concept appeared somewhat earlier.

On culture and conservation once again
P.J. Owoc, 1973

AIM / The author extended the earlier work of Greenfield (1966).

SUBJECTS / N = 449, with an age-range from 6 years through 18 years. The Nigerian Ss were selected according to Schooling / Non-schooling and urban / rural areas.

METHOD / The typical Piagetian liquid conservation task was administered and all testing was conducted in the subjects' own language — Yoruba, Efik or Hausa.

RESULTS / Conservation operativity was related to age — as age level increased, so did the percentage of subjects who showed conservation attainment. 'More specifically, what has been determined . . . re-emphasizes the divergence in ability between schooled and unschooled subjects. Even the extension of the sample to include adults did nothing more than to magnify to statistical significance a trend already evident at the nine to 11 age level. In fact, among unschooled groups, the levelling off of cognitive development began to occur as early as ages eight to nine for children living in urban as well as rural settings. If as Piaget suggests, the search for psychological equilibration is the only necessary and sufficient condition for the development of intellectual structures (Boyle, 1969) the information derived from studies using gross kinds of classificatory variables can only identify some settings as being more fruitful than others for encountering the kinds of situations which will produce cognitive discrepancies', p. 254.

Product and process in cognitive development: some comparative data on the performance of school age children in different cultures
H. Philp and M. Kelly, 1974

AIMS / Three hypotheses were formulated as follows:
(a)   To determine whether some of the results of Bruner and Piaget would 'stand up' in non-western children;
(b)   The relationship between the results of Piagetian and Brunerian investigations among Western and non-Western children;
(c)   The implications of both (a) and (b) above, for curriculum development.

SUBJECTS / N = 1536. This comprised children living in New South Wales (N = 656); children of non-English Speaking migrants living in New South Wales (N = 448); and children from three different areas in Papua and New Guinea (N = 432). Subjects ranged in age from six years five months to 15 years.

METHOD / The various tasks selected for administration evaluated either 'product' or 'process' dimension. ' . . . we accepted the distinction made by Bruner (1963) between knowledge as "product" (Piaget's "connaissance") and the "process" of acquiring knowledge or of attacking (although not necessarily solving) problems', p. 251. The tests were as follows:

A. *Product-Type Tasks* — Mainly derived from Piaget (i) Conservation of quantity, (ii) Conservation of length, (iii) Formal operations (the four chemical test, Inhelder and Piaget, 1958), (iv)/(v) Nine block matrix (based on Bruner and Kenney, 1966).

B. *Process-Type Tasks* — Mainly derived from Bruner (vi) / (vii) Problem solving. These tests were a modification of the Olson bulb board (Bruner *et al.*, 1966). (viii) / (ix) Classification of stimuli according to degree of inclusiveness and basis of classification (patterned after Olver and Hornsby, 1966). (Details of the above tests are given in Philp and Kelly, 1974, pp. 251–253; Bruner *et al.*, 1966; Bruner and Kenney, 1966; Olver and Hornsby, 1966, Inhelder and Piaget, 1958; and Huntsman, 1974).

As far as possible all testing was carried out with English as the medium of instruction. However, with the Papua-New Guinea subjects, village children (i.e. those who had no schooling) were tested in the vernacular.

RESULTS / The results were as follows:

(a) Piagetian and Brunerian behaviours were shown by Papua-New Guinea children (schooled and non-schooled), as well as New South Wales subjects (migrant and non-migrant). However Piagetian formal operations were not evidenced among any of the Papua-New Guinea subjects.

(b) 'The order of appearance of what we have called product behaviours is the same in all our samples, although median ages of appearance differ from one group to another. The fact that formal operations did not appear among our Papua-New Guinea children does not invalidate this statement, since it is the highest point in the Piagetian hierarchy of cognitive skills', p. 263.

(c) Piagetian product-type and Brunerian product-type tasks were identical in their order of appearance.

(d) 'The Brunerian process-type tasks present a somewhat different picture. It is important to distinguish between the scale which Bruner describes as "enactive, ikonic, symbolic" and that which his colleagues, Olver and Hornsby, derived from the classification of equivalence material. It would appear that these two scales are measuring somewhat different things, although they were correlated. Given this the New South Wales children and the migrant children (. . . they are in the main Western Europeans) behave in much the same way as did children in the American samples described by Bruner . . . However, in Papua-New Guinea the ikonic-transitional-symbolic process runs against a Brunerian hypothesis . . . ', p. 263. Identical results appeared in the equivalence tasks.

(e) Schooled Papua-New Guinea children behaved like the unschooled children on the process-type tasks as the tests increased in difficulty.

(f) 'The migrant children fall between the New South Wales children and the Papua-New Guinea school children on most tasks, but they are much more like the New South Wales group, especially as difficulty increases', p. 264.

Finally the authors conclude, ' . . . comment on relationship between the Piaget and the Bruner models. Both of these models work for product-type tasks . . . children in every culture . . . do the same kinds of things as they do in the samples described by both these theorists. On the other hand, the Brunerian model does not work in all cultures for process-type tasks . . . because different languages process the world in different sorts of ways . . . We are not, by any means, suggesting that Sapir and Whorf (Hoijer, 1954) were right', p. 264.

Left—right orientation among Hausa children: a methodological note
D.R. Price-Williams and R.A. Levine, 1974

AIM / To examine left—right orientation among Hausa children and to compare the results with previous studies.

SUBJECTS / N = 53. Ss were Hausa (Nigerian) children within the age range from four to 11 years inclusive (22 boys and 31 girls).

METHOD / Two tasks of left—right orientation were administered: (a) identification of left and right hands on the child's own body and on the body of an E facing the S, and (b) subtracting from a group composed of a large middle doll with two smaller dolls each side of it, first the middle and the smaller on the right, and then the middle and the smaller on the left. The S was asked to identify which doll was the left and which was the right. (Details of the experimental procedure are given in LeVine and Price-Williams, 1974.)

RESULTS / The results and methods are compared with studies using a similar approach: Benton (1959), Binet (1911), Elkind (1961), Galifret-Granjon (1960), Laurendeau and Pinard (1970), Piaget (1928), and Terman (1916). Generally, the Hausa children performed at about the same level as the Swiss children (Piaget, 1928) and children examined by Elkind (1961). 'The inclusion of the child's legs in both those studies (Piaget and Elkind) and our omission of them, however, reduce the comparability of the findings. We gave the children a task that is probably somewhat easier than that of other studies . . . and all of the youngest Hausa children were able to do it. This may be due to factors other than the ease of the task: e.g., the small and sex-skewed sample, and possibly early training of Hausa children in differentiating their right and left hands as part of Islamic toilet training', p. 358. With respect to the doll questions, there was a clear increase with age in performance on both items, after age seven, but a high percentage of correct response among the four- to five-year-olds was also observed.

The effect of cross-cultural contact
C. Reich and M. Purbhoo, 1975

AIM / The authors hypothesized that greater cross-cultural contact would result in greater generalized cross-cultural role-taking ability and more favourable attitudes toward ethnic groups in general.

SUBJECTS / The subjects in the study were 11th grade students in the two groups of schools. 'One group of four schools, called the HiD (i.e., High Density) schools, was characterized by a high proportion of New Canadians. A second group of five schools, called the Lo D (i.e., Low Density) schools had a relatively low proportion of New Canadians. The proportion of New Canadians in the Hi D schools ranged from .62 to .67 with a mean of .65. Lo D schools ranged from .21 to .43 New Canadians, with a mean of .29. Proportion of New Canadians in a school represents cross-cultural interaction potential rather than interaction per se', p. 316.

METHOD / Ss' socioeconomic status was measured through the administration of the Blishen's (1967) scale. The ethnic background was designated as Canadian (i.e., native speaker of English, born in Canada) or New Canadian (i.e., not a native speaker and / or not born in Canada). There were over 40 different ethnic groups represented by the label New Canadian. The hypothesis was tested by comparing students in schools with a high proportion of New Canadians (Hi D,$\bar{\chi}$ = .65) with students in a matched group of schools having a relatively low proportion of New Canadians (Lo D, $\bar{\chi}$ = .29) on tests aimed at evaluating cross-cultural role-taking ability, tolerance for diversity in society, and on performance on the Prisoners' Dilemma Game. The measure of role-taking ability was based on Feffer and Gourevitch (1960); measures of attitude—social diversity was patterned after Adelson (1968) and Adelson and O'Neil (1966); and measures of attitude—prisoner's Dilemma Game (Swingle, 1969). (Fuller details of the experimental procedures including scoring techniques are given in Reich and Purbhoo, 1975, pp. 317–320.)

RESULTS / The Canadian and New Canadian students in Hi D schools performed at the higher levels when compared to students in Lo D schools on the cross-cultural role-taking test. However, only New Canadians demonstrated greater tolerance in Hi D than in Lo D schools. No support was evident for the hypothesis from results of the Prisoner's Dilemma Game. Reich and Purbhoo concluded, 'The present study has demonstrated that the type of cognitive development in which the individual is increasingly able to integrate different perspectives in dealing with the physical world (Piaget) and with the social world (Feffer, Kohlberg) occurs as well in his ability to deal with the ethnological world. Values, however, are more resistant to change. Perhaps it is because, as most researchers in the area have assumed, they have a motivational and emotional as well as a cognitive component . . . ', (*ibid.*, p. 325).

The development of some mathematical concepts among Iraqi children seriation and serial correspondence*
S. Safar, 1974

AIM / This is a genetic cross-sectional study of concept formation among Iraqi children. It is concerned with the formation of the concepts of seriation and serial correspondence and the effect of coaching on the acceleration of concept formation.

SUBJECTS / N = 341 kindergarten and primary school children, from the lower middle class. The age group ranged from four–12 years. They were grouped according to their ages and forty subjects were drawn from each group with the exception of the kindergarten children. They were all taken as a sample of an age group.

METHOD / The children were interviewed individually by the research worker who used objects that were familiar to the children such as dolls, sticks and rulers. At the same time children were asked standardized questions, avoiding Piaget's clinical method.
1. *Serial correspondence*: The child is given nine dolls of varying heights; and along with them he is given nine sticks of varying lengths. These objects are arranged in a number of positions. The child is requested to arrange the dolls in accordance with their heights, and to ascribe to each doll its proper stick. The elements are presented haphazardly, reversed, or dispersed for each child. He is then requested

---

* Written and prepared by the author for inclusion in this volume. Gratitude is extended to Dr Samia Safar of the University of Baghdad.

to alot to each doll its proper stick.

2. *Seriation*: The child is given ten rulers of varying lengths, he is asked to arrange them 'like a stairs', beginning from the shortest element, when the task is completed, the child is given a middle length ruler and requested to introduce it into the stairs in its proper place. Coaching: children who fail to complete the task are given the principles upon which seriation is built i.e. the pattern that is established on the basis of the relationships among the elements. Then he is requested to do the task beginning from the shortest element, the longest element and the middle.

RESULTS / Results indicated that the concept of seriation and serial correspondence develops gradually in children. And the process of growth has three stages: The first stage is between four- / eight-years-old where the concept is not shown; the second, between eight to 11 is a transitional stage, while the third stage, in which the concept formation is complete, starts at 11 years of age.

Results obtained through following a special teaching method confirmed the possibility of accelerating the growth of the seriation concept provided the child is in a transitional stage.

DISCUSSION / The sample group lags about three years of growth behind the western children of the same age. Perhaps this could be attributed to the environmental differences. It was also found that the girls were about six months ahead of the boys regarding the growth of the serial correspondence concept only.

A study of the relationship between school experience, socio-economic status, and conservation attainment in first grade boys and girls
N. Schorr, 1975

AIM / To examine the relationship between two types of early school experience and the attainment of conservation in Orthodox Jewish children.

SUBJECTS / N = 76 children within the age range from six years three months and six years nine months. 'Children from the restricted school experience came from Hasidic homes and attended Hasidic schools in New York City. Children from the enriched schools attended private Jewish day schools and came from Orthodox Jewish home backgrounds'. Only Ss who scored within one standard deviation above and below the test mean (Columbia Mental Maturity Scale) participated.

METHOD / All children were administered the Concept Assessment Kit — Conservation, Forms A and B (Goldschmid and Bentler, 1968b).

RESULTS / The following hypotheses were supported at the .01 level of significance: '(a) children from the enriched school experience showed greater conservation attainment than children from the restricted school experience; (b) children from middle socioeconomic background showed greater conservation attainment than lower socio-economic children; (c) there was no significance in the conservation performance of boys and girls; (d) there was a significant interaction effect between school and socioeconomic status. It was found that middle SES children in the enriched school experience showed greater conservation attainment than lower SES children in the same type of school . . . Further studies should be undertaken with other culturally and educationally isolated milieus within the United States, in order to determine the milieu effects on conservation attainment', Schorr (1975, p. 2112—A).

The use of Piagetian derived categories to analyse children's social language during selected preschool experiences*
M.E. Smart, R.J. Dahl and C.J. Wetzstein, 1975

PROBLEM / At the University of Southern California School for Early Childhood Education, the primary goal of research has been to identify ways of fostering the development of representational thought in young children. A hypothesized condition contributing to the development of representational thought is the linguistic environment (Sigel, 1970). Empirical evidence is lacking with respect to the significance of curricular experiences typically included in pre-school programmes on the development of representational thought as reflected by children's socialized language. What influences do selected aspects of the traditional curriculum have on the quantity and complexity of language as a function of age, ethnicity, and sex? Do they affect children's use of language which denotes temporal, spatial, numerical, causal, and other Piagetian derived concepts?

PROCEDURES / Subjects were 82 three-, four-, and five-year-olds enrolled at the University of Southern California School for Early Childhood Education (USC SECE) in the fall, 1974 (38 Mexican-

* Reprinted by kind permission of the authors. Gratitude is expressed to Professor Margaret E. Smart, Dr Richard Dahl and Dr Connie J. Wetzstein of the University of Southern California, School for Early Childhood Education.

Americans, 35 Black, 9 White / Other). Children were assigned to each of six classrooms using stratified random sampling procedures to control for sex, age, and ethnicity. Two classrooms, combined into a single treatment group, presented each activity for twelve consecutive days until each group had participated in the three treatments (cooking, intellectual kits, water play).

Data were obtained by trained observers recording actions and language (English or Spanish) of each subject for a total of nine three-minute samples.

Analysis of data was predicted on Piaget's early work in language and thought (1955). Major classifications were (1) spontaneous adaptive information, (2) elicited adaptive information, and (3) questions as based upon an earlier study (1974).

FINDINGS / 1. Across the three treatments there was a significant difference in the amount of language for the three major classifications favoring spontaneous (66 per cent).

2. A significant difference (.05 level) was found only in the amount of spontaneous language as a function of the three treatments. Cooking accounted for more than either water play or intellectual kits.

3. Although there were no significant differences between the three language classifications as a function of sex and age, there was one trend noticed: a. The total amount of spontaneous language was equivalent for boys and girls, but the boys responded differentially to each treatment, favouring cooking.

4. There was significance in amount of spontaneous language as a function of ethnicity: Mexican-American children verbalized less than the other groups. There was a tendency to verbalize spontaneously more frequently during water play for Blacks and during cooking for Mexican-Americans.

CONCLUSIONS / The development of representational thought as reflected by children's socialized language is influenced by the linguistic environment of the pre-school child. Support for cooking and water play as experiences capable of evoking spontaneous socialized language is evidenced in the findings.

Children's cognition of territory: a study of Piaget's spatial stages
J.P. Stoltman, 1972

AIM / The author maintains that Piaget's theory of spatial stages postulates that between six and 12 years of age children territorially decentrate from their immediate town or city to a local comprehension of their nation and its territorial relationships with subnational territories. The study attempted a verification of Piaget's theory (Piaget and Inhelder, 1956).

SUBJECTS / = 204 children stratified by grade (one to six), sex, race, and urban—rural residence.

METHOD / Stoltman devised an evaluation instrument incorporating Piagetian tasks based on Piaget and Inhelder (*op. cit.*).

RESULTS / Subjects did not conform to the Piagetian stages. 'Significant differences . . . were found between observed frequencies of children and the theoretically expected. Close conformity between the observed and expected occurred with those children eight years of age and younger . . . the decentration of the American sample was slower than that theorized by Piaget. The mean scores on the evaluation instrument were tested for significant differences between males—females, rural—urban children, and blacks—whites. No significant differences were attributed to the main effect of sex and rural—urban residence. A significant difference . . . was found between the black and white subjects. The data analysis suggests this difference is probably attributed to the socioeconomic variable rather than an effect of race. Age of the child and socioeconomic variable rather than an effect of race. Age of the child and socioeconomic status of parents were significantly related to the children's conception of territory . . . The multiple relationship between the independent variables, age and SES, and performance on the evaluation instrument was .71 . . . '.

Prediction of Piagetian conservation for second grade Mexican-American and Anglo-American children
M.T. Swize, 1972

AIM / The author was intent 'to determine the possible relationship between the ability of selected second grade students to perform six Piagetian conservation tasks and the resulting composite score and the following predictor variables — subjects and subject level, ethnic background, primary language used in the home, nursery school, New Nursery School, Head Start, kindergarten, CA, MA, IQ, sex, arithmetic, spelling and reading achievement'.

SUBJECTS / N = 70 second grade children from elementary schools of Mexican-American and Anglo-American parentage.

METHOD / The following tests were administered: (a) Intelligence quotient and mental age were obtained through giving the Colombia Mental Maturity Scale; (b) The Concept Assessment Kit-Conservation comprised tasks of two-dimensional space, number, substance, continuous quantity, weight and discontinuous quantity (Goldschmid and Bentler, 1968b); (c) Arithmetic, Spelling and Reading Achievement scores were determined by the Metropolitan Achievement Test; (d) CA, sex, pre-school experiences, ethnic background, and language used in the home were made available through the school — and (e) subject and subjects level was determined by Warner's Index of Status Characteristics.

RESULTS / The data were subjected to Pearson product-moment correlation and multiple linear regression. Attendance in the New Nursery School and Head Start correlated significantly but negatively at the .05 level with the ability to conserve two-dimensional space. No predictor variables related significantly with the ability to conserve number. Attendance in the New Nursery School correlated significantly but negatively at the .01 level with substance. High scores on Arithmetic and Reading Achievement correlated significantly at the .05 level with the ability to conserve continuous quantity. Enrolment in Head Start related significantly positively at the .05 level with continuous quantity. Boys performed better (.05 level) than girls with this conservation task. Enrolment in nursery schools and higher mental age related significantly with the ability to conserve weight. Enrolment in the New Nursery School was negatively and significantly related to ability to weight conservation operativity. Attendance in the New Nursery School and Head Start correlated negatively and significantly at the .05 level with the ability to conserve discontinuous quantity. Higher scores on Reading achievement related significantly at the .05 level with the composite score. 'In the regression analysis ... the criterion variable weight was significant at the .05 level. When the individual variables were tested, only socioeconomic level and primary language used in the home yielded a significant and positive specific contribution to the prediction of the criterion weight'.

*Three dimensions of intellectual functioning in Australian Aboriginal and disadvantaged European children**
L.J. Taylor and P.R. de Lacey, 1974

AIM / The study examines the relationship among three modes of

*   Gratitude is extended to Dr P.R. de Lacey of the University of Wollongong for sending his work to be abstracted.

intellectual functioning in disadvantaged children.

SUBJECTS / N = 60. Thirty were Aboriginal and 30 low-socioeconomic European children, aged six, eight and ten.

METHOD / The three modes of intellectual functioning were: verbal intelligence, operational thinking, and divergent thinking. The Peabody Picture Vocabulary Test (PPVT) (Dunn, 1965) served as the test of verbal intelligence. Taylor *et al.* (1972) found the PPVT to be a highly reliable test for European and part-Aboriginal children. Operational thinking was evaluated through Piagetian-type tests of classification (Inhelder and Piaget, 1964). DeLacey (1970a) has shown the suitability of such tests for Aboriginal and low socioeconomic European children. The Nixon Test and the Matrices Test were administered in a manner identical to those reported by de Lacey (1970b). Divergent thinking was measured through the administration of the Rorschach Ink Blots and Uses Tests. Vernon (1971, p. 254) report that 'the Rorschach Ink Blots, patterns, uses, similarities and consequences constitute the most satisfactory battery which will operate over a wide age range'.

RESULTS / The data were subjected to correlational techniques, t-tests and analyses of variance. The positive correlation for the two samples, between the PPVT and Nixon test substantiate those reported by (deLacey, 1970a), as did the correlation between the PPVT and Matrices Test for the Aboriginal sample. However, the nonsignificant negative correlation between the Matrices Test and PPVT, for European subjects contradicted those of deLacey (1970b). The t-tests supported significant differences between the Aboriginal and European subjects on the PPVT. There were no significant differences between Aborigines and Europeans on either the operational or divergent thinking tasks. ' . . . has important implications as it suggests areas of relative strength in Aboriginal children which may be capitalized upon to enable greater success in society, especially the existing educational system. If educators were to restructure the curriculum to take advantage of operational and divergent thinking abilities, they would create a situation in which a wider range of abilities could be focused on a problem and hopefully increase the chances of a successful solution. By designing an experimental curriculum in this fashion, it could be discovered whether encouraging the growth of divergent and operational thinking processes improves academic performance', p. 57.

Linguistic subsystems and concrete operations
M.D. Tenezakis, 1975

AIM / Sinclair-de-Zwart's (1967, 1969) findings on relationships between cognitive and linguistic development were compared with data gathered in Sydney, Australia from Greek-English bilinguals and English monoglots.

SUBJECTS / N = 298 were drawn from grades one, two and three in two public schools located in two working class suburbs. The sample comprised '136 "old Australian" monolingual children. . . and their 162 Greek classmates'. Median ages ranged from 6 years 3 months to 8 years ten months.

METHOD / Tests included language production, quantity conservation and language comprehension (details are given in Tenezakis, 1975).

RESULTS / On the conservation task, 'the proportion of conserving Ss was the same for Australians, Greeks tested in Greek and Greeks tested in English. (2) On the language comprehension task, conservers and non-conservers were, with some exceptions, not significantly different from one another. (3) On the language production task, the results provided no data directly contrary to the Genevan results. Where a difference occurred between conservers and non-conservers, the difference was in the predicted direction. On several measures, however, the difference was not as large as in the Genevan study, or did not occur.'

Performance on a Piagetian task and reading ability: a study of Punjabi children in an English primary school.[1] *
H.V. Vyas, 1976

The recent years have seen a considerable upsurge of interest in developmental psychology, especially in the Piagetian theory (Lunzer, 1970; Modgil, 1974). The literature which has been growing has gone a long way to strengthen the empirical foundations of the theoretical formulations; and has also explored various hunches and peripheral issues arising from them. A critical question appears to be whether the

---

* Written and prepared by the author for inclusion in this volume. Gratitude is extended to Harshad V. Vyas of the North East London Polytechnic.

[1] The author gratefully acknowledges the willing cooperation accorded by the Headteacher of Holy Trinity Church of England Primary School, Gravesend, Mr Cyril Ford and the members of his staff in carrying out this investigation.

theories are capable of being tested cross-culturally. The extent of evidence available (Modgil, 1974, pp. 226–257) would suggest that the support for the theory, while being implicit in researches, is in need of further research and development. One direction in which development could proceed is in the refinement of research methodology (Ashton, 1975). Also, one single factor which appears to influence the performance on Piagetian tasks is the contribution made by differential cultural experiences. The issue needs to be extended to include what can be termed bi-cultural experience. This relates to a particular cultural group's exposure to a second culture. A bi-cultural study is qualitatively different from a cross-cultural study in that in the former an individual is exposed to two sets of cultural experiences whereas in a cross-cultural study, the performance on a particular task is judged within the framework of criteria laid down by the first or the second culture. Immigrant communities which have settled in this country provide examples of the groups who have a firm base in their own culture; and are undergoing a new acculturation process in this country. It seems that research is lacking in this particular field; and there should be some preliminary work along these lines to extend the perspectives. It should be noted, in parenthesis, that Haynes (1971) considered the performance on concept formation tasks of Punjabi children attending a junior school in England. Her concern, however, was to establish a base for prediction of learning ability; and the concept formation tests consisted of six sorting tasks designed to elicit responses indicating formation of 'sets'.

There are two important issues related to the education of Asian pupils in England. One – isolated by Haynes (1971) – is the educational assessment of pupils based on performance tasks which are relevant to the school situation. The other is the progress the Asian pupils make in the learning of English as a second language and its relationship with pupils' progress in various aspects of the curriculum. The implications of Piagetian theory for the traditional curriculum subjects have been studied (Peel, 1972; Modgil, 1974, pp. 258–274); but lesser-known curriculum subjects like the learning of English as a second language has not received similar attention.

In providing psychological explanations of foreign language learning ability, some writers have recently been turning to the Piagetian theory of cognitive development. What they have put forward are specific hypotheses which are in obvious need of testing. The early stage of child language, for example, described as Stage I speech, is regarded as consisting of either relations or propositions concerning the sensorimotor world; and seems to represent the expression of sensorimotor intelligence (Lovell and Dixon, 1965). In second language learning in particular, it has been suggested (Bugelski, 1956, quoted by

Jacobovits, 1970) that 'child learning' is mostly concerned with building up 'behaviour elements', 'reaction systems' or 'cognitive schemas'. Jacobovits (1975) goes on to add 'some of these strategies will prove helpful in organizing the facts about the second language but others, will be misleading and inapplicable'. This explanation of what second language learning might involve is similar to the twin concepts of 'assimilation' and 'accommodation' in Piagetian theory.

What is being suggested for language learning in general could possibly apply with more force to specific aspects of language learning, e.g. learning to read. Abstract categories like 'word', 'sound' and 'letter' have been shown to hinder five-year-olds learning to read (Downing, 1970). From the experiment he has cited, it becomes clear that 'the concrete aids facilitated motor and verbal responses' as against a solely verbal approach. This finding suggests that development of linguistic categories through sensorimotor approaches is appropriate to the five-year-olds learning to read in so far as it earmarks the stage of sensorimotor intelligence. Clearly, this finding has implications for learning to read in a foreign language. It has been suggested in a paper by M.J. Paine (1976), summarized in the IATEFL Newsletter, that the problems of the initial EFL reader might be due to allographic differences in the English language. Robins (1964, p. 131) provides the following explanation of the term 'Allophone'. 'Members of phonemes are often called phones or allophones and it is a common practice to write phonetic symbols between square brackets and the symbols of a broad transcription between oblique brackets. For example [t] and [t^h] are allophones of the / t / phoneme. (Allograph is the term used for an allophone in a written text). M.J. Paine further suggests that problems in discriminating between allographic differences might be related to the Piagetian concepts of 'reversibility' and 'conservation'.

The above considerations point to a possible relationship between the development of reading ability in the learners of English as a second language and cognitive development in Piagetian terms. The aim of this study was to analyse this relationship and its implications.

SUBJECTS / The sample consisted of 55 Punjabi-speaking children in the age range of seven to 11 years attending a Church of England Aided Primary school. The school has 240 children on roll. The Punjabi children form 45 per cent of the school population. There is no special provision for the teaching of English to non-English speaking children. There is, however, provision for remedial work for which one teacher has a responsibility. The emphasis is on teaching of reading; and some of the children attend the remedial sessions on a rota basis. In the headteacher's opinion, the Punjabi children's progress was 'sluggish' up to the age of 8 years; but appeared to 'accelerate' from age 8 upwards.

The sample was drawn from the junior classes and was random. All the Punjabi children who completed tests were included. The children were grouped in age bands of 7+ (N = 9), 8+ (N = 15), 9+ (N = 20) and 10+ (N = 11). The Kingston Test of Silent Reading yields Reading Quotients up to the chronological age of ten years eleven months. This meant that the children falling outside this age limit could not be included in the sample. The Table below provides information about the distribution of scores for each age group.

Table 1:

Age	N	M	SD	M	SD
		Reading Quotients		*Conservation Task*	
7+	9	98.00	7.87	54.44	6.85
8+	15	89.46	7.41	56.00	15.41
9+	20	76.95	16.99	56.50	17.86
10+	11	87.00	10.76	65.45	19.71

These statistics are based on an assumption of similarity between the spread in scores for boys and girls. This is done in order to obtain the picture of the group as a whole. Thus, in the case of 7+age group, for instance, means and standard deviations are based upon a single mean score for the two groups. This assumption is not entirely unwarranted as would be shown in the next part of the analysis. It should be noted while examining this table that the Reading Quotients begin from a base of 100, 87, 78 and 70 for 7-, 8-, 9- and 10-year-olds respectively. The conservation scores begin from a base of 10 in all cases.

METHOD / In line with the view that 'studies investigating interrelationships among a variety of tasks measuring different processes are required' (Ashton, 1975), a simple correlational design was selected. The rationale for the selection of measures may now be stated. In view of the preference in many junior school classes for a formal approach to the curriculum, it seemed that a reading test administered in a group situation might be appropriate. Additionally, the emphasis placed on reading through remedial provision in school, meant that reading ability would be an important area of performance to be investigated. The Kingston Test of Silent Reading (Hebron, 1954) appeared to be the most appropriate. This was administered by class teachers to the whole classes from which the data pertaining to the sample were extracted.

The Piagetian task selected for this investigation was that of conservation of solid substance, better known as the 'plasticine problem'. The protocol used was patterned after Elkind (1961) but only related to the conservation of substance. Two balls of plasticine, identical in shape, size and weight were shown to the subject. Each subject was individually questioned. The first question put was 'Do these two balls have the same amount of plasticine in them?'. If the subject said 'No', he was allowed extra quantity to make the two balls the same. The second question was the prediction question. 'If I roll one of the balls into a sausage, will there be as much plasticine in the sausages as in the ball?'. The prediction was noted down. Before putting the third question, the experimenter rolled one ball into a sausage shape. The third question was: 'Is there as much plasticine in the sausage as in the ball?'. The answer was noted down. Finally, the subject was asked a justification for the answer: 'Why is that?'. The scoring procedure for questions 1, 2 and 3 was the same. 'Yes' was a conservation answer in each case and was assigned a mark of 2. 'No' was a non-conservation answer and carried one mark. The justification answer was marked on the basis of the categories reported by Elkind (1961). Accordingly the following four types were used: 'Romancing' (one mark), Perceptual (two marks), specific (three marks) and general (four marks). This marking procedure yielded a total score of 10. This was multiplied by 10 (maximum score = 100) for ease of computation in relation to the other standardized score.

RESULTS / As the sample is composed of 30 boys and 25 girls, the first question to consider is whether there is a significant difference on the two tests between the two groups. This is particularly important in view of the assumption regarding the homogeneity of the two groups incorporated in Table 1. For this analysis, the mean scores are based on the treatment of two groups as independent samples.

Table 2: Reading quotients

Sex	N	M	SD	SE	CR
Boys	30	89.00	8.53	2.79	.95
Girls	25	91.64	11.59		

The critical ratio of .95 suggests that approximately 67 per cent of the cases will fall outside the normal distribution limits. This suggests that the difference between the two groups is by 'chance fluctuations'. The groups can therefore be regarded as random and as representing the Punjabi children in the school as a whole.

Table 3: Conservation task

Sex	N	M	SD	SE	CR
Boys	30	56.00	48.48	12.21	.27
Girls	25	59.33	42.05		

Now we examine the performance of these children in the conservation task. The critical ratio of .27 suggests that here again the difference between the performance of groups is much more emphatically by 'chance fluctuations' and the similar fluctuations may be found in approximately 89 per cent of the cases. A conclusion to be drawn from these two sets of data is that the groups of boys and girls are alike in their performance on the two measures.

The next question to consider is about the nature of relationship between the performance on the conservation task and reading ability.

Table 4: Correlations

Age	N	r	t	df	Level of significance
7+	9	−.21	.74	7	NS
8+	15	.26	1.35	13	NS
9+	20	.15	.63	18	NS
10+	11	.61	2.14	9	.010

No significant relationship exists between the two measures except for the 10+ age group. As some of the samples in the analysis reported in Table 4 are small, the relationship was also considered by taking the group in its entirety. As demonstrated earlier, there is evidence to suggest that the groups are homogeneous in their performance on the two measures. For the sample as a whole (N = 55), the mean score for the Reading Quotient was 90.20 with a standard deviation of 9.53. For the same group, the mean score on the conservation task was 58.00 with a standard deviation of 14.67. The r between the two measures was .21 (t = .12, 53 df) and was not significant.

In the final part of the analysis, the sex differences at each age level in the performance on the two measures were examined. This is of particular interest in that the overall picture (Tables 2 and 3) revealed no significant differences between boys and girls in the groups as a whole. In any case, the evidence in Tables 2 and 3 is in need of further analysis as 7+ to 10+ age range could mask important developmental differences. These analyses now follow.

Table 5: Reading quotients

Age	Sex	N	M	Difference	t	df	Level of Significance
7+	Girls	3	102.00	6.00	1.05	7	NS
	Boys	6	96.00				
8+	Boys	7	90.42	1.80	.50	13	NS
	Girls	8	88.62				
9+	Girls	8	96.50	12.50	2.80	18	.002
	Boys	12	84.00				
10+	Boys	5	90.60	6.60	1.44	9	NS

It may be noted from the above table that in all cases except the girls in 8+ group, the differences are not significant.

Table 6: Conservation task

Age	Sex	N	M	Difference	t	df	Level of Significance
7+	Girls	3	56.66	3.33	.33	7	NS
	Boys	6	53.33				
8+	Boys	7	60.00	7.50	1.99	13	.010
	Girls	8	52.50				
9+	Girls	8	58.75	3.50	.68	18	NS
	Boys	12	55.00				
10+	Boys	5	76.00	19.34	1.58	9	NS

In case of the conservation task, too, there are no differences between the sexes except for the boys in 8+ group.

A brief mention may now be made about the achievement of conservation in the sample. Of the 55 children, only three boys were found to be conservers. These were one boy (age 8 years five months, Reading quotient 106 — highest in the age group), one boy (age 10 years six months with a Reading quotient of 82) and one boy (age ten years and Reading quotient of 106 — highest in the age group). Most of the subjects provided a perceptual explanation for the sausage shape having more plasticine in them in their opinion. This judgment was based on sausage shape being 'fatter', 'thicker', 'like a cylinder' and 'taller when standing'. Some also came to this conclusion because they saw sausage shape to be 'fatter on the edges'.

DISCUSSION / The study has produced some interesting information. Although the group appeared homogeneous on the basis of statistical evidence, very high probability of chance differences meant that it was not possible to obtain normal distribution by taking only one school as a sample. This is another way of saying that each school, no matter what percentage of immigrant children it contains, will still be reflecting the school type, neighbourhood, and many other sociological features. It is possible that the failure to achieve conservation by the majority of the children may be in part due to this select character of the sample.

This point of school type may be extended a little further. It was noted earlier that the formal approach to the curriculum appeared to be preferred in school and that the non-English speaking children received help through remedial provision, especially in reading. It is possible that children need to involve themselves more in their own learning. It is likely that formal methods demand 'accommodation' from the children as opposed to 'assimilation' which would occur in play and in all active participation. The nature of the Indian child's cultural experience and how that determines his particular mode of perception may provide another basis for understanding the children's failure. It is interesting that Lannoy (1971), although not writing about Indian children in an educational context, has this observation to make: 'The Indian child learns about his environment more by observation than through explicit parental instruction. This is thought to be the only really adequate way for him to find his way in the world, superior even to formal education'. An Indian child's chosen mode of behaviour would seem to be through perception and observation and the culturally-induced overemphasis on this mode may have resulted in the phenomenon of 'centering' and preoccupation with one variable in the perceptual field. It is to be noted development in language skills will have influence on conservation. In the evidence cited in Table 4, there is a significant relationship between reading ability and the conservation task. Downing (no date) has put forward a cognitive clarity theory of reading which suggests that the learner of reading moves from a state of cognitive confusion to a state of cognitive clarity about the reading task. The children in the 10+ age group probably represent the children whose cognitive clarity is demonstrated in their reading quotients as well as in the conservation task.

The superiority of the nine-year-old girls over boys in the reading test is interesting. This result, as well as the eight-year-old boy's superiority over girls in the conservation task, are difficult to explain in absence of any other supporting evidence. A number of observations have already been made about the select nature of the sample. It is highly likely that at specific age levels the samples, apart from being small, are relatively more select.

A number of conclusions may be drawn from the above discussion. The correlational evidence reported here although limited, is promising. The work is needed in the bi-cultural field using more complex correlational and regression designs. As noted earlier, Piagetian theories could provide explanations of foreign language learning. The test construction exercises in English as a second language should consider the correlations of various language tests with Piagetian tasks. It would seem that psychometrics provide the best scope for understanding the processes underlying development of language and concepts. One direction in which Piagetian research could profitably proceed is in correlations of Piagetian tasks with teaching styles and strategies of individual teachers. This may be especially important from the point of view of the education of Asian children in that these children very often have to make their adjustments to the learning situation within the school due to their earlier experience of formal schooling.

*Mexican American preschoolers' acquisition of English in a Piagetian oriented preschool**
C.J. Wetzstein and M.E. Smart, 1976

PROBLEM / There is little evidence in the literature on the acquisition of English by monolingual Spanish speaking children from a Piagetian viewpoint. This study is an attempt to answer some explorative questions regarding this language acquisition process. How does a child three- to five-years-old, who is still learning Spanish in his home, acquire knowledge of the English code? For what purposes do they use English or Spanish, in the school environment? How does their usage of the two linguistic codes change qualitatively and quantitatively over one calendar year?

*   Reprinted by kind permission of the authors. Gratitude is expressed to Dr Connie J. Wetzstein and Professor Margaret E. Smart of the University of Southern California, School for Early Childhood Education.

PROCEDURES / Subjects: Mexican American children who had been in attendance at the University of Southern California School for Early Childhood Education (USC SECE) from the Spring of 1974 to the Spring of 1975, excluding summer sessions. As of May 1974, the five boys and three girls ranged in age from three years nine months to four years nine months. Typically, they were first generation children of Mexican American homes in which both parents were present. The families had low incomes and resided in the immediate neighborhood of the university.

The children's daily school experiences included multiple opportunities to use sensory materials which invited their exploration. The planned environment encouraged children to use language (Spanish or English) for their own purposes. English is modeled by the teacher during small group activities in a natural conversational setting.

Data were obtained by observers trained in language techniques developed by Smart, Theimer, and Dahl (1974). Verbatim language samples of each child were recorded, accompanied by detailed situational and interactive descriptions. Each child was randomly observed during different parts of the pre-school day. The observers were trained to the 95 per cent level of interrater reliability. Piaget's (1955) categories, egocentric and social language and his subcategories, spontaneous adaptive information and commands, were used to analyze the data. In addition, the utterances were assessed in terms of selected psychological and sociological linguistic aspects.

FINDINGS / The findings were as follows: (1) Language used for egocentric purposes, i.e., monologue and repetition, was typically in English. (2) When the child communicated with others, he used English or Spanish depending on whom he addressed and on the topic discussed. (3) The amount of socialized language depended on the child's developmental stage. Increased amount of spontaneous adaptive information and decreased amount of commands were noted as indices of decentration. (4) The appearance of adjectives, adverbs and the presence of analogies in English marked qualitative linguistic gains as well as an increased ability to represent verbally social and physical reality (Carroll, 1964). (5) Very little 'code switching' as defined by Gumperz (1972) occurred from one language to another within one utterance.

DISCUSSION / The acquisition of any language is highly dependent on the social and physical milieu within which the child develops intellectually. Language was internalized when a meaningful context was provided within the school environment.

Factors affecting Piagetian classification and seriation skills in a sample of Mexican-American and Anglo-American children
R.H. Wisener, 1976

AIM / The author was intent to assess the development of classification and seriation skills in a sample of Mexican-American and Anglo-American children: whether verbal ability, sex, grade, and age predicted success on these tasks.

SUBJECTS / N = 60 Anglo- and Mexican-Americans, from each of the grades of kindergarten through third grade.

METHOD / Peabody Picture Vocabulary Test (PPVT) (Dunn, 1965) scores were used as the predictor variable in order to assess the effects of possible differences in verbal ability between the test groups on task performance. Eight Piagetian tasks of classification and three transitivity Piagetian tasks were administered. All Ss were tested individually and the protocols recorded verbatim.

RESULTS / Verbal ability, sex, grade, and age were successful in predicting the composite classification score. 'However, the predictor variables, both as a group and singly, were not effective in predicting performance on transitivity tasks. The predictor variables of ethnic background, age, grade, and sex were not found to be effective predictors of classification task performance when taken in isolation. Instead, the single best predictor of classification performance was found to be verbal ability', Wisener (1976, p. 3587–B).

Judgment and imaging aspects of operations: a Piagetian study with Korean and Costa Rican children
J. Youniss and A. Dean, 1974

Experiment One
AIM / To explore the possibility that 'an additional important factor in milieu studies may be the process through which a solution to a task is achieved rather than the content of the operations to which the task relates', p. 1020.

SUBJECTS / N = 64. Half of the Ss were between eight- and nine-years-old while the other half were between 11 and 12 years. Subjects were drawn from both urban and rural environments.

METHOD / Five tasks were administered drawn from Piaget and

Inhelder (1971). Four were given under two conditions, anticipation and judgment. The fifth was an anticipatory imagery task. The tests were the conservation of length, area, substance, seriation, and rotation. (Details of the experimental procedures are also described in Youniss and Dean, 1974, pp. 1021–1022.)

Experiment Two

AIM / To assess judgment and imaging aspects 'beyond conservation or seriation situations with tasks at a more advanced level in concrete operational intelligence', p. 1024.

SUBJECTS / N = 160. The younger group of Ss had an age range from eight to nine years 11 months; and the older group ranged in age from 11 years to 12 years 11 months.

METHOD / The tasks administered were: inferential size judgment (patterned after Youniss and Murray, 1970), inferential size manipulation, probability concepts (modelled after Ross, 1966), combinational pairing (Goodnow, 1962), and country naming.

RESULTS / Eleven- and 12-year-old Ss performed at the higher levels than eight- to nine-year-olds with judgment procedures, and Ss from rural mileus performed like their urban age peers. However, with imaging procedures, rural children demonstrated impairments in comparison with urban children. The findings showed the absence of milieu differences in judgment tasks of operations as well as the presence of milieu differences on imaging problems. The authors finally draw three implications. 'Operations should not be constructed as simply present or absent but as representing successive structurings by the child. Judgmental tasks may signify early structuring, and imaging versions of these same operations may represent more complete structuring. Second, to understand progressive structuring, a better grasp of the role of processes (strategies, planning, successive production) is necessary. A more complete description of developing intelligence needs to bring in imaging processes as complements to structural analyses. Finally, understanding of milieu effects requires on the one hand more explicit understanding of operations and on the other hand more far-reaching cultural analyses than we or most psychologists are equipped to provide', p. 1031.

ABBREVIATIONS USED IN THE BIBLIOGRAPHY
(under the series *Piagetian Research*, Vols. 1–8)

Acta Psychol.	Acta Psychologica (Holland)
Adol.	Adolescence
Aging and Hum. Develop.	Aging and Human Development
Alberta J. Ed. Res.	Alberta Journal of Educational Research
Am. Ed. Res. Assoc.	American Educational Research Association
Am. Ed. Res. J.	American Educational Research Journal
Am. J. Ment. Def.	American Journal of Mental Deficiency
Am. J. Orthopsych.	American Journal of Orthopsychiatry
Am. J. Psych.	American Journal of Psychology
Am. J. Soc.	American Journal of Sociology
Am. Psych.	American Psychologist
Am. Psych. Assoc.	American Psychological Association
Am. Soc. Rev.	American Sociological Review
Ann. Rev. Psych.	Annual Review of Psychology
Arch. Dis. Child.	Archives of the Diseases of Childhood (UK)
Archiv. Gen. Psychiat.	Archives of General Psychiatry
Arch. de Psychol.	Archives de Psychologie
Aust. J. Psych.	Australian Journal of Psychology
Aust. J. Soc. Issues	Australian Journal of Social Issues
Brit. J. Clin. & Soc. Psych.	British Journal of Clinical and Social Psychology
Brit. J. Ed. Psych.	British Journal of Educational Psychology
Brit. J. Psych.	British Journal of Psychology
Brit. J. Stat. Psych.	British Journal of Statistical Psychology
Brit. J. Psych. Stat.	British Journal of Psychology – Statistical Section
Brit. J. Soc.	British Journal of Sociology
Brit. Med. Bull.	British Medical Bulletin
Brit. J. Med. Psych.	British Journal of Medical Psychology
Bull. Danish Inst. for Ed. Res.	Bulletin of the Danish Institute for Educational Research
Calif. J. Ed. Res.	Californian Journal of Educational Research
Can. Educ. Res. Dig.	Canadian Educational and Research Digest
Can. J. Behav. Sci.	Canadian Journal of Behavioural Science
Can. J. Psych.	Canadian Journal of Psychology
Can. Psychol.	Canadian Psychology
Child. Developm.	Child Development (USA)
Child Study Journ.	Child Study Journal
Childhood Psych.	Childhood Psychology (UK)
Cogn.	Cognition
Cogn. Psych.	Cognitive Psychology
Contemp. Psych.	Contemporary Psychology (USA)
Dev. Psych.	Developmental Psychology (USA)

Abbreviations   *205*

Diss. Abstr.	Dissertation Abstracts (USA)
Educ. of Vis. Handicap.	Education of the Visually Handicapped
Educ. & Psych. Measmt.	Educational and Psychological Measurement (USA)
Ed. Res.	Educational Research (UK)
Ed. Rev.	Educational Review (UK)
Educ. Stud. Maths.	Educational Studies in Mathematics
El. Sch. J.	Elementary School Journal (USA)
Eug. Rev.	Eugenics Review (UK)
Excep. Child.	Exceptional Children
Forum Educ.	Forum Education
Gen. Psych. Mon.	Genetic Psychological Monographs (USA)
Harv. Ed. Rev.	Harvard Educational Review
Human Developm.	Human Development (Switzerland)
Hum. Hered.	Human Heredity
Inst. Child Welf. Monogr.	Institute of Child Welfare Monographs
Int. J. Psych.	International Journal of Psychology (France)
Int. Rev. Educ.	International Review of Education (Germany)
Int. Soc. Sci. Bull.	International Social Science Bulletin (France)
Jap. J. Ed. Psych.	Japanese Journal of Educational Psychology
Jap. Psych. Res.	Japanese Psychological Research
J. Abnorm. Soc. Psych.	Journal of Abnormal and Social Psychology (USA)
Journ. Amer. Acad. Child Psychiat.	Journal of American Academy of Child Psychiatry
J. Am. Stat. Assoc.	Journal of American Statistical Association
J. App. Psych.	Journal of Applied Psychology (USA)
J. Compar. Psychol.	Journal of Comparative Psychology
J. Comp. and Physiolog. Psych.	Journal of Comparative and Physiological Psychology
J. Child Psych. Psychiatr.	Journal of Child Psychology and Psychiatry
J. Clin. Psych.	Journal of Clinical Psychology (USA)
J. Consult. Psych.	Journal of Consultant Psychology (USA)
J. Cross. Cult. Psych.	Journal of Cross-Cultural Psychology (USA)
J. Ed. Psych.	Journal of Educational Psychology (USA)
J. Ed. Res.	Journal of Educational Research (USA)
J. Ed. Stud.	Journal of Educational Studies (USA)
J. Exp. Child Psych.	Journal of Experimental Child Psychology (USA)
J. Exp. Educ.	Journal of Experimental Education
J. Exp. Psych.	Journal of Experimental Psychology

J. Gen. Psych.	Journal of Genetic Psychology (USA)
J. Gerontol	Journal of Gerontology
J. Home Econ.	Journal of Home Economics
Journ. Learn. Disabil.	Journal of Learning Disabilities
J. Math. Psych.	Journal of Mathematical Psychology
J. Ment. Sub.	Journal of Mental Subnormality
J. Negro Ed.	Journal of Negro Education (USA)
J. Pers.	Journal of Personality (USA)
J. Pers. Soc. Psych.	Journal of Personality and Social Psychology (USA)
J. Pers. Assessm.	Journal of Personality Assessment (USA)
J. Psych.	Journal of Psychology (USA)
J. Res. Maths. Educ.	Journal of Research in Mathematics Education
J. Res. Sci. Teach.	Journal of Research in Science Teaching (USA)
J. Soc. Iss.	Journal of Social Issues (USA)
J. Soc. Psych.	Journal of Social Psychology (USA)
J. Soc. Res.	Journal of Social Research
J. Spec. Ed.	Journal of Special Education (USA)
Journ. Struct. Learn.	Journal of Structural Learning
J. Teach. Ed.	Journal of Teacher Education (USA)
J. Verb. Learn. Verb. Behv.	Journal of Verbal Learning and Verbal Behaviour (UK/USA)
J. Youth Adolesc.	Journal of Youth and Adolescence
Math. Teach.	Mathematics Teacher (USA)
Maths. Teach.	Mathematics Teaching
Merr.-Palm. Quart.	Merrill-Palmer Quarterly (USA)
Mon. Soc. Res. Child Dev.	Monographs of the Society for Research in Child Development (USA)
Mult. Beh. Res.	Multivariate Behavioural Research
New Zealand Journ. Educ. Stud.	New Zealand Journal of Educational Studies
Ped. Sem.	Pedagogical Seminary
Pedag. Europ.	Pedogogica Europaea
Percep. Mot. Skills	Perceptual and Motor Skills
Psych. Absts.	Psychological Abstracts
Psych. Afric.	Psychologica Africana
Psych. Bull.	Psychological Bulletin (USA)
Psych. Iss.	Psychological Issues
Psych. Mon.	Psychological Monographs (USA)
Psych. Mon. Gen. and Appl.	Psychological Monographs: General and Applied (USA)
Psychol. Rec.	Psychological Record
Psych. Rep.	Psychological Reports (USA)
Psych. Rev.	Psychological Review (USA)
Psychol. Sch.	Psychology in Schools
Psych. Sci.	Psychological Science (USA)
Psychomet.	Psychometrika
Psy.-nom. Sc.	Psychonomic Science
Psy. Today	Psychology Today
Publ. Opin. Quart.	Public Opinion Quarterly (USA)

Quart. J. Exp. Psych.	Quarterly Journal of Experimental Psychology (UK/USA)
Rev. Educ. Res.	Review of Educational Research
R. Belge de Ps. Ped.	Review Belge de Psychologie et de Pédagogie (Belgium)
Rev. Suisse Psych.	Revue Suisse de Pschologie (Switzerland)
Scan. J. Psych.	Scandinavian Journal of Psychology
Sch. Coun. Curr. Bull.	Schools Council Curriculum Bulletin
Sch. Sci. Maths.	School Science and Mathematics
Sci.	Science
Sci. Americ.	Scientific American
Sci. Ed.	Science Education (USA)
Scot. Ed. Stud.	Scottish Educational Studies
Sem. Psychiat.	Seminars in Psychiatry
Soc. Psychi.	Social Psychiatry
Soviet Psych.	Soviet Psychology
Teach. Coll. Contr. Ed.	Teachers' College Contributions to Education (USA)
Theo. into Pract.	Theory into Practice
Times Ed. Supp.	Times Educational Supplement
Train. Sch. Bull.	Training School Bulletin
Vita. Hum.	Vita Humana
WHO Mon.	World Health Organization Monographs
Wiener Arb. z. pad. Psychol.	Wiener Arbeiten zur pädagogischen Psychologie (Austria)
Yearbook Journ. Negro Educ.	Yearbook of the Journal of Negro Education
Zeitschr. f. ang. Psychol.	Zeitschrift für angewandte Psychologie und Charakterkunde (Germany)
Zeitschr. f. pad. Psychol.	Zeitschrift für pädagogische Psychologie und Fugendkunde (Germany)

ABRAVANEL, E. (1975) 'Perceptual set induction in young children: cross-cultural support for the role of active classification', *Intern. J. Psych.*, 10, 3, 159–164.

ADELSON, J. (1968) 'Adolescent perspectives on law and government'. Paper read at the American Psychological Association Annual Meeting.

ADELSON, J. and O'NEILL, R.P. (1966) 'Growths of political ideas in adolescence: the sense of community', *J. Pers. Soc. Psych.*, 4, 295–306.

ADJEI, K. (1973) Maternal Behaviours and Cognitive Development. Unpublished PhD thesis, University of Strathclyde.

AL-FAKHRI, S. (1975) 'The development of the concept of spatial co-ordinate system: concept of perpendicular and horizontal', Personal communication.

AL-FAKHRI, S. (1975a) 'The development of the concept of length among Iraqi children', Personal communication.

AL-FAKHRI, S. (1975b) 'The development of the concept of class-inclusion among Iraqi children', Personal communication.

AL-FAKHRI, S. (1975c) 'The concept of the conservation of continuous quantity among Iraqi children', Personal communication.

AL-FAKHRI, S. (1975d) 'The formation of the concept of measurement amongst Iraqi children', Personal communication.

AL-FAKHRI, S. (1975e) 'The development of some concepts relevant to natural phenomena among Iraqi children', Personal communication.

ALMY, M. (1967) 'The psychologist looks at spatial concept formation: children's concept of space and time', *Res. Needs in Geog. Educ.*, 7, 23–40.

ALMY, M., DAVITZ, J., and WHITE, M.A. (1970) *Studying School Children in Uganda: Four Reports of Exploratory Research*. New York: Teachers College Press.

AL-SHAIKH, A.A. (1973) An experimental study of the development of the concept of quantitative conservation: substance, weight and volume in Iraqi children. Unpublished MA thesis, University of Baghdad.

AL-SHAIKH, A.A. (1974) 'The development of the concept of conservation of length among Iraqi school children', *J. College Arts*, 18, 110–136.

ANASTASIOW, N.J. and HANES, M.L. (1974) 'Cognitive development and the acquisition of language in three subcultural groups', *Dev. Psych.*, 10, 703–709.

ASHBY, B., MORRISON, A., and BUTCHER, H.J. (1970) 'The abilities and attainments of immigrant children', *Res. Educ.*, 4, 73–80.

ASHTON, P.T. (1975) 'Cross-cultural Piagetian research: an experimental perspective', *Harv. Ed. Rev.*, 4, 475–506.

AYISI, C.H. (1972) 'Performance of Ghanaian Children on Some Piagetian Conservation Tasks,' Research Report, School of Education, University of Cape Coast.

BALDWIN, A.L., BALDWIN, C.P., HILTON, J.M. and LAMBERT, N.W. (1969) 'The measurement of social expectations and their development in children', *Monog. Soc. Res. Child Dev.*, 34, (4, Serial No. 128).

BARKAI, H. (1971) *The Kibbutz: An Experiment in Microsocialism.* Hebrew University, Dept of Economics, Research Report No. 34.

BEARD, R.M. (1963) 'The order of concept development studies in two fields, II. Conceptions of conservation of quantity among primary school children', *Educ. Rev.*, 15, 228–37.

BEARD, R.M. (1968) 'An investigation into mathematical concepts among Ghanaian children', *Teach. Educ. New Countries*, 9, 3–14, 132–45.

BEARISON, D.J. (1969) 'Role of measurement operations in the acquisition of conservation', *Dev. Psych.*, 1, 654–60.

BENTON, A.L. (1959) *Right–left Discrimination and Finger Localization.* New York: Hoeber.

BERNSTEIN, B. (1961) 'Social class and linguistic development: a theory of social learning'. In: HALSEY, A.H., FLOUD, J. and ANDERSON, C.A. (Eds.), *Education, Economy and Society.* New York: Free Press.

BERRY, J.W. (1965) 'Temne and Eskimo perceptual skills', *Int. J. Psych.*, 1, 207–229.

BERRY, J.W. (1969) 'On cross-cultural comparability', *Int. J. Psych.*, 4, 119–28.

BERRY, J.W. (1971) 'Ecological and cultural factors in spatial skill development', *Can. J. Behav. Sci.*, 3, 324–36.

BERRY, J.W. (1974) 'Radical cultural relativism and the concept of intelligence'. In: BERRY, J.W., and DASEN, P.R. (Eds.), *Culture and Cognition.* London: Methuen, pp. 225–230.

BERRY, J.W. (1975) 'An ecological approach to cross-cultural psychology', *Nederlands Tijdschrift voor de Psych.*, 30, 51–84.

BETTELHEIM, B. (1969a) *The Children of the Dream.* London: Macmillan.

BETTELHEIM, B. (1969b) 'Personality formation in the kibbutz', *Am. J. Psychoanal.*, 29, 3–9.

BINET, A. (1911) 'Nouvelles recherches sur le mesure du niveau intellectuel chez les enfants d'ecole', *Annee Psycholog*, 17, 145–201.

BLACKETH, R.E. and REYMENT, R.A. (1971) *Multivariate Morphometrics*. London: Academic Press.

BLISHEN, B.B. (1967) 'A socio-economic index for occupations in Canada, *Canad. Rev. Soc. Anthrop.*, 4, 41–53.

BOVET, M.C. (1971) Etude interculturelle des processus du raisonnement. Notions de quantités physiques et relations spatiotemporelles chez des enfants et des adultes non-scolarisés. PhD thesis, Geneva University.

BOVET, M.C. (1974) 'Cognitive processes among illiterate children and adults'. In: BERRY, J.W., and DASEN, P.R. (Eds.), *Culture and Cognition*. London: Methuen, pp. 311–334.

BOVET, M.C. and OTHENIN-GIRARD, C. (1975) 'Etude Piagétienne de quelques notions spatio-temporelles dans un milieu africain', *Inter. J. Psych.*, 10, 1, 1–17.

BOWD, A.D. (1975) 'Note on conservation differences for Indian and White children', *Percep. Mot. Skills*, 41, 361–362.

BOYLE, D.G. (1969) *A Students' Guide to Piaget*. Oxford: Pergamon Press.

BRAINERD, C.J. (1973) 'Order of acquisition of transitivity, conservation and class-inclusion of length and weight', *Dev. Psych.*, 8, 105–116.

BROWN, A.L. (1973) 'Conservation of number and continuous quantity in normal, bright, and retarded children', *Child Developm.*, 44, 376–379.

BROWN, D.G. (1956) 'Sex-role preference in young children'. *Psych. Mon.*, 70, 1–19.

BRUNER, J.S. and KENNEY, H.J. (1965) 'Representation and mathematics learning'. In: MORRISETT, L.N. and VINSONHALER, J. (Eds.), 'Mathematical learning', *Monog. Soc. Res. Child Developm.*, 30 (1, Serial No. 99), 50–59.

BRUNER, J.S., OLVER, R.R., and GREENFIELD, P.M. (1966) *Studies in Cognitive Growth*. New York: Wiley.

BUCK-MORSS, S. (1975) 'Socio-economic bias in Piaget's theory and its implications for cross-cultural Studies', *Human Developm.*, 18, 35–49.

BUGELSKI, B.R. and ALAMPAY, D.A. (1961) 'The role of frequency in developing perceptual set', *Can Journ. Psych.*, 15, 205–211.

BURKE, C.F. (1900) 'The collecting instinct', *Pedagog. Sem.*, 7, 179–207.

BURROUGHS, G.E.R. (1971) 'Design and Analysis in Educational Research', *Educ. Mono.* No. 8, Birmingham University.

BUTCHER, H.J. (1972) 'Comments on Jensen's paper', *Educ. Res.*, 14, 2, 94.

CALHOUN, L.G. (1971) 'Number conservation in very young children: the effect of age and mode of reasoning', *Child Developm.*, 42, 561—72.

CAMPBELL, D.T. and FISKE, D. (1959) 'Convergent and discriminant validation by the multitrait—multimethod matrix', *Psych. Bull.*, 56, 81—105.

CAMPBELL, D.T. and STANLEY, J.C. (1966) *Experimental and Quasi-Experimental Designs for Research*. Chicago: Rand McNally Company.

CARLSON, J. (1975) 'Kulturvergleichende Forschung sensu Piaget: einige Perspektiven'. In: WALTER, H. (ed) *Sozialforschung, Band III, Sozialökologie — neue Wege in der Sozialforschung*. Stuttgart: F. Frommann Verlag, pp. 283—312.

CARLSON, J. (1976) 'Cross-cultural Piagetian research: what can it tell us?' In: RIEGEL, K. and MEACHAM, J. (Eds.), *The Developing Individual in a Changing World*. The Hague: Mouton.

CAROTHERS, J.C. (1971) 'Discussion: criteria of stages of mental development'. In: TANNER, J.M. and INHELDER, B. (Eds.), *Discussions on Child Development*. New York: Inter. Universities Press.

CASATI, I. and LEZINE, I. (1968) *Les étapes de l'intelligence sensori-motrice Manual*. Paris: Centre de psychologie appliqué.

CASE, R. (1975) 'Social class differences in intellectual development: a Neo-Piagetian investigation', *Can. Journ. Behav. Sci.*, 7, 3, 244—261.

CELLARD, J. Mon lieutenant, (1975) 'J'ai raté mon train', *Le Monde*, Sélection hebdomadaire, Nov. 19, p. 14.

CHENG TSU-HSIN, and LEE MEI-KE (1960) 'An investigation into the scope of the conception of numbers among 6- to 7-year-old children', *Acta Psychol.*, (Sinica) 1, 28—35, (*Psych. Abstr.*, 35, 4710).

CHIU, LIAN-HWANG (1972) 'A cross-cultural comparison of cognitive styles in Chinese and American children', *Int. J. Psych.*, 7, 235—243.

COLE, M. and BRUNER, J.S. (1971) 'Cultural differences and inferences about psychological processes', *Am. Psych.*, 26, 867—76.

COLE, M. and SCRIBNER, S. (1974) *Culture and Thought: A Psychological Introduction*. New York: Wiley.

COLE, M., GAY, J., GLICK, J.A. and SHARP, D.W. (1971) *The Cultural Context of Learning and Thinking*. London: Methuen.

COUSINS, D. and ABRAVANEL, E. (1971) 'Some findings relevant to the hypothesis that topological spatial features are differentiated prior to Euclidean features during growth', *Brit. J. Psych.*, 62, 475—79.

COWLEY, J.J. and MURRAY, M. (1962) 'Some aspects of the development of spatial concepts in Zulu children', *J. Soc. Res.*, 13, 2—18.

CREPAULT, J. (1975) *Contribution a l'Etude de la genèse des Structures cinématiques. La Notion de simultanéité.* Paris: Travaux du Centre d'Etudes des Processus Cognitifs et du Langage, no 5.

DANZINGER, K. (1958) 'Children's earliest conceptions of economic relationships', *J. Soc. Psych.*, 47, 231—240.

DARCY, N.T. (1963) 'Bilingualism and the measurement of intelligence: a review of a decade of research', *J. Gen. Psych.*, 103, 255—82.

DASEN, P.R. (1970) Cognitive development in Aborigines of Central Australia: concrete operations and perceptual activities. Unpublished PhD thesis, Australian National University.

DASEN, P.R. (1972) 'Cross-cultural Piagetian research: a summary', *J. Cross-Cult. Psych.*, 3, 1, 23—39.

DASEN, P.R. (1972a) 'The development of conservation in Aboriginal children: a replication study', *Int. J. Psych.*, 7, 2, 75—85.

DASEN, P.R. (1973) 'Preliminary study of sensori-motor development in Baoulé children', *Early Child Develop and Care*, 2, 345—54.

DASEN, P.R. (1973a) 'Biologie ou Culture? La Psychologie inter-ethnique d'un point de vue Piagetien', *Can. Psychol.*, 14, 2, 149—66.

DASEN, P.R. (1974) 'The influence of ecology, culture and European contact on cognitive development in Australian Aborigines'. In: BERRY, J.W. and DASEN, P.R. (Eds.), *Culture and Cognition: Readings in Cross-Cultural Psychology.* London: Methuen.

DASEN, P.R. (1974a) 'Le développement psychologique du jeune enfant africain', *Arch. de Psych.*, 41, 164, 341—61.

DASEN, P.R. (1974b) 'Piagetian Research in Central Australia'. In: *The Psychology of Aboriginal Australians.* Sydney: Wiley.

DASEN, P.R., (1975) 'Le développement des opérations concrètes chez les Esquimaux Canadiens', *J. Int. Psych.*, 10, 3, 165—80.

DASEN, P.R. (1975a) 'Concrete operational development in three cultures', *J. Cross-Cult. Psych.*, 6, 2, 156—72.

DASEN, P.R. (1976) (Ed) *Piagetian Psychology: Cross-Cultural Contribution.* To be published by Gardner Press, New York. Also personal communication.

DASEN, P.R. (1976a) 'Moderate malnutrition and cognitive development: the choice of the dependent variable'. In: *Proceedings of the 8th International Meeting 'Nutrition and Psyche: A multi-disciplinary study group on nutrition, body and mind',* in press. Also personal communication.

DASEN, P.R. (1976b) 'A contribution to cross-cultural Piagetian psychology'. In: WARREN, N. (Ed.) *Studies in Cross-Cultural Psychology*. Volume One. London Academic Press, in press.

DASEN, P.R. (1976c) 'Cross-cultural cognitive development: the cultural aspects of Piaget's theory', personal communication. Also paper presented at the New York Academy of Sciences Conference on Issues in Cross-cultural Research. Oct. 1–3, 1975.

DASEN, P.R. (In press) 'Cross-cultural data on operational development: asymptotic development curves'. In: *Proceedings of the CERI–CNRS Conference on 'Dips in Learning and Development Curves'*, edited by J. Mehler and T. Bever. Also personal communication.

DASEN, P.R. (In press) 'Concrete operations and sensorimotor intelligence'. In: *Proceedings of the Centre for African Studies, University of Cambridge*, Conference on 'Universals of Human Thought: Some African Evidence', edited by B. Lloyd and J. Gray. Also personal communication.

DASEN, P.R. and INHELDER, B. (In press) 'Piaget's Theory in cultural context. In: TRIANDIS, H.C. (Ed.) *Handbook of Cross-Cultural Psychology*. New York: Allyn and Bacon, in press. Also personal communication.

DASEN, P.R., and SEAGRIM, G.N. (1969–76) *Inventory of Cross-Cultural Piagetian Research*. Published yearly, private circulation.

DASEN, P.R., BOVET, M. and INHELDER, B. (1974) 'Les Etapes de l'intelligence sensori-motrice chez l'Enfant Baoulé. Etude preliminaire', *Arch. de Psych.*, 41, 164, 363–86.

DASEN, P.R., de LACEY, P.R., and SEAGRIM, G.N. (1974) 'An investigation of reasoning ability in adopted and fostered Aboriginal children'. In: KEARNEY, G.E., de LACEY, P.R. and DAVIDSON, G. (Eds.), *The Psychology of Aboriginal Australians*. Sydney: John Wiley.

DAWSON, J.L.M. (1967) 'Cultural and physiological influences on spatial-perceptual processes in West Africa', *Int. J. Psych.*, 115–128 (I) and 171–185 (II).

De LACEY, P.R. (1969) Milieu, race and classificatory ability in Australia. Unpublished PhD thesis, University of New England, Armidale, N.S.W.

De LACEY, P.R. (1970) 'A cross-cultural study of classificatory ability in Australia', *J. Cross-Cult. Psych.*, 1, 293–304.

De LACEY, P.R. (1970a) 'Classificatory performance among Aboriginal and White Australian children'. Report to the AIAS, Canberra.

DE LACEY, P.R. (1971) 'Verbal intelligence, operational thinking and environment in part-Aboriginal children', *Aust. J. Psych.*, 23, 145–49.

DE LACEY, P.R. and NURCOMBE, B. (1972) 'The reliability of the Peabody Picture Vocabulary Test', *Aust. Psych.*, 7, 3, 167.

DeLEMOS, M.M. (1966) The development of the concept of conservation in Australian Aboriginal children. Unpublished PhD thesis, Australian National University, Canberra.

DeLEMOS, M.M. (1968) 'A study of the effects of experience and materials in a series of Piaget conservation tests', *ACER Bull. for Psychology*, 8, 1—4.

DeLEMOS, M.M. (1969)'The development of conservation in aboriginal children', *Int. J. Psych.*, 4, 255—69.

DeLEMOS, M.M. (1969a) 'Conceptual development in Aboriginal children: implications for Aboriginal education'. Cited in DUNN. S.S. and TATZ, C.M. (Eds.), *Aborigines and Education*. Melbourne: Sun Books.

DeLEMOS, M.M. (1970) 'The current debate on race and intelligence: a summary'. Paper presented at ACER Staff seminar, July 10, ACER, Melbourne.

DeLEMOS, M.M. (1972) 'The development of spatial concepts in Zulu children'. In: BERRY, J.W. and DASEN, P.R. *Culture and Cognition: Readings in Cross-Cultural Psychology*. London: Methuen.

DEMPSEY, A.D. (1971) 'Time conservation across cultures', *Int. J. Psych.*, 6, 115—20.

DEREGOWSKI, J.B. (1972) 'Pictorial perception and culture', *Sc. Amer.*, 227 (5), 82—88.

DEREGOWSKI, J.B. and SERPELL, R. (1971) 'Performance on a Sorting Task: A Cross-cultural Experiment', *Int. J. Psych.*, 6, 273—81.

DEVEREUX, E.C., SHOUVAL, R., BRONFENBRENNER, U., RODGERS, R.R., KAV-VENAKI, S., KIELY, E., and KARSON, E. (1974) 'Socialization practices of parents, teachers, and peers in Israel: the Kibbutz vs. the city', *Child Developm.*, 45, 269—81.

DODWELL, P.C. (1960) 'Children's understanding of number and related concepts', *Can. J. Psych.*, 14, 191—205.

DODWELL, P.C. (1961) 'Children's understanding of number concepts: characteristics of an individual and of a group test', *Can. J. Psych.*, 15, (1) 29—36.

DODWELL, P.C. (1962) 'Relations between the understanding of the logic of classes and of cardinal number in children', *Can. J. Psych.*, 16, (II), 152—60.

DOOB, L.W. (1974) 'Eidetic images among the Ibo'. In: BERRY, J.W. and DASEN, P.R. (Eds.), *Culture and Cognition: Readings in Cross-Cultural Psychology*. London: Methuen.

DOWNING, J. (1970) 'Children's concepts of language in learning to read', *Educ. Res.* 12, 106—112.

DOWNING, J. (no date) 'A summary of evidence related to the cognitive clarity theory of reading' for the Bullock Committee.

DUNN, L.M. (1965) *Peabody Picture Vocabulary Test: Manual.* Circle Pines, Minn: American Guidance Service.

DUROJAYE, M. (1972) 'Conservation in six cultures'. Paper presented at the 20th Intern. Congr. of Psych., Tokyo, August.

EDNEY, J. (1974) 'Human territoriality', *Psych. Bull.*, 81, 959—75.

ELKIND, D. (1961) 'Children's discovery of the conservation of mass, weight, and volume: Piaget replication study II' *J. Gen. Psych.*, 98, 219—27.

ETUK, E. (1967) The development of number concepts: an examination of Piaget's theory with Yoruba-speaking Nigerian children. Unpublished DEd dissertation, Columbia University (order No. 67—12, 685).

EVANS, J.L. (1970) *Children in Africa: a review of psychological research.* New York: Teachers College Press.

EVANS, J.L., and SEGALL, H.M. (1969) 'Learning to classify by colour and by function: a study of concept discovery by Ganda children', *J. Soc. Psych.*, 77, 35—53.

EYSENCK, H.J. (1971) *Race, Intelligence and Education.* London: Temple-Smith.

FAIGIN, H. (1958) 'Social behavior of young children in the kibbutz', *J. Abnorm. Soc. Psych.*, 56, 117—29.

FEFFER, M.H. (1959) 'Cognitive aspects of role-taking in children', *J. Person.*, 27, 152—68.

FEFFER, M.H. (1970) 'Developmental analysis of interpersonal behaviour', *Psych. Rev.*, 77, 3, 197—214.

FEFFER, M.H., and GOUREVITCH, V. (1960) 'Cognitive aspects of role-taking in children', *J. Person.*, 28, 383—96.

FELDMAN, C.F. *et al.* (1974) *The Development of Adaptive Intelligence.* NY: Jossey-Bass Inc.

FIRLIK, R.J. (1975) 'Mixed-age grouping and performance on standard conservation tasks', *Diss. Abstr.*, 35, 8, 4751A—5579A, (4858A).

FITZGERALD, L.K. (1970) Cognitive development among Ga children: Environmental correlates of cognitive growth rate within the Ga tribe. Unpublished PhD thesis, University of California, Berkeley.

FJELLMAN, J. (1969) 'Methods of investigating cognitive development of children in rural Kenya: some Kamba results'. Mimeographed: Bureau of Educational Research, University of Nairobi.

FJELLMAN, J.S. (1971) The myth of primitive mentality: A study of semantic acquisition and modes of categorization in Akamba children of South Central Kenya. Unpublished thesis, Stanford

University, Stanford, California.

FLAVELL, J.H. (1963) *The Developmental Psychology of Jean Piaget.* Princeton, N.J.: Van Nostrand.

FLAVELL, J.H. (1968) *The Development of Role-Taking and Communication Skills in Children.* New York: Wiley.

FLAVELL, J.H. (1971) 'Stage-related properties of cognitive development', *Cogn. Psych.*, 2, 421–53.

FLAVELL, J.H., and WOHLWILL, J.F. (1969) 'Formal and functional aspects of cognitive development'. In: ELKIND, D. and FLAVELL, J. *Studies in Cognitive Development.* NY: Oxford University Press.

FOGELMAN, K.R. (1970) *Piagetian Tests for the Primary School.* Windsor: NFER.

FUJINAGA, T., SAIGA, H., and HOSOYA, J. (1962) 'The developmental study of the children's number concept by the method of experimental education', *Jap. J. Ed. Psych.*, 11, 18–26.

FURBY, L. (1971) 'A theoretical analysis of cross-cultural research in cognitive development: Piaget's conservation task', *J. Cross-Cult. Psych.*, 2, 3, 241–55.

FURBY, L. (1974) 'Socialization practices with respect to possession and ownership: A study using the Human Relations Area Files', *Oregon Research Institute Research Bulletin*, 14, 20.

FURBY, L. (1975) 'A proposal for behavioral observational studies of possessiveness in young children', *Oregon Research Institute Research Bulletin*, 15, 9.

FURBY, L. (1976) 'The socialization of possession and ownership among children in three cultural groups: Israeli kibbutz, Israeli city and American', personal communication.

FURBY, L. (1976a) Collective possession and ownership: A developmental, cross-cultural study of its characteristics', *Oregon Research Institute Research Bulletin*, 16, 9.

FURBY, L. (1976b) 'Inequalities in personal possessions: Explanations for and judgments of the unequal distribution of material goods among children and adults in three cultural groups', *Oregon Research Institute Research Bulletin*, 16, 11.

FURBY, L. (1976c) 'Possessions: Their meaning and function throughout the life span'. In: BALTES, P. (Ed.), *Life-span Development and Behaviour.* Vol 1. in press.

FURBY, L. (1976d) 'Possessiveness in human beings: A study of its meaning and motivation', *Oregon Research Institute Research Bulletin*, 16, 14.

FURBY, L. (1976e) 'Sex differences and similarities in personal possessions among children and adults', *Oregon Research Institute Research Bulletin*, 16, 12.

FURBY, L. (1976f) 'Sharing: A developmental, cross-cultural study of decisions and moral judgments about letting others use one's possessions', *Oregon Research Institute Research Bulletin*, 16, 13.

FURBY, L. (1976g) 'The acquisition of personal possessions among children and adults', *Oregon Research Institute Research Bulletin*, 16, 10.

FURBY, L. (1976h) 'The psychological foundations and functions of possession and ownership', *Oregon Research Institute Research Monograph*, 16, 3.

FURBY, L. (1976i) 'The role of personal possessions in one's independence and identity among adolescents', *Oregon Research Institute Research Bulletin*, 16, 15.

FURBY, L., HARTER, S., and JOHN, K. (1975) 'The nature and development of possession and ownership: A cognitive-attitudinal study of 5 to 21 year-olds,' *Oregon Research Institute Research Monograph*, 15, 4.

GALIFRET-GRANJON, N. (1965) 'Batterie Piaget-Head (tests d'orientation gauche-droite)'. In: ZAZZO, R. (Ed.), *Manuel pour l'Examen psychologique de l'Enfant*. Neuchatel et Paris: Delachaux et Niestlé.

GALLAGHER, G. (1971) 'Some findings on the role of language in the acquisition of operational structures: performance on Piagetian conservation tasks by bilingual Greek children', *Victoria Education Department Research Report*, R.R5 / 71.

GARRETT, H.E. (1953) *Statistics in Psychology and Education*. London: Longmans.

GAUDIA, G. (1972) 'Race, social class, and age of achievement of conservation on Piaget's tasks', *Dev. Psych.*, 6, 158–65.

GAY, J., and COLE, M. (1967) *The New Mathematics and Old Culture*. New York: Holt, Rinehart and Winston.

GEBER, M. (1971) 'Gesell tests on African children', *Pediatrics*, Springfield, 20, 1055–1065.

GHUMAN, P.A.S. (1974) A cross-cultural study of the basic thinking processes of English, 'British' Punjabi and Indigenous Punjabi boys. PhD thesis, Birmingham University.

GHUMAN, P.A.S. (1975) *The Cultural Context of Thinking: A Comparative Study of Punjabi and English boys*. Windsor: NFER, pp. 136.

GHUMAN, P.A.S. (1976) 'A cross-cultural study of the basic thinking processes of English, "British" Punjabi and Indigenous Punjabi boys'. Personal Communication.

GLICK, J. (1975) 'Cognitive development in cross-cultural perspective'. In: HOROWITZ, T.D. *et al.* (Eds.), *Review of Child Development Research*. Chicago: University of Chicago Press, pp. 595–654.

GOFFMAN, E. (1972) *Relations in Public*. New York: Harper.

GOLDEN, M., and BIRNS, B. (1968) 'Social class and cognitive development in infancy', *Merr.-Palm. Quart.*, 14, 139—149.

GOLDSCHMID, M.L. (1967) 'Different types of conservation and their relation to age, sex, IQ, MA and vocabulary', *Child Developm.*, 38, 1229—46.

GOLDSCHMID, M.L., and BENTLER, P.M. (1968b) *Manual: Concept Assessment Kit—Conservation*. San Diego, California: Educational and Industrial Testing Service.

GOLDSCHMID, M.L., BENTLER, P., DEBUS, R., KOHNSTAMM, G., MODGIL, S.L. *et al.* (1973) 'A cross-cultural investigation of conservation', *J. Cross-Cult. Psych.*, 4, 1, 49—75.

GOLDSMITH, et. al. (1972) *Blueprint for Survival*. Stacey.

GOODMAN, L.W. and LEVER, J. (1971) 'Children's toys and socialization to sex roles'. Paper presented at the Meeting of the Society for the Study of Social Problems, August.

GOODNOW, J. (1962), 'A test of milieu differences with some of Piaget's tasks', *Psych. Mon.*, 76, No. 36 (whole No. 555).

GOODNOW, J. (1969) 'Problems in research on culture and thought'. In: FLAVELL, J.H. and ELKIND, D. (Eds.), *Studies in Cognitive Development*. London: Oxford University Press.

GOODNOW, J. (1970) 'Cultural variations in cognitive skills'. In: HELLMUTH, J. (Ed.), *Cognitive Studies*, Vol. I. Brunner / Mazel publishers. Also in WILLIAMS, R.D. (Ed.) (1969) *Cross-Cultural Studies*. Penguin Books.

GOODNOW, J., and BETHON, G. (1966) 'Piaget's tasks: the effects of schooling and intelligence', *Child Developm.*, 37, 573—82.

GOW, B.N. (1971) The effect of familiarity on learning and generalization of conservation tasks. Honours thesis, University of Newcastle, New South Wales.

GREENFIELD, P.M. (1966) 'On culture and conservation'. In: BRUNER, J.S., OLVER, R.R. and GREENFIELD, P.M. (Eds.), *Studies in Cognitive Growth*. New York: Wiley, pp. 225—256.

GREENFIELD, P.M. (1974) 'Comparing dimensional categorization in natural and artificial contexts: a developmental study among the Zinacantecos of Mexico', *J. Soc. Psych.*, 93, 157—171.

GREENFIELD, P.M. (1976) 'Cross-cultural research and Piagetian theory: paradox and progress'. In: RIEGEL, K., and MEACHAM, J. (Eds.), *The Developing Individual in a Changing World*. The Hague: Mouton.

GREENFIELD, P.M. and BRUNER, J. (1966) 'Culture and cognitive growth', *Intern. J. Psych.*, 1, 89—107.

GREENFIELD, P.M., and BRUNER, J.S. (1971) 'Learning and language', *Psychol. Today*, 5, 40.

GREENFIELD, P.M., REICH, C., and OLVER, R.R. (1966) 'On culture and equivalence'. In: BRUNER, J., and OLVER, R.R., and GREENFIELD, P.M. (Eds.), *Studies in Cognitive Growth*. New York: Wiley.

GUMPERZ, J.J., and EDWARD, H. (1972) 'Bilingualism, bidialectalism and classroom interaction'. In: CAZDEN, C. (Ed.), *Language in the Classroom*. New York: Teachers Press.

GUYLER, K.R. (1969) The effects of some Task and Subject Variables on the Accuracy and Process of Seriation of Length: A Comparison between Infant and Junior Children Based on the Original Work of Jean Piaget. Unpublished MA (Education) Thesis, University of London.

HAERTEL, G.D. (1976) 'A construct validation of Jensen's Level I and Level II Intelligence using a sample of fifth grade children', *Diss. Abstr.* 36, 9, 5603A—6342A, (p. 5945A).

HAMZA, A.Y. (1976) 'Piaget's concept of conservation: a comparative study of Libyan and American children's conservation status', *Diss. Abstr.*, 36, 7, 3135B—3685B (p. 3301—B).

HARTLEY, R.E. (1960) 'Children's concepts of male and female roles'. *Merr.-Palm Quart.*, 6, 83—91.

HAYNES, J.M. (1971) *Educational Assessment of Immigrant Pupils*. Windsor: NFER.

HEBRON, M.E. (1954) *The Kingston Test of Silent Reading*. London: Harrap.

HENDRIKZ, E. (1966) A cross-cultural investigation of the number concepts and level of number development in five-year-old Urban Shona and European children in Southern Rhodesia. Unpublished MA (Psychology) Thesis, University of London.

HERON, A. (1971) 'Concrete operations, "g" and achievement in Zambian children', *J. Cross-Cult. Psych.*, 2, 325—36.

HERON, A. (1974) 'Cultural determinants of concrete operational behaviour'. In: DAWSON, J.L.M. and LONNER, W.J. (Eds.), *Readings in Cross-Cultural Psychology*. Hong Kong University Press, pp. 94—101.

HERON, A. and DOWEL, W. (1973) 'Weight conservation and matrix-solving ability in Papuan children', *J. Cross.-Cult. Psych.*, 4, 207—19.

HERON, A. and DOWEL, W. (1974) 'The questionable unity of the concrete operations stage', *Int. J. Psych.*, 9, 1, 1—9.

HERON, A. and KROEGER, E. (1974) 'The effects of training on uneven concrete operational development in Yugoslav migrant children', Selected Proceedings, 2nd International Congress of Cross-Cultural Psychology. Now published as 'A preliminary study of the effects of training on uneven concrete operational development in Yugoslav migrant children. In: BERRY, J.W. and LONNER W.J. (Eds.), *Applied Cross-Cultural Psychology*. Amsterdam: Swets and Zeitlinger, 1975.

HERON, A. and SIMONSSON, M. (1969) 'Weight conservation in Zambian children', *Int. J. Psych.*, 4, 281–92.

HOIJER, H. (1954) 'The Sapir-Whorf hypothesis'. In: HOIJER, H. (Ed.), *Language in Culture*. Chicago: University of Chicago Press.

HOLTZMAN, W.H. (1968) 'Cross-cultural studies in psychology', *Int. J. Psych.*, 3, 83–91.

HUDSON, W. (1960) 'Pictorial depth perception in sub-cultural groups in Africa', *J. Soc. Psych.*, 52, 183–208.

HUDSON, W. (1962) 'Pictorial perception and educational adaptation in Africa', *Psych. Afric.*, 9, 226–239.

HUNTSMAN, R.W. (1974) 'Some aspects of children's ability to form equivalence categories', *Papua and New Guinea J. Ed.*, 9, 1.

HYDE, D.M. (1959) An investigation of Piaget's theories of the development of the concept of number. Unpublished doctoral thesis, University of London.

INGLE, R.B., and SHAYER, M. (1971) 'Conceptual demands in Nuffield O-Level chemistry', *Educ. Chem.*, 8, 182–83.

INHELDER, B. (1971) 'Developmental theory and diagnostic procedures'. In: GREEN *et al.* (Eds.), *Measurement and Piaget*. N.Y. McGraw Hill.

INHELDER, B. and PIAGET, J. (1958) *The Growth of Logical Thinking from Childhood to Adolescence*. New York: Basic Books.

INHELDER, B. and PIAGET, J. (1964) *The Early Growth of Logic in the Child*. London: Routledge and Kegan Paul.

IRWIN, H.M. and McLAUGHLIN, D.H. (1970) 'Ability and preference in category sorting by Mano school children and adults', *J. Soc. Psych.*, 82, 15–24.

JACOBOVITS, L.A. (1970) 'Motivation in foreign language learning'. In: TURSI, J.A. (Ed.) *Foreign Languages and the "New" Student*, pp.31–104.

JAHODA, G. (1970) 'A cross-cultural perspective in psychology', *The Advancement of Sc.*, 27, 1, 14.

JAHODA, G. (1971) 'Retinal pigmentation, illusion susceptibility and space perception', *Int. J. Psych.*, 6, 99–208.

JAHODA, G., DEREGOWSKI, J.B., and SINHA, D. (1974) 'Topological and Euclidean spatial features noted by children: a cross-cultural study', *Int. J. Psych.*, 9, 3, 159–72.

JENSEN, A.R. (1968) 'Patterns of mental ability and socio-economic status', *Proc. Nat. Acad. Sc.*, 60, 1330–1337.

JENSEN, A.R. (1970) 'Level I and Level II performance in low and middle class SES elementary school children'. In: JENSEN, A.R. and

ROWHER, W.D. (Eds.) *An Experimental Analysis of Learning Abilities in Culturally Disadvantaged Children.* Final Report # 2404, Office of Economic Opportunity.

JENSEN, A.R. (1971) 'Do schools cheat minority children?', *Ed. Res.*, 14, 1, 3—28.

JENSEN, A.R. (1972) *Genetics and Education.* London: Methuen.

JENSEN, A.R. (1973) 'Level I and Level II abilities in three ethnic groups', *Am. Ed. Res. J.*, 10, 263—276.

JENSEN, A.R. (1973a) *Educability and Group Differences.* London: Methuen and Company Limited.

JENSEN, A.R. (1974) 'Interaction of Level I and Level II abilities with race and socioeconomic status', *J. Ed. Psych.*, 66, 99—111.

KAGAN, J. and MOSS, H.A. (1962) *Birth to Maturity.* New York: Wiley.

KAMARA, A.A. (1971) Cognitive development among school age Themne children of Sierra Leone. Unpublished PhD thesis, University of Illinois, Urbana-Champaign.

KAMARA, A., and EASLEY, J.A. (jnr) (1973) 'Is the rate of cognitive development uniform across cultures? — A methodological Critique with new evidence from Themne children'. In: MAEHR, M.S. and STALLINGS, W.M. (Eds.), *Culture, Child and School.* Brooks / Cole Pub.

KAMARA, A., and EASLEY, J.A. (1976) Cited in DASEN, P.R. (Ed.) *Piagetian Psychology: Cross-Cultural Contributions.* To be published by Gardner Press, NY.

KEATS, D.M., and KEATS, J.A. (1974) 'The effect of language on concept acquisition in bilingual children', *J. Cross-Cult. Psych.*, 5, 1, 80—99.

KEATS, D.M., KEATS, J.A. and RAFAEI, W. (1976) 'Concept acquisition in Malaysian Bilingual children *J. Cross-Cult. Psych.*, 7, 1, 87—99.

KELLAGHAN, T.P. (1965) The study of cognition in a non-Western society with special reference to the Yoruba of South Nigeria. Unpublished PhD thesis, Belfast University.

KELLAGHAN, T.P. (1968) 'Abstraction and categorisation in African children', *Int. J. Psych.*, 3, 115—50.

KELLY, M.R. (1970) 'Some findings in the area of language and cognition'. Paper presented to the Australian Association for Research in Education Founding Conference, Sydney, New South Wales, November.

KELLY, M. (1976) Cited in DASEN, P.R. (Ed.), *Piagetian Psychology: Cross-Cultural Contributions.* To be published by Gardner Press, NY.

KELLY, M. and PHILP, H. (1975) 'Vernacular test instructions in relation to cognitive task behaviour among highland children of

Papua New Guinea', *Brit. J. Ed. Psych.*, 45, 189—97.

KELLY, M., TENEZAKIS, M., and HUNTSMAN, R. (1973) 'Some unusual conservation behaviour in children exposed to two cultures', *Brit. J. Ed. Psych.*, 43, 181—2.

KERLINGER, F.N. (1969) *Foundation of Behavioural Research.* London: Holt Rinehart and Winston.

KESSLER, C. (1971) *The Acquisition of Syntax in Bilingual Children.* Washington, D.C.: George University Press.

KILGORE, W.J. and SULLIVAN, B. (1975) 'Academic values and the Jensen — Shockley controversy.' *J. Gen. Ed.*, 27, 3, 177—87.

KIMINYO, D.M. (1973) A cross-cultural study of the development of conservation of mass, weight, and volume in Kenyan children. Unpublished PhD thesis, University of Alberta.

KIMINYO, D.M. (1976) Cited in: DASEN, P.R. (Ed.), *Piagetian Psychology: Cross Cultural Contributions.* To be published by Gardner Press, New York.

KIRK, L. (1975) 'Estimating the ages of children in nonliterate populations: a field method', *J. Cross-Cult. Psych.*, 6, 2, 238—49.

KLIPPEL, M.D. (1976) 'A cross-ethnic study of language and cognitive ability', Personal communication. First phase of this research to be presented as a paper at the 47th ANZAAS Congress at Hobart, Australia, May.

KOHLBERG, L. (1968) 'Early education: a cognitive-developmental view', *Child Developm.*, 39, 1013—62.

KOHLBERG, L. (1969) 'Stage and sequence: cognitive-developmental approach to socialization.' In: GOSLIN, D.A. (Ed.), *Handbook of Socialization Theory and Research.* Rand McNally.

KOHLBERG, L. (1971) 'From is to ought. How to commit the naturalistic fallacy and get away with it in the study of moral development'. In: MISCHEL, T. (Ed.), *Cognitive Development and Epistemology.* New York: Academic Press.

LABOV, W. (1970) 'The logic of nonstandard English'. In: WILLIAMS, F. (Ed.), *Language and Poverty.* Chicago: Markham.

LAMBERT, W.E. and MACNAMARA, J. (1969) 'Some cognitive consequences of following a first grade curriculum in a second language', *J. Ed. Psych.*, 60, 86—96.

LANGER, J. (1969) 'Disequilibrium as a source of development'. In: MUSSEN, P., LANGER, J. and COVINGTON, M. (Eds.), *Trends and Issues in Developmental Psychology.* New York: Holt, Rinehart and Winston.

LANNOY, R. (1971) *The Speaking Tree.* London: Oxford Univ. Press.

LAURENDEAU-BENDAVID (1976) Cited in DASEN, P.R. (Ed.) *Piagetian Psychology: Cross-Cultural Contributions.* To be published by Gardner Press, New York.

LAURENDEAU, M. and PINARD, A. (1962) *Causal Thinking in the Child*. New York: International Universities Press.

LAURENDEAU, M., and PINARD, A. (1970) *The Development of the Concept of Space in the Child*. New York: International Universities.

LAWLESS, S.R. (1974) Levels of reasoning in mapwork shown by school children in Malawi. MPhil thesis, Nottingham University, also personal communication.

LEHMAN, H.C. and WITTY, P.A. (1927) 'The present status of the tendency to hoard', *Psych. Rev.*, 34, 48–56.

LESTER, B.M. and KLEIN, R.E. (1973) 'The effect of stimulus familiarity on the conservation performance of rural Guatemalan children', *J. Soc. Psych.*, 90, 197–205.

LeVINE, R.A. (1970) 'Cross-cultural study in child psychology'. In: MUSSEN, P.H. (Ed.), *Carmichael's Manual of Child Psychology*. New York: John Wiley.

LEZINE, I., STAMBAK, M. and CASATI, I. (1969) *Les etapes de l'intelligence sensori-motrice*. Monographie Number I. Paris: Centre de psychologie appliquée.

LLOYD, B.B. (1971) 'Studies of conservation with Yoruba children of differing ages and experiences', *Child Developm.*, 42, 415–28.

LLOYD, B.B. (1971a) 'The intellectual development of Yoruba children: a re-examination', *J. Cross-Cult. Psychol.*, 2, 29–38.

LLOYD, F. and PIDGEON, D.A. (1961) 'An investigation into the effects of coaching on non-verbal test material with European, Indian and African children', *Brit. J. Ed. Psych.*, 31, 145–151.

LOVELL, K. (1965) *The Growth of Basic Mathematical and Scientific Concepts in Children*. University of London Press.

LOVELL, K. and DIXON, E.M. (1965) 'The growth of grammar in imitation, comprehension, and production', *J. Child Psych. Psychiatr.*, 5, 1–9.

LOVELL, K. and OGILVIE, E. (1961) 'The growth of the concept of volume in junior school children', *J. Child Psych. Psychiatr.*, 2, 118–26.

LOVELL, K. and SLATER, A. (1960) 'The growth of the concept of time: a comparative study', *J. Child Psych. Psychiatr.*, 1, 179–90.

LOVELL, K., HEALEY, D., and ROWLAND, A.D. (1962) 'The growth of some geometrical concepts', *Child Developm.*, 33, 4, 751–767.

LUNZER, E.A. (1960) *Recent Studies in Britain Based on the Work of Jean Piaget*. Slough: NFER. (New Edition, 1973).

LUNZER, E.A. (1970) 'Children's thinking', In: BUTCHER, H.J. and PONT, H.B. (Eds.) *Educational Research in Britain*. Vol I. University of London Press, pp.69–100.

LURIA, A.R. (1961) *The Role of Speech in the Regulation of Normal and Abnormal Behaviour*. London: Pergamon Press.

MacARTHUR, R. (1973) 'Some ability patterns: central Eskimos and Nsenga Africans', *Int. J. Psychol.*, 8, 239—47.

MACCOBY, M. and MODIANO, N. (1966) 'On culture and equivalence, I'. In: BRUNER, J., OLVER, R.R., and GREENFIELD, P.M. (Eds.), *Studies in Cognitive Growth*. New York: Wiley.

MACCOBY, M. and MODIANO, N. (1969) 'Cognitive styles in rural and urban Mexico', *Human Developm.*, 12, 1, 22—33.

MacNAMARA, J. (Ed.) (1966) *Bilingualism in Primary Education*. Edinburgh: Edinburgh University Press.

MAHAR, J.S. and UDAI, J. (1969) 'Development of conservation in rural and urban school children: an experimental study', *Int. Psych Rev.*, 6, 45—49.

MAISTRIAUX, R. (1955) 'La sous-évolution des noirs d'Afrique: Sa nature, ses causes, ses remèdes', *Rev. de la Psych. des Peuples*, 10, 397—456.

MARON, S. (1971) 'Equality'. In: *Kibbutz: A new society*. Tel Aviv: Ichud Habonim.

McFIE, J. (1961) 'The effect of education on African performance in a group of intellectual tests', *Brit. J. Ed. Psych.*, 31, 232—240.

MERMELSTEIN, E. and SHULMAN, L.S. (1967) 'Lack of formal schooling and the acquisition of conservation', *Child Developm.*, 38, 39—51.

MILLER, S.A. (1973) 'Contradiction, surprise, and cognitive change: the effects of disconfirmation of belief on conservers and nonconservers', *J. Exp. Child Psych.*, 15, 47—62.

MMARI, G.R.V. (1974) 'Tanzania's experience in and efforts to resolve the problems of teaching mathematics through a Foreign Language', UNESCO, ED—74 / CONF. 808.

MODGIL, S.L. (1965a) An investigation into the development of the concept of substance in a group of children aged ten. Part I. Unpublished thesis, Newcastle University.

MODGIL, S.L. (1965b) An investigation into the development of the concept of weight in a group of children aged ten. Part II, unpublished thesis, Newcastle University.

MODGIL, S.L. (1965c) An investigation into the development of the concept of volume in a group of children aged ten. Part III, unpublished thesis, Newcastle University.

MODGIL, S.L. (1974) *Piagetian Research: A Handbook of Recent Studies*. Windsor: NFER.

MOHSENI, N. (1966) La comparison des réactions aux epreuves d'intelligence en Iran et en Europe. Unpublished thesis, University of Paris.

MONTANGERO, J. (1974) Le double aspect "logique" et "physique" de la notion de durée. Thése de doctorat, Univ. de Genève

(Neuchâtel: Delachaux et Niestlé, sous presse).

MWANGANGI, R.J.W. (1975) 'The cognitive development of Kenya African children as shown by their performance on selected Piagetian tasks of conservation'. *Diss. Abstr.*, 35, 8, pp. 4757A to 5579A, (p. 5001A).

NEUBAUER, P.B. (1965) *Children in Collectives: Child-rearing aims and practices of the Kibbutz.* Springfield Ill.: Charles C. Thomas.

NORO, S. (1961) 'Development of the child's conception of number', *Jap. J. Ed. Psych.*, 9, 230—9, (*Child Developm., Abstr.* 38, 115).

NURCOMBE, B. (1970) 'Precausal and paracausal thinking: concepts of causality in Aboriginal children', *Aust.—New Zealand J. Psychiatr.*, 4, 70—81.

NYITI, R.M. (1973) Intellectual development in the Meru children of Tanzania. Unpublished PhD thesis, University of Illinois, Urbana-Champaign.

OHUCHE, R.O. (1971) 'Piaget and the Mende of Sierra Leone', *J. Exp. Educ.*, 39, 75—78.

OHUCHE, R.O. (1972) 'The uses of real numbers in traditional Sierra Leone'. Mimeographed, Library, Njala University College.

OHUCHE, R.O. (1973) 'Geometry, estimation and measurement in traditional Sierra Leone', Report of research in Commonwealth Countries, London: Education Division, Commonwealth Secretariat.

OHUCHE, R.O., and PEARSON, R.E. (1974) 'Piaget and Africa: a survey of research involving conservation and classification in Africa', Paper presented at the Seminar entitled, 'The development of Science and Mathematics concepts in young children in African countries', University of Nairobi, 17th to 27th Sept., organized by UNESCO and UNICEF. Also personal communication.

OKONJI, M.O. (1970) 'The effect of spatial training on the classificatory behaviour of some Nigerian Ibo children', *Brit. J. Ed. Psych.*, 40, 1, 21—6.

OKONJI, M.O. (1971a) 'Culture and children's understanding of geometry', *Brit. J. Psych.*, 6, 121—28.

OKONJI, M.O. (1971b) 'A cross-cultural study of the effects of familiarity on classificatory behaviour', *J. Cross-Cult. Psych.*, 2, 39—49.

OKONJI, M.O. (1972) Cultural variables in cognition. PhD thesis, jointly with Makerere University and Strathclyde University.

OKONJI, M.O. (1974) 'The development of logical thinking in preschool Zambian children: classification', *J. Gen. Psych.*, 125, 247—255.

OLVER, R.R. and HORNSBY, J.R. (1966) 'On equivalence'. In: BRUNER, J., OLVER, R.R. and GREENFIELD, P.M. (Eds.), *Studies in Cognitive Growth.* New York: Wiley.

OMARI, I.M. (1972) The development of Piagetian spatial concepts among Pare African children in Tanzania. PhD thesis, Columbia University.

OMARI, I.M. (1975) 'Developmental order of spatial concepts among school-children in Tanzania', *J. Cross-Cult. Psych.*, 6, 4, 444—56.

OMARI, I.M. (1976) 'Cognitive egocentrism: age and environmental variables in spatial decentration among Tanzanian children'. Paper presented at Second Panafrican Conference on Psychology, Nairobi, January 5th.

OMARI, I.M. and COOK, H. (1972) 'Differential cognitive cues in pictorial depth perception', *J. Cross-Cult. Psych.*, 3, 321—25.

OMARI, I.M. and MacGINITIE, W.H. (1974) 'Some pictorial artifacts in studies of African children's pictorial depth perception', *Child Developm.*, 45, 535—39.

OMOTOSO, H.M. (1975) 'Conservation, seriation and classification as factors in the acquisition of mathematics in Nigerian children', *Diss. Abstr.*, 36, 3, 1133A—1868A (p. 1398—A).

OPPER, S. (1976) Cited in Dasen, P.R. (Ed.) *Piagetian Psychology: Cross-Cultural Contributions*. To be published by Gardner Press, N.Y.

OTAALA, B. (1971c) 'A preliminary investigation of the conservation abilities of schooled Iteso adults', *Uganda J.*, 35(1) 63—7.

OTAALA, B. (1971d) 'The classification ability of unschooled rural Iteso adults', *Uganda J.*, 35(2) 189—94.

OTAALA, B. (1972) *Conservation Abilities of Primary School Children in Five Ethnic Areas of Uganda*. Kampala: Makerere University, Faculty of Education.

OTAALA, B. (1973) *The Development of Operational Thinking in Primary School Children*. New York: Teacher's College Press.

OVERTON, W.F., WAGNER, J., and DOLINSKY, H. (1971) 'Social class differences and task variables in the development of multiplicative classification', *Child Developm.*, 42, 1951—58.

OWOC, P.J. (1973) 'On culture and conservation once again', *Int. J. Psych.*, 8, 4, 249—54.

PAGE, H.W. (1971) 'Locating a point in a two-dimensional space: an experiment with Zulu youths', *J. Behav. Sci.*, 1, 3, 131—35.

PAGE, H.W. (1973) 'Concepts of length and distance in a study of Zulu youths', *J. Sc 1. Psych.*, 90, 9—16.

PAINE, M.J. (1976) 'Cognitive ability and the initial EFL reader' International Association of Teachers of English as a Foreign Language, *Newsletter*, No. 41, January.

PASTALAN, L. (1970) 'Privacy as an expression of human territoriality'. In: PASTALAN, L.A. and CARSON, D.H. (Eds.), *Spatial Behavior of Older People*. Ann Arbor, Mich.: University of

Michigan Press.

PEARSON, R.E. and OHUCHE, R.O. (1974) 'Piaget and Africa: a survey of research involving conservation and classification in Africa'. Paper presented at the Seminar entitled, 'The Development of Science and Mathematics Concepts in Young Children in African Countries', University of Nairobi, 17th to 27th Sept., organized by UNESCO and UNICEF. Also personal communication.

PEEL, E.A. (1972) (Ed.) 'The quality of thinking in secondary school subjects', *Ed. Rev.*, 24, 3, Birmingham University School of Education.

PEEL, E.A. and LAMBERT, W.E. (1962) 'The relation of bilingualism to intelligence', *Psych. Mon.*, 76, 1—23.

PELUFFO, N. (1962) 'Les notions de conservation et de causalité chez les enfants prévenant de differentes milieux physiques et socio-culturels', *Archives de Psychologie*, 38, 75—90.

PELUFFO, N. (1964) 'N.la nozione de conservazione del volume e le operazione de combinazione come indici di suiluppe del pensiero operatorio in suggetti appartnenti and ambieuti fisici e socioculturati diversi', *Riviste de Psicol Sociale*, 11, 99—132.

PELUFFO, N. (1965) 'Problemi cognitivi strategie, piant di soluzione', *Riviste de Psicol Sociale*, 12, 91—103.

PELUFFO, N. (1967) 'Culture and cognitive problems', *Int. J. Psych.*, 2, 187—98.

PHILLIPS, J.L. (Jr.) (1969) *The Origins of Intellect: Piaget's Theory*. San Francisco: Freeman.

PHILP, H. and KELLY, M. (1974) 'Product and process in cognitive development: some comparative data on the performance of school age children in different cultures', *Brit. J. Ed. Psych.*, 44, 3, 248—65.

PIAGET, J. (1928) *Judgment and Reasoning in the Child*. London: Routledge and Kegan Paul.

PIAGET, J. (1932) *The Moral Judgment of the Child*. London: Kegan Paul, Trench, Trubner & Co.

PIAGET, J. (1952b) *The Child's Conception of Number*. London: Routledge and Kegan Paul.

PIAGET, J. (1954) *The Construction of Reality in the Child*. New York: Basic Books.

PIAGET, J. (1955) *The Language and Thought of the Child*. New York: The World Publishing Company. (1926 French Edition).

PIAGET, J. (1956) *Logic and Psychology*. Manchester University Press.

PIAGET, J. (1966) 'Nécessité et signification des recherches comparatives en psychologie génétique', *Int. J. Psychol.*, 1, 3—13.

PIAGET, J. (1967) *Biologie et Connaissance*. Paris: Gallimard.

PIAGET, J. (1970) *The Child's Conception of Time*. New York: Basic Books.

PIAGET, J. (1971) *Biology and Knowledge*. Chicago: University of Chicago Press.

PIAGET, J. (1972) 'Intellectual evolution from adolescence to adulthood', *Human Developm.*, 15, 1–12.

PIAGET, J. (1974) 'Need and significance of cross-cultural studies in genetic psychology'. In: BERRY, J.W., and DASEN, P.R. (Eds.), *Culture and Cognition*. London: Methuen, pp. 299–310.

PIAGET, J. and INHELDER, B. (1941) *Le Developpement des Quantités Chez l'Enfant*. Neuchatel, France: Delachaux et Niestlé.

PIAGET, J. and INHELDER, B. (1956) *The Child's Conception of Space*. London: Routledge and Kegan Paul.

PIAGET, J. and INHELDER, B. (1969) *The Psychology of the Child*. New York: Basic Books.

PIAGET, J., INHELDER, B., and SZEMINSKA, A. (1960) *The Child's Conception of Geometry*. New York: Basic Books.

PILLER, M. (1971) 'Recherche de psychologie sur une population d'adultes analphabétes de la Côte d'Ivorie'. Unpublished Report, Geneva University.

PINARD, A., MORIN, C., and LEFEBVRE, M. (1973) 'Apprentissage de la conservation des quantités liquides chez des enfants Rwandais et Canadiens – Francais', *Int. J. Psych.*, 8, 15–23.

PONZO, E. (1966) 'Acculturazione e detribalizzazione', *Rivista de Psicologia Sociale*, 13, 41–107.

POOLE, H.E. (1968) 'The effect of urbanisation upon scientific concept attainment among the Hausa children of Northern Nigeria', *Brit. J. Ed. Psych.*, 38, 57–63.

PRATOOMRAJ, S., and JOHNSON, R.C. (1966) 'Kinds of questions and types of conservation tasks as related to children's conservation responses', *Child Developm.*, 37, 343–53.

PREISWERK, R. (1976) 'Jean Piaget et l'étude des relations interculturelles'. Manuscript.

PRICE-WILLIAMS, D.R. (1961) 'A study concerning concepts of conservation of quantity among primitive children', *Acta Psychologia*, 18, 297–305.

PRICE-WILLIAMS, D.R. (1962) 'Abstract and concrete modes of classification in a primitive society', *Brit. J. Ed. Psych.*, 32, 50–61.

PRICE-WILLIAMS, D.R. (Ed.) (1969) *Cross-cultural Studies*. Harmondsworth: Penguin Books Ltd.

PRICE-WILLIAMS, D.R. (1975) *Exploration in Cross-Cultural Psychology*. San Francisco: Chandler and Sharp.

PRICE-WILLIAMS, D.R., and GORDON, W. (1968) 'Manipulation and conservation: a study of children from pottery-making families in Mexico', unpublished paper.

PRICE-WILLIAMS, D.R., GORDON, W., and RAMIREZ, M. (1969)

'Skill and conservation: a study of pottery-making children', *Dev. Psych.*, 1, 6, 769. Also published in BERRY, J.W. and DASEN, P.R. (Eds.) (1974) *Culture and Cognition*. London: Methuen.

PRINCE, J.R. (1968) 'The effect of western education on science conceptualization in New Guinea', *Brit. J. Ed. Psych.*, 33, 64—74.

PRINCE, J.R. (1969) *Science Concepts in a Pacific Culture*. Sydney: Angus and Robertson.

PRINCE, J.R. (1969) 'Views on physical causality in New Guinea students'. Paper presented at 41st ANZAAS Congress, Adelaide, August.

PROSKURA, (1971) 'Teaching and formation of serial orders by preschool children'. (Symp. 32. 184. 186). In: AL-HAMDANI, M. *Psychological Studies from Socialist Countries*. Baghdad, Ministry of Information, pp. 124—127.

RAPAPORT, D. (1958) 'The study of kibbutz education and its bearing on the theory of development', *Am. J. Orthopsychiatr.*, 28, 587—97.

RAVEN, J.C. (1963) *Guide to Using Coloured Progressive Matrices*. London: H. K. Lewis and Company.

REICH, C., and PURBHOO, M. (1975) 'The effect of cross-cultural contact', *Canad J. Behav. Sci.*, 7, 4, 313—327.

REID, J. (1970) 'Reliability assessment of observation data. A possible methodological problem', *Child Developm.*, 41, 1143—50.

RHEINGOLD, H.V. and COOK, K.L. (1975) 'The contents of boys and girls rooms as an index of parents' behaviour', *Child Developm.*, 46, 459—63.

ROBINS, R.H. (1964) *General Linguistics: an introductory survey*. London: Longmans.

ROLL, S. (1970) 'Conservation of number: A comparison between cultures and subcultures', *Revta. Interam. Psicol.*, 4 (1), 13—18.

ROSE, S., HAMBLEY, J., and HAYWOOD, J. (1973) 'Science, Racism and Ideology', *The Socialist Reg.*, 235—260.

ROSS, B.M. (1966) 'Probability concepts in deaf and hearing children', *Child Developm.*, 37, 917—927.

SAFAR, S. (1974) The development of some mathematical concepts among Iraqi children. Unpublished M.A. thesis, Baghdad University.

SCHORR, N. (1975) 'A study of the relationship between school experience, socio-economic status, and conservation attainment in first grade boys and girls', *Diss. Abstr.*, 36, 4, 1869A — 2458A (p. 2111A).

SCHWARTZ, R.D. (1958) 'Some problems of research in Israeli settlements', *Am. J. Orthopsychiatr.*, 28, 572—76.

SCRIBNER, S. (1976) 'Modes of thinking and ways of speaking: culture and logic reconsidered'. Manuscript.

SCRIBNER, S., and COLE, M. (1973) 'Cognitive consequences of formal and informal education', *Sc.*, 182, 553—59.

SEAL, H.L. (1964) *Multivariate Statistical Analysis for Biologists.* London: Methuen.

SECHREST, L., FAY, T.L. and ZAIDI, S.M.H. (1972) 'Problems of translation in cross-cultural research', *J. Cross-Cult. Psych.*, 3, 41—56.

SEEGMILLER, B.R. (1972) 'Conservation of quantity: a cross-cultural investigation. Unpublished PhD thesis, New York University.

SERPELL, R. (1969a) 'Cultural differences in attentional preference for colour over form', *Int. J. Psychol.*, 4, 1—8.

SERPELL, R. (1969b) 'The influence of language, education and culture on attentional preference between colour and form', *Int. J. Psychol.*, 4, 183—194.

SERPELL, R. (1976) *Culture's Influence on Behaviour.* London: Methuen.

SHAYER, M. (1972) 'Conceptual demands in the Nuffield O-Level physics course', *Sch. Sci. Rev.* 54, 26—34.

SHEPPARD, J.L. (1971) 'The acquisition of class-inclusion using the elements of a grouping'. Paper presented to Australian Conference on Cognitive Development, Canberra.

SIEGEL, A.W., and KRESH, E. (1971) 'Children's ability to operate within a matrix: a developmental study', *Dev. Psych.*, 4. 2, 232—9.

SIGEL, I.E. (1970) 'The distancing hypothesis: a causal hypothesis for the acquisition of representational thought'. In: JONES, M.R. (Ed.), *Effects of Early Experience.* Coral Gables, Florida: University of Miami Press.

SIGEL, I.E., and HOOPER, F.H. (Eds.) (1969) *Logical Thinking in Children.* New York: Holt, Rinehart and Winston.

SIGEL, I.E., and MERMELSTEIN, E. (1965) 'Effects of nonschooling on Piagetian tasks of conservation'. Paper presented at the meeting of the American Psychological Association, Chicago, September.

SIMPSON, E.L. (1974) 'Moral development research: a case study of scientific cultural bias', *Human Developm.*, 17, 81—106.

SINCLAIR-DE-ZWART, H. (1967) *Acquisition du Langage et Développement de la Pensée.* Paris: Dunod.

SINCLAIR-DE-ZWART, H. (1969) 'Developmental psycholinguistics'. In: ELKIND, D. and FLAVELL, J. (Eds.), *Studies in Cognitive Development: Essays in Honour of Jean Piaget.* New York: Oxford University Press.

SMART, M.E., DAHL, R., and WETZSTEIN, C.J. (1975) 'The use of Piagetian derived categories to analyse children's social language during selected preschool experiences'. Paper presented at the fifth annual symposium of the Jean Piaget Society, Philadelphia. Also personal communication.

SMART, M.E., THEIMER, W.E., and DAHL, R.J. (1974) 'The use of Piaget's categories to analyse the language of Black and Mexican American preschool children'. Paper read at the fifth Annual UAP Conference on Piagetian Theory and the Helping Professions. Los Angeles, California: Univ. of Southern California, January 29th.

SPIRO, M.E. (1955) 'Education in a communal village in Israel' *Am. J. Orthopsychiatr.*, 25, 283–92.

SPIRO, M.E. (1965) *Children of the Kibbutz*. Cambridge, Mass: Harvard Univ. Press.

STEINER, G. (1974) 'On the psychological reality of cognitive structures: a tentative synthesis of Piaget's and Bruner's theories', *Child Developm.*, 45, 891–99.

STOLTMAN, J.P. (1972) 'Children's conception of territory: a study of Piaget's spatial stages', *Diss. Abstr.*, Order No. 72–11047, Xerox University Microfilms.

STOTT, D.H. (1960) 'Interaction of heredity and environment in regard to measured intelligence'. In: BUTCHER, J.H. and LOMAX, E.B. (Eds.), *Readings in Human Intelligence*. London: Methuen.

STRODTBECK, F.L. (1964) 'Considerations of meta-method in cross-cultural studies', *Am. Anthrop*, Special Publication, 66, 223–29.

SWINGLE, P.G. (1969) 'Ethnic factors in interpersonal bargaining', *Can. J. Psych.*, 23, 136–146.

SWIZE, M.T. (1972) 'Prediction of Piagetian conservation for second grade Mexican-American and Anglo-American children', *Diss. Abstr.*, Order No. 72–13331, (5624A), Xerox University Microfilms.

SZEMINSKA, A. (1965) 'The evolution of thought: some applications of research findings to educational practice', *Monogr. Soc. Res. Child Developm.*, 30(2), 47–57.

TAIWO, C.O. (1968) 'Primary school mathematics in African Societies'. Commonwealth Conference on Mathematics in Schools. London: Commonwealth Secretariat.

TALMON, Y. (1972) 'Secular asceticism: patterns of ideological change'. In: TALMON, Y. (Ed.) *Family and Community in the Kibbutz*. Cambridge, Mass: Harvard University Press.

TAYLOR, J.A., and WALES, R.J. (1970) 'A developmental study of form discrimination in pre-school children', *Quart. J. Exp. Psych.*, 22, 720–34.

TAYLOR, L.J., and DeLACEY, P.R. (1974) 'Three dimensions of intellectual functioning in Australian Aboriginal and disadvantaged European children', *J. Cross-Cult. Psych.*, 5, 1, 49–58.

TAYLOR, L.J., NURCOMBE, B. and DeLACEY, P.R. (1973) 'Research note: classification in Aboriginal children: a re-evaluation', *Aust. Psych.*, 8, 246–49.

TENEZAKIS, M.D. (1975) 'Linguistic subsystems and concrete operations', *Child Developm.*, 46, 430–36.

TERMAN, L. (1916) *The Measurement of Intelligence* Boston: Houghton Mifflin.

TRIANDIS, H.C. (1974) 'Psychologists on culture and thought', *Revs. Anthrop.*, 1, 484–92.

TUDDENHAM, R.D. (1969) 'A Piagetian test of cognitive development'. Paper presented at the Symposium on Intelligence, Ontario, Toronto, May. Published in The Toronto Symposium 1969 on Intelligence, W.B. Dockrell, (Ed.), 1970.

UZGIRIS, I.C. (1964) 'Situational generality of conservation', *Child Developm.*, 35, 831–841.

VERNON, P.E. (1965a) 'Ability factors and environmental influences', *Am. Psych.*, 20, 723–33.

VERNON, P.E. (1965b) 'Environmental handicaps and intellectual development', *Brit. J. Ed. Psych.*, 35, 1–12.

VERNON, P.E. (1966) 'Educational and intellectual development among Canadian Indians and Eskimos', *Ed. Rev.*, 18, 79–91 and 186–95.

VERNON, P.E. (1967) 'Administration of group intelligence tests to East African pupils', *Brit. J. Ed. Psych.*, 37, 282–91.

VERNON, P.E. (1969) *Intelligence and Cultural Environment*. Methuen's Manuals of Modern Psychology, London: Methuen.

VERNON, P.E. (1969a) 'Abilities and educational attainments in an East African environment', *J. Spec. Edu.*, 4, 335–45.

VERNON, P.E. (1971) 'Effects of administration and scoring on divergent thinking tests', *Brit. J. Psych.*, 41, 245–257.

VOYAT, G. (1970) 'Cross-cultural study of cognitive development on the Pine Ridge Indian Reservation', *Public Health Service Indian Bulletin*, No. 11, January.

VOYAT, G. (1970a) 'IQ: God-given or man-made?', *Saturday Rev., 1969*, 52, 74–5. Reprinted in: HELLMUTH, J. (Ed.), *Disadvantaged Child.* Volume 3, 158–162. New York: Brunner-Mazel.

VYAS, H.V. (1976) 'Performance on a Piagetian task and reading ability: a study of Punjab; children in an English Primary School.' Personal communication.

VYGOTSKY, L.S. (1962) *Thought and Language*. Cambridge: The MIT Press (Originally published, 1934).

WADDELL, V. (1966) 'Some cultural considerations on the development of the concept of conservation'. Unpublished paper presented to a genetic epistemology seminar, Australian National University.

WARREN, N. (1972) 'African infant precocity', *Psych. Bull.*, 78, 5, 353–67.

WERNER, E.E., (1972) 'Infants around the world. Cross-cultural studies of psycho-motor development from birth to two years', *J. Cross-Cult. Psych.*, 3, 111—134.

WERNER, O. and CAMPBELL, D.T. (1970) 'Translating, working through interpreters, and the problem of decentering'. In: NAROLL, R. and COHEN, R. (Eds.), *A Handbook of Method in Cultural. Anthropology.* New York: The Natural History Press, pp. 398—420.

WEST, H. and ABRAVANEL, E. (1972) 'Evidence for class-concept mediation of perceptual sets in preschool children', *Child Developm.*, 43, 1242—1248.

WETZSTEIN, C.J., and SMART, M.E. (1976) 'Mexican American preschoolers acquisition of English in a Piagetian oriented preschool'. Paper read at the Sixth Annual Seminar of Piagetian Theory and its implications for the Helping Professions. Los Angeles, California: University of Southern California, January 30th. Also personal communication.

WILTSE, S. and HALL, G.S. (1891) 'Children's collections', *Ped. Sem.*, 1, 234—37.

WISEMAN, S. (1966) *Correlation Methods.* Manchester University Press.

WISENER, R.H. (1976) 'Factors affecting Piagetian classification and seriation skills in a sample of Mexican-American and Anglo-American children', *Diss. Abstr.*, 36, 7, 3135B—3685B (p. 3587—B).

WITKIN, H.A. (1966) 'Cognitive styles and cross-cultural research', *Int. J. Psych.*, 2, 233—249.

WITKIN, H.A. et al. (1974) 'Social conformity and psychological differentiation', *Int. J. Psych.*, 9, 1, 11—31.

WITKIN, H.A., DYK, R.B., FATERSON, H.F., GOODENOUGH, D.R., and KARP, S.A. (1962) *Psychological Differentiation.* New York: Wiley.

WOBER, M. (1969) 'Distinguishing centri-cultural from cross-cultural tests and research', *Percept. Mot. Skills*, 28, 488.

WOHLWILL, J.F. (1968) 'Piaget's system as a resource of empirical research'. In: SIGEL, I.E. and HOOPER, F.E. (Eds.), *Logical Thinking in Children.* New York: Holt, Rinehart and Winston.

WOHLWILL, J.F. (1970) 'The place of structural experience in early cognitive development', *Interchange*, 1, 13—27.

WORCHEL, S., LEE, J. and ADEWOLE, A. (1975) 'Effects of supply and demand on ratings of object value', *J. Pers. Soc. Psych.*, 32, 906—14.

YOUNISS, J. and DEAN, A. (1974) 'Judgment and imaging aspects of operations: a Piagetian study with Korean and Costa Rican children', *Child Developm.*, 45, 1020—1031.

YOUNISS, J. and MURRAY, J.R. (1970) 'Transitive inference with non-transitive solutions controlled', *Dev. Psych.*, 2, 169–175.

ZA'ROUR, G.I. (1971) 'The conservation of number and liquid by Lebanese school children in Beirut', *J. Cross-Cult. Psych.*, 2, 165–72.

ZA'ROUR, G.I. (1971a) 'Conservation of weight across different materials by Lebanese school children in Beirut', *Sci. Ed.*, 55 (3), 387–94.

INDEX